Young Children's Personal, Social and Emotional Development

Third Edition

Marion Dowling

SAGE
Los Angeles | London | New Delhi
Singapore | Washington DC

First edition published 2000
Second edition published 2005
Reprinted 2008
Third edition published 2010

SAGE Publications Ltd
1 Oliver's Yard
55 City Road
London EC1Y 1SP

SAGE Publications Inc.
2455 Teller Road
Thousand Oaks, California 91320

SAGE Publications India Pvt Ltd
B 1/I 1 Mohan Cooperative Industrial Area
Mathura Road
New Delhi 110 044

SAGE Publications Asia-Pacific Pte Ltd
33 Pekin Street #02–01
Far East Square
Singapore 048763

Library of Congress Control Number: 2009924943

British Library Cataloguing in Publication data

A catalogue record for this book is available from
the British Library

ISBN 0 978-1-84860-105-5
ISBN 0 978-1-84860-106-2 (pbk)

Typeset by Dorwyn, Wells, Somerset
Printed in Great Britain by T.J. International Ltd, Padstow, Cornwall
Printed on paper from sustainable resources

Mixed Sources
Product group from well-managed
forests and other controlled sources
FSC www.fsc.org Cert no. SGS-COC-2482
© 1996 Forest Stewardship Council

Contents

Foreword by Lillian Katz

In the four years since the publication of the second edition of this very welcome book, the importance of getting children off to a good start, and the risks involved in failing to do so, have become even more clear, ever more urgent. The increasing flow of developmental studies and research continues to alert us to the important long-term effects of early social and emotional development. The evidence accumulates almost daily, that unless children achieve at least a minimal level of socio-emotional competence by roughly about six years of age, they are at risk in many important ways for the rest of their lives. Furthermore, it is clear that if we address the social and emotional needs and difficulties experienced by some under-sixes, we can make a difference for their whole lives fairly easily. If we wait until the children with such difficulties are ten years old or are teenagers, we will need the services of the whole staff of a whole local authority mental health agency – and it still may be too late.

In this third edition, Marion Dowling continues to enlighten us fully concerning useful and appropriate strategies for addressing this aspect of development and thus for ways of enhancing the effectiveness and quality of provisions for our youngest children.

Dowling's wisdom, insight, and knowledge are placed fully in the context of recent government mandates and provisions. These include recognition of the significant contribution of staff training, development, and support in helping young children's personal, social and emotional development. As she points out, the agenda facing the UK, as is also the case for many other nations, is extensive and complex. Certainly, addressing these many issues effectively requires competent and confident staff.

Each chapter begins with a summary of its contents. In this way reading and study of the chapter are greatly facilitated. As in the two previous editions, all the basic issues are addressed and clear practical suggestions and strategies, based on recent research studies, are described and explained. In addition, practice-oriented insights into the fundamentals of children's development in the social and emotional domains are offered. Guidelines for the careful observation of young children in order to formulate appropriate teaching strategies are explained. The case studies depicting the typical and frequent predicaments faced by teachers will be especially helpful for newcomers to the field. These case studies are accompanied by important and useful practical suggestions. In addition, directions for how readers can locate other possible sources of information and insight are also offered.

If we can encourage parents of young children to examine this highly readable book, we can also increase its contribution to the present and future well-being of all our children.

Lilian G. Katz, Ph.D.
Professor Emerita &
Co-Director of the Clearinghouse on Early Education and Parenting
University of Illinois
51 Gerty Drive
Champaign, IL 61820

Preface

I write this third edition amidst a climate of concern for the world, notably the effects of climate change, the current financial crisis, continuing poverty and ever-increasing violence both in local communities and across continents. The cumulative affect of all of this make it too easy to become negative about the suffering of others and the impact on our own lives. We also cannot help being worried for the future of our youngest children. The Good Childhood report provides powerful evidence of how trends in today's society cause a range of problems for children of all ages (1). At the start of their lives there should be everything to play for but as children grow up today many odds seem stacked against them.

Nevertheless I am confident that there is no more important time than now to recognise young children's personal needs and to emphasise the messages in this book. Given an environment of love, recognition and support, children will be helped to grow resilient and stand a chance of making their way in the world; regardless of their competencies they are likely to become eager learners. Sir Christopher Ball stressed in the influential and well known Start Right report that 'the art of learning is concerned with the "super skills and attitudes" of which motivation, socialisation and confidence are the most important. These are the fruits of early learning' (2). If we take this wise message seriously, attention to young children's personal, social and emotional development becomes the priority. The messages are addressed in the principles of the Early Years Foundation Stage and considered throughout this book. The Cambridge Primary Review's latest report takes this forward and recommends a primary framework which is based on the early years principles (3).

Parents and early years practitioners have the privilege and responsibility of helping to shape the lives of young children. This book calls attention to the need to respect all that makes each child a unique person and to nurture the positive aspects of their personal development. Having faith in our children and making sure that they grow up strong into the world of tomorrow will surely help us to have faith in the future.

The chapter headings in this book remain broadly the same but with more emphasis on the needs of babies and children under three and the realities of cultural diversity. There are updated references throughout, including reference to the Early Years Foundation Stage Framework. I have also included expanded sections on attachment and key person, early brain development and young children thinking and how this relates to their confidence and independence. Once again I am tremendously grateful to all the staff and children with whom I have been fortunate enough to work and who have provided the material for the pen portraits included.

For the sake of simplicity I use the following general terms and phrases:

- Parent is used for any person who assumes parental responsibility for a child. The term can apply to birth parents or other relatives, foster or adoptive parents, childminders or other carers who are deemed responsible for the child.
- Setting/early years setting is used to cover any provision that offers education and care for children and support for parents.
- Practitioner/early years practitioner/staff are used as general terms to cover any person who works in an early years setting. In some of the case studies I refer to a particular professional.

However, in using these umbrella terms to describe the provision and the staff, I do not wish to boil everything down to a common denominator. There continue to be massive differences in early years provision and across the country children and their families still receive very dissimilar services. Moreover, it is not helpful to pretend that by calling everyone and everything by the same name this makes them the same. Nevertheless, the messages in this book are intended for all who work with children in their earliest years; indeed, most of the messages can apply to those who work with other age groups. Some readers will be experienced and highly qualified, others just starting out on their careers and training. I firmly believe that, whatever the stage of their professional development, successful practitioners need to understand what lies behind young children's behaviour and be equipped to help them to grow into worthwhile people.

Once again my thanks to all the numerous friends and colleagues who encouraged me to complete this third edition. I particularly appreciate the generosity of Lillian Katz in re-writing the Foreword.

REFERENCES

1. Layard, R. and Dunn, J. (2009) *A Good Childhood: Searching for Values in a Competitive Age*. London: The Children's Society.
2. Ball, C. (1994) *Start Right: The Importance of Early Learning*. London: RSE, para 2.17.
3. Cambridge Primary Review (2009) *Towards a New Primary Curriculum. A Report from the Cambridge Primacy Review*. Esmée Fairbairn Foundation/University of Cambridge, Faculty of Education, www.primaryreview.org.uk.

Acknowledgements

The author and publishers would like to thank the following for permission to reproduce items in this book:

Daniel Dowling and Tiffany Gordon for the photograph of Ruby on p. 80.

Thanks for the photograph of Emily on p. 143, taken at the Washwood Heath Children's Centre as part of the Moonbeams Project (Birmingham City Council, Children, Young People and Families). Image by Debi Keyte-Hartland (2006) Artist Educator.

Bridgwater College Early Excellence Centre for photographs of their Forest School on p. 182.

Stay and Play Session, Sure Start Links 4, Links 4 Children's Centre, Huddersfield, for the photograph on p. 85.

Introduction: The Significance of Young Children's Personal, Social and Emotional Development

Since I wrote the second edition of this book, young children and their families continue to be at the top of the political agenda and new initiatives are both multiple and far-reaching. In this introduction, some of the recent major developments will be examined briefly in so far as they affect the well-being of young children and their families.

There continues to be substantial financial investment in early years. The Department for Education and Science, now the Department for Children, Schools and Families spent £2.1 billion on Sure Start Children's Centres up to 2006 and from 2006–2008 it allocated a further £1.8 billion. Since 1997 the numbers of daycare places have increased more than threefold. There were 1,000 children's centres in September 2006 and a target for local authorities to raise this to 3,500 centres by 2010 (1). Resources continue to pour into early years – some impressive new buildings and good quality resources are now evident in settings, particularly in areas of the greatest need.

Concerns about the welfare and safety of young children have intensified following the tragic death of Baby P. The government is now requiring all local authorities to establish Children's Trust boards which aim to prevent abuse of children by bringing different agencies to set a clear strategy for child development. These were first established on a voluntary basis following Lord Laming's report on the appalling death of eight-year-old Victoria Climbié only five years previously. However, there was wide variation in how the trusts were applied and with little evidence today that the trusts were being effective. It remains to be seen if this new measure will improve matters. Social workers are recognised to have a hugely complex and demanding role in ensuring child protection and sadly there is a view that the steps taken by the government cannot ensure that such tragedies will not happen again (2).

POLICY INITIATIVES

To date the most far-reaching changes to the care and education of children have been brought about by the Green Paper *Every Child Matters* (3), and the Children Act 2004 which provides the legal framework for the programme of reform (4). These two documents are impressive in principle: they place young children and their families at the heart of policy; different agencies are required to work together to ensure a fully co-ordinated and swift approach to dealing with concerns. For the first time the government revealed a long-term vision for children and families. Following consultation, the agenda for change was set out and linked to five outcomes intended to ensure that all young children enjoy happy and fulfilling lives now and in the future. In 2006 the Childcare Act (5) required local authorities to improve these outcomes for all young children, namely:

- being healthy
- staying safe
- enjoying and achieving
- making a positive contribution
- achieving economic well-being.

The Children's Plan (2007) fits in with the agenda of *Every Child Matters*. It set out a number of ambitions in all areas for children, for example to halve child poverty by 2010 and eradicate it by 2020. Another aim is for all children to be ready for school with at least 90 per cent of children by age five developing well across all areas of the Early Years Foundation Stage (6). One year following its introduction a progress report was issued with new priorities for 2009. These include a staged approach to end child poverty by 2020, a new child health strategy and a response to review the impact of commercialisation on child well-being (7). The Independent Review of the Primary Curriculum (currently at draft stage) raises the status of early years by emphasising the role of play as a valuable means of learning and stressing the need for children to experience smooth transitions based on play-based learning as they move into Year 1 (8). These major policy initiatives are ambitious in scope and have triggered massive activity within local authorities.

SUPPORT FOR FAMILIES AND CHILDREN

The integration of services to support families and children in a unified way is gaining momentum across the country and there is evidence that it is having a positive impact (see Chapter 10). Rafts of guidance documents are available to support practice and websites proliferate. Most of the material is well presented and useful if only staff have the time to search for, read and digest it.

The two national guidance documents, the *Curriculum Guidance for the Foundation Stage* and *Birth to Three Matters* are merged with the National Standards into one mandatory Framework which covers the age group 0–5. The Early Years Foundation Stage emphasises the central place of young children's personal, social and emotional development. No longer is it simply regarded as 'good practice' to nurture these aspects, but a requirement placed on all practitioners. Apart from personal, social and emotional development being one of the areas of learning, children's personal development is highlighted in commitments within the four principles of the Framework. These are also highlighted in each of the chapters in this book.

The government now appears to recognise that working with young children is a skilled and demanding job and in 2006 the Children's Workforce Development Council (CWDC) was set up to bring about early years workforce reform.

> The Children's Workforce Development Council aims to improve the lives of children and young people. It does this by ensuring that the people working with children have the best possible training, qualifications, support and advice. It helps children and young people's organizations and services to work together so that the child is at the centre of all our services (9).

As from September 2009 a new simplified Qualifications List required for practitioners working within the EYFS becomes mandatory and ensures that all staff members hold full and relevant qualifications (10).

Professional Development Programmes

All early years practitioners now have access to a programme of professional development; funds have been invested since 2007 through the Graduate Leader Fund (previously the Transformation Fund) to support a clear route through training to achieve Early Years Professional (EYP) Status which is deemed to be equivalent to NVQ level 6. A three-year evaluation is planned to look at the impact of the status and already anecdotal evidence shows some interesting benefits for settings and centres, for example in work with parents and support for staff to become more self-reflective (11).

All early years provision is now regulated against a set of common standards. Inspection is now regarded as a shared and active enterprise. Settings and schools now complete a self-evaluation form (SEF) which allows them to offer their own reflections of their provision. Although the SEF is still optional for private and voluntary provision, increasingly settings understand the benefits of providing evidence of what they offer and evaluating the impact of their work.

No Room for Complacency

This impressive range of developments should be fully and warmly acknowledged. The government continues to show unprecedented commitment to invest in children's services and this has produced some very good outcomes for young families. Nevertheless there is no room for complacency. The investment is not enough; the new initiatives are often not well thought out and, indeed, those same early years workers who recognise the benefits of government intervention share concern that some of the developments have worrying consequences for the personal development of young children.

Despite the increase in daycare places, some of the most vulnerable families are not benefitting. A Childcare and Early Years Providers Survey found that families in the least deprived areas had the highest use of formal childcare – 47 per cent – while in the most deprived districts it was just 36 per cent (12). Moreover an Ofsted review showed that less advantaged families have less access to good quality care from childminders or daycare (13).

New buildings and resources can offer exciting opportunities for children and support for their learning; however this will only have impact if staff understand how to use space and equipment to best effect and recognise their own role in meeting young children's needs. Too often there is little chance for practitioners to discuss this as a team, and come to understand how they might help children to be confident and independent in using what is on offer. The appointment of a Children's Commissioner in 2005 was always tempered by the reality of the post carrying restricted powers; the commissioner cannot investigate individual cases of child abuse and has no power to take or support legal action on children's behalf. Current law in England and Wales allows parents and some other carers to justify common assault of children as reasonable punishment (14). This remains in stark contrast to what happens in other European countries. For example, in Sweden, Finland, Denmark, Norway, Austria, Cyprus, Croatia and Latvia, any physical assault on a child is expressly forbidden; the decision is based on affording children the same rights as adults (15). The fact that our government has not gone down this road only contributes to the larger query about whether recent measures proposed by the government are sufficiently strong to protect children.

The proposals in *Every Child Matters* and subsequently in the government's ten-year strategy are unquestionably exciting but the agenda is huge. Although one cannot argue with the intentions, translating them into effective practice is another matter. Although great strides have been made, the implementation of fully co-ordinated practice is still far off in many local authorities. Anning highlights a major problem: 'For many professionals who have been catapulted into multi-professional teamwork, the emotional aspects of coping with changes in their working lives are underestimated both in the preparation and training offered to members of multi-professional teams' (16).

Need for Reflection and Consolidation

Practice in early years has undoubtedly been supported by a wealth of guidance available nationally and from local authorities. For example, the Social and

Emotional Aspects of Development (SEAD) document which relates to young children's personal development includes useful case studies which help practitioners to recognise practical ways of nurturing children's personal growth (17). Other examples are cited throughout this book. But there is a general feeling of overload. Senior staff almost drown in the flurry of new initiatives and there is little sign of the paperless workplace! One worrying result is that amidst all this activity there is an emerging erosion of confidence from all but the most resilient of our wonderful practitioners. Less confident staff are confused by mixed messages and are reluctant to use their initiative for fear of doing the 'wrong thing'. Without a strong leader, practitioners work within a culture of permission as they ask a recurring question: 'Are we allowed to do that'? There is a genuine need for a calm time of consolidation and encouragement for practitioners to recognise that rather than blindly following dictates from above, they still have a degree of autonomy in their work based on their secure knowledge of what is right for young children.

The Early Years Foundation Stage (EYFS) had a rocky introduction but most early years practitioners recognise that it is a document based on clear principles and it does support the child's development and learning from 0–5 years. However, some expectations for children's achievements remain pitched too high, namely two of the literacy goals. Also, in the rush of training to familiarise practitioners with the Framework, some staff have picked up wrong messages. For example, there have been worrying misunderstandings about how to observe children and use this information to promote their welfare and learning and also how to use the Development Matters section in the Framework as a steer rather than a checklist. All staff want to do a good job and they can best be helped by practical and bespoke support which opens their eyes to the possibilities of best practice.

Some messages in the EYFS appear to be contradicted by the interim findings of the Review of the Primary Curriculum. For example, the emphasis on the Unique Child in the EYFS is not acknowledged in the Review, where the recommendation is for a single point of entry for all children to the reception class (18). Importantly, findings from the recently published Cambridge Primary Review reveal a miserable prospect for children in their primary years as they face a narrow and utilitarian curriculum which concentrates too heavily on numeracy and literacy (19).

Improving Standards of Care/Status of Professionals

The government acknowledges the need for workforce reform and has introduced the single qualifications framework, which sets out basic skills and knowledge that all staff should achieve (20). Despite this the present minimum requirement of a Level 2 sets an abysmally low basic standard to work with children. Crucially, ministers still ignore the poor pay and conditions of service which exist for the majority of practitioners. Too often private providers of childcare, working on tight budgets and to required staffing ratios, employ the cheapest staff possible – young, inexperienced staff who have few other options and often have little interest in pursuing a career with young children. These young adults often do not have the appropriate skills, nor do they model desirable behaviour to impressionable children. Moreover, fatigue and poor wages lead to staff feeling unsupported and undervalued; in these circumstances they have little to offer young children. It is not sufficient to rely on staff doing the work because of the intrinsic rewards of working with young children. High-level recruitment and retention of the best people are also dependent on them being paid a realistic salary and working reasonable hours.

The introduction of EYP status has raised the levels of expertise of many practitioners but many who have achieved the status have not received increased salaries or any change in their job descriptions. The equivalence of EYP status and qualified teacher status also remains unclear.

The above issues urgently need to be resolved to ensure that all adults working with children are properly respected and supported in their particular roles.

Regulation of provision is accepted as wholly necessary but Ofsted inspections are very brief. Moroever, inspector training involves only a cursory introduction to the EYFS, which is hardly adequate to support them in their responsibility to issue judgements on provision and outcomes in settings. Given that settings and local authority officers place high value on the outcome of an Ofsted inspection, it is essential that the exercise is carefully conducted by personnel of the highest calibre. Staff and officers testify that this is sometimes the case but by no means always.

Until recently the huge push was to expand provision. While this has been successful, it has often been at the expense of providing the best for our youngest children. Certainly, examples of high quality care and education are evident – very often built on the foundations of nursery schools and former early excellence centres. Nevertheless, some provision is simply not good enough. Anecdotal evidence gathered from a range of local authority officers reveal examples of:

- young babies being cared for by poorly trained and often inexperienced practitioners who fail to recognise the fascinating unique characteristics of each of their key children
- very young four-year-olds, in a cramped reception class with a teacher still not trained in early years and accountable to senior managers who also have no understanding of child development
- practitioners struggling to achieve good practice in private daycare, where owners are predominantly concerned with making a profit and so cut costs to the margin.

All of these examples add up to young children's well-being being jeopardised and we cannot be proud of that.

Quality Improvement

To be fair the government is now turning its attention to issues of quality. The National Children's Bureau is leading work on quality improvement and has worked with leaders in national organisations and local authorities to issue a set of principles which local authorities and settings can use to help affirm their practice and recognise how it can be bettered (21).

On a broader front, a searching review from the Innocenti Research Centre, published by Unicef and focused on countries in the OECD, has also confronted the issue of quality as it highlights two movements in the developed world.

> Today's rising generation is the first in which a majority are spending a large part of early childhood in some form of out-of-home care.

> At the same time, neuroscientific research is demonstrating that loving, stable, secure, and stimulating relationships with caregivers in the earliest months and years of life are critical for every aspect of a child's development (22).

Given these developments the stark question is whether provision in settings out-of-home will prove to be a force for good or ill for today's children and tomorrow's world.

The review attempts for the first time to evaluate and compare early childhood services in ten developed countries against ten benchmarks which set minimum standards for protecting the rights of children in their most vulnerable and formative years. England meets the criteria for five of the benchmarks (although these findings have been questioned by the government as being out of date) and was placed in the middle of the 'league table'. This unquestionably shows progress from previous years but there remains much to be done. The study stresses that early childhood programmes will not benefit children if they fall below certain levels of cost and quality.

Adults are the Key

Against this background early years practitioners continue their work. In the following chapters the adult is seen as the key to helping children develop sound qualities and attitudes. Regardless of background, the early years practitioner stands as a model for the child. Leo Tolstoy describes personal responsibility very powerfully in his account of the experimental primary school he set up on his estate:

> If we come to understand that we can educate others only through ourselves, the question of education is made void, and only the question of life is left. 'How must I live myself?' I do not know a single act in the education of children which is not included in the education of oneself (23).

A headteacher of a nursery school once told me that the main aim in her school was to 'follow the child with love and help to grow the adequate person.' I agree with her wholeheartedly. Most of us would agree with the idea of an 'adequate person'. We all appreciate and admire people who have good interpersonal skills, live their lives by a clear moral code, and are able to show their own feelings and have empathy with the feelings of others. These individuals are usually confident when they take decisions in life and are brave in facing up to difficult situations; they are enthusiastic and show sticking power in seeing things through both at work and in their personal lives. Regardless of their intellectual abilities, these individuals appear equipped both to get the most out of life and to deal with problems. These are rough and ready definitions of 'adequacy' but it is surely these qualities that we want to demonstrate, encourage and promote in our young children. The type of person we become colours all else we do in life. The small baby lies ready to reciprocate and blossom in our loving care.

There are clearly grounds for optimism. In this country there is now a strong and established political searchlight on children aged under five. What is more, there is a pervasive acknowledgement from research, which is being carried into practice, that we are educating and caring for more than a child's intellect. If early years settings foster children's personal, social and emotional qualities they are surely opening doors for them to live a life of personal fulfilment whatever their other achievements. However, it is unrealistic and unfair to place this requirement on settings alone. Society as a whole must take ultimate responsibility for children's personal development. When we see examples of child exploitation and abuse, and some of the negative models of adult behaviour to which they are exposed personally and through the media, it is difficult to see that this responsibility is being regarded. In the conclusion to her book *Children First*, Penelope Leach argues powerfully for every one of us to face up to the fact that the responsibility is ours:

> Neither 'society' nor 'social attitudes' can ultimately let individuals off their own moral obligations, because there is no society that is separate from us. The whole complicated, conservative, consumerist collective is nothing but the children we were, the children we have had, the children we have now and those they will have in the future. The people who work, care and are cared for are the same people. There is nobody else to turn the social tide (24).

REFERENCES

1. Select Committee on Public Accounts Thirty Eighth Report (2006) *Sure Start Children's Centres.* House of Commons on Public Accounts, www.parliament.the-stationery- office.com/pa/cm20.
2. Curtis, P. (2008) Balls was irresponsible to propose that Baby P case will not happen again, *The Guardian,* main sections, 12 December, p. 17.
3. HM Treasury (2003) *Every Child Matters.* London: The Stationery Office.
4. Department for Education and Skills (DfES) (2004) *The Children Act.* www.publications.parliament.
5. Department for Education and Skills (DfES) (2006) *The Childcare Act.* www.publications.parliament.
6. Department for Education and Skills (DfES) (2007) *Children and Young People Plan:*

Building Better Futures. London: DfES.

7. Gaunt, C. (2008) New priorities set for Children's Plan, *Nursery World*, 18 December, p. 4.
8. Department for Children, Schools and Families (DCSF) (2008) Independent Review of the Primary Curriculum (Interim report). London: DCSF.
9. Children's Workforce Development Council (2006) Home Page www.cwdcouncil.org.uk.
10. Children's Workforce Development Council (2008) Qualifications List. www.qualificationslistcwdcouncil.org.uk.
11. EYP Update (2008) in *Nursery World,* 30 October, pp. 23–6.
12. Vevers, S. (2008) Poorest provision is in deprived areas, *Nursery World,* 9 October, p. 10.
13. Ofsted (2008) *Early Years: Leading to Excellence,* www.ofsted.gov.uk.
14. Department for Education and Skills (DfES) (2004) The Children Act, chapter 31, section 58. London: HMSO.
15. BBC News, World Edition (2004) *Report on the Decision of the House of Lords to Reject an Amendment to the Children Bill on Smacking,* 6 July.
16. Anning, A., Cottrell, D., Frost, N. Green, J., and Robinson, M. (2006) *Developing Multiprofessional Teamwork for Integrated Children's Services,* Open University Press, McGraw Hill Education, p. 93.
17. Department for Children, Schools and Families (DCSF)/The National Strategies Early Years (2008) *Social and Emotional Aspects of Development Guidance for Practitioners working in the Early Years Foundation Stage.* London: DCSF.
18. Department for Children, Schools and Families (DCSF) (2008) Independent Review of the Primary Curriculum (Interim report). London: DCSF, p. 51.
19. Cambridge Primary Review (2009) *Interim Findings of the Cambridge Primary Review,* Esmée Fairbairn Foundation/University of Cambridge, Faculty of Education.
20. Department for Education and Skills (DfES) (2005) Common core of skills and knowledge for the children's workforce. Non-statutory guidance. London: HMSO.
21. National Quality Improvement Network (2008) *Quality Improvement Principles: A Framework for Local Authorities and National Organisations to Improve Quality Outcomes for Children and Young People.* London: National Children's Bureau.
22. UNICEF (2008) *The Childcare Transition,* Innocenti Report Card 8, UNICEF Innocenti Research Centre, Florence, p. 1.
23. Quoted in McAllister, W.J. (1931) *The Growth of Freedom in Education.* London: Constable, p. 399.
24. Leach, P. (1994*) Children First.* London: Michael Joseph, p. 265.

1

The Seeds of Confidence

Summary of contents

- Confidence is a catalyst in supporting early personal growth. The young child develops confidence through becoming aware of herself as a separate and worthwhile person, as well as having a realistic view of what she can achieve.
- Children gain their self-esteem initially from the love and recognition that they receive from their family and other significant people in their lives including their practitioner who is their key person.
- When they move into an early years setting they will gain confidence if their questions and comments are understood, their interests are recognised and strengthened as schemes of thought. They also become aware of themselves, what they are capable of doing and what is approved behaviour.
- Children's self-esteem and self-knowledge are closely linked to the ways in which they see themselves as learners. This leads them to show either 'mastery' or 'helpless' patterns of behaviour. Their success as learners is dependent on them feeling secure and also having opportunities to experiment in play contexts and try things out for themselves.

Early childhood is such a momentous time of life. Gazing at a newborn baby we can never be sure of how she will develop – what potential she has within her – but we know that there is everything to play for. And watching her grow up it is impossible to separate the different strands of development, as they are all inter-related. Increased physical movement leads to possibilities for growing independence which in turn means that the baby extends her horizons, and strengthens her curiosity to discover more. But studies strongly suggest that the catalyst for these amazing achievements is the child's growing confidence (1, 2, 3).

Confidence is a characteristic valued by all and one that parents most want for their children. We may hear of parents who deliberately send their young children to certain settings or schools or arrange for them to join clubs 'in order to give them confidence'. Many parents see that the prime role of care and education is to help children to acquire social skills and become confident before entering mainstream school. The confident person is well equipped to deal with life, whether in school or work or in social situations. Conversely, under-confident people find coping with these aspects of life often difficult and painful. Above all, truly confident people are comfortable with themselves and have insights into their own strengths and weaknesses. This distinguishes them from over-confident people, who although they think well of themselves may lack self-insight and have a false sense of optimism of what they can achieve. In a world that demands so much of them, children do need to become confident from an early age. It is necessary for their early success in life and also for the future. In a 60-year study of more than a thousand men and women of high intelligence followed through from childhood to retirement, those most confident in their early years were most successful as their careers unfolded (4). What then is required to achieve this precious personal attribute, and how can we help young children to develop it?

An interesting question is whether confidence is an inherited trait and whether some babies are blessed with it at birth. To some extent this might be true: very small babies show clear signs of personality traits; for example, sociable and shy behaviours. However, being outgoing does not necessarily link with a good level of confidence, while low key, seemingly unassuming persons can be quietly sure of themselves. So as Lillian Katz suggests, perhaps it is not what we are born with that counts so much but what we are allowed to do and who we are encouraged to be (5). Thus young children's levels of confidence are coloured by their early experiences and successes and failures, the thoughts they have about themselves and other people's reactions to them. Most people would admit that their confidence ebbs and flows according to the people they are with and the situations demanded of them. However, a person's confidence is linked closely to three factors. These are: becoming aware of oneself (self-concept); developing a view of oneself, either positive or negative (self-esteem); and getting to know about one's strengths and weaknesses (self-knowledge). Children become aware of the first two at a very early stage of their lives; their experiences in the nursery will influence powerfully all three factors.

BECOMING AWARE OF ONESELF

The Early Years Foundation Stage recognises that 'being acknowledged and affirmed by important people in their lives leads to children gaining confidence and inner strength through secure attachments with these people' (6).

We begin to recognise ourselves from early on. After about 18 months a toddler has a pretty good idea that the reflection shown in a mirror is a representation of herself. Before that even, babies will build a picture of themselves from the way in which they are regarded and treated, particularly by those people who are closest to them. Young babies start to form this picture from their mothers, whose loving acceptance of them is the first signal that they are a person who matters. Rosemary Roberts describes this beautifully:

> The mother's face and body are like a mirror to the baby. This very early mirroring process which can reflect the mother's acceptance, forms the basis of the baby's self-concept; the mother's responses are the first 'brush strokes' for the developing picture (7).

This image of oneself as a distinct person is crucial in order to establish a sense of identity; initially it is most strongly established through ongoing contact with one person (see also Chapters 2 and 3). Dorothy Selleck argues that only the presence of a parent or committed regular key person which is now a requirement for every child in an early years setting can provide the continuity, attention and sensuous pleasure that a baby needs to make sense of his experiences and set in motion the process of mental development (8). For children under two, particularly those who are placed in daycare, their key person offers an essential warm attachment and the assurance that, despite being one of a number, that baby or toddler is special and unique. Young babies who have been institutionalised from birth and who lack regular contact with one carer may fail to recognise the 'brush strokes' described by Roberts. In certain circumstances a person's sense of 'self' can be eroded – for example, adults imprisoned in conditions of harsh confinement. Terry Waite wrote movingly of his long period in captivity and of the times when he wondered who he was: 'How I yearn with a childish, selfish longing to be understood and cared for. I am frightened. Frightened that, in growing up, my identity may slip away' (9).

Attachment relationships are discussed in Chapter 4 where they are linked to children's emotional development. However, sound attachments are fundamental to a child's overall healthy development; a baby will gain confidence in her identity when a few loving and significant people recognise and respond to her. Maria Robinson describes this process as attunement. She stresses the importance of learning to interpret the baby's signals and suggests that the parent is then able to attune their own responses to those of the baby. This responsive affirmation helps the child learn more about mum or dad and strengthens belief in himself (10). As the toddler develops into the pre-school years, other people contribute to a broader view of her identity. Through their different behaviours these people will help a child to know who she is. For example, Alison knows that she is dad's little daughter and she makes him laugh; her baby brother's loving older sister when she cuddles him and gives him his bottle; her older brother's noisy little sister when she dances and sings to his records; and Alison the artist at nursery when her teacher admires her paintings. By becoming aware of the way in which others view us we build up a composite picture of ourselves. We also learn to behave in character; we get a picture of how other people regard us and then adapt our behaviour to fit this picture. Because of their immaturity, young children are very open to the opinions and views of other more experienced adults, particularly those adults who are familiar and loved, members of their immediate family, and later those others who care for and work with them. Children who feel that they belong are likely to recognise themselves as distinctive.

Figure 1.1 Yuichi's family provide her with a sense of personal continuity

The stable family provides the child with a sense of personal continuity. Young children love to hear stories of when they were babies or to share recall of past family events. They are also keen to share and listen to predictions of 'what will happen when you are a big girl'. These shared experiences and concerns help young children to start to have a sense of self within the larger family.

The family, then, has a powerful effect on each child's sense of identity, but when the child moves to an early years setting the practitioners share this responsibility.

SELF-ESTEEM

When a child establishes her identity she is simply becoming aware of how others see her. Once we talk about self-esteem we start to place a value on that identity. Children do not gain a clear view of their self-worth until they are around six years of age but their early experiences within the family and in early years settings provide the basis for them to make a judgement about themselves. Self-esteem is not fixed; it can change according to the people we are with and the situations that we find ourselves in. Alison's self-esteem is mainly secure as she recognises that she is valued in different ways by her father, by her baby brother, and in the nursery. She has a lower esteem though when she is with her older brother, who makes it clear that she is often intrusive and a nuisance to him. So the views of others not only help a young child to recognise herself as a person who is seen in different ways; they also contribute to the regard she has for herself. And again it is the people who are closest to the child and who have an emotional link who will have the most profound effect on her self-esteem. These are described as the 'significant others' and they include the family and primary carers, the key person and other practitioners who have early contacts with the child.

One of the most important gifts we can offer young children is a positive view of themselves. Without this gift they will flounder throughout life and be constantly seeking reassurance from others as they cannot seek it from within. However, as Siraj-Blatchford points out, positive self-esteem depends on whether children feel that others accept them and see them as competent and worthwhile (11).

Case study 🗁

Four-year-old Eva had poor eyesight and after three weeks in her new reception class she was prescribed spectacles to wear. Eva was extremely self-conscious about her glasses and that same day was found weeping in the cloakroom after one child asked her why she was wearing 'masks over her eyes'. From that moment all efforts from her teacher Anna and later her mum could not persuade Eva to wear her spectacles in school although she clearly had visual difficulties with mark making and when looking at picture books.

Four days later, Anna arrived in school wearing a pair of quite ornate spectacles (with clear glass in the lens as she had perfect sight). As she had anticipated the children noticed the difference and this interest gave Anna the opportunity she wanted. At story time she asked the children what they thought about her new purchase – all thought them very pretty. Anna stressed how pleased she was with the spectacles and how well she could see with them. She involved other children in the class who also wore glasses and said how smart they looked. Eva said nothing but was clearly listening. The following day she hesitantly came into the class wearing her spectacles. Anna complimented Eva on her appearance and Eva was delighted to be able to identify and describe some fine detail in the picture storybook they shared in a group.

Comment

Having to wear spectacles severely affected Eva's self-esteem – she felt vulnerable and different. Anna's sensitive move to show wearing spectacles in a positive light and to model this herself was clearly effective. Eva resumed wearing the spectacles because she no longer felt different, but was finally persuaded of their benefit when she realised that she could now see things more easily.

When children constantly demand attention or boast about their achievements this is sometimes wrongly interpreted as an over-developed self-esteem. However, we should recognise that self-esteem is not conceit and this type of behaviour is more likely to reflect a lack of self-regard and a basic insecurity. In an article which stresses that self-esteem is basic to a healthy life, Murray White looks at the possible problems in later school life arising from its lack:

> If teachers examine what causes bullying and other chronic misbehaviours – the showing off, the fighting and the failure which some children have adopted – they will discover that low self-esteem is at the root of it. These children behave as they do because of strong feelings of inadequacy and internal blame, a belief that they do not possess the ability or intelligence to succeed (12).

SELF-ESTEEM IN THE EARLY YEARS SETTING

The value that we place on ourselves is also affected by how secure we feel. Both adults and children are usually secure with people they know but also when they are in familiar situations. When we start a new job or a new course of learning, most of us feel very vulnerable being placed in the position of a novice. We do not even know where to get a cup of coffee, let alone really understand aspects of new work or how others will work with us.

Studies of young children at home show them to be comfortable and in control with mum or the main carer safely in sight. A one-year-old is usually wary of any-one who comes between her and her mum and will use her parent as a secure base to explore wider territory (13). Tizard and Hughes' well-known study of four-year-old girls conversing and questioning with their mothers gives a picture of children in a situation when they feel they are on sure territory (14). In nearly all families young children recognise that there are loving adults who know them and care about them. This knowledge in itself helps the child to feel secure.

When starting in an early years setting the young child faces new experiences including developing contact with people who are unknown to her and to whom she is unknown. She is placed in a similar position to an adult starting a new job but has much less experience of life to support her. Consequently the move to a group setting can be a momentous event in the child's life which for some can result in considerable self-doubt; even the most confident child can find this move intimidating. When they start school, children's expectations of what it will be like often does not match the reality.

> Those with older siblings or those who play with pupils from school may have acquired some understanding of school values and systems vicariously. Within role play they may have developed 'script knowledge' (Gura, 1996: 37) while they were exploring make-believe school ... However, for the first-born and for many others, school will be a completely new experience. In presenting their picture of school, parents, siblings and friends shape children's thinking but on arriving at school children may find the reality to be different (15).

The setting plays a key role in maintaining children's self-esteem when they are learning to work and play in a different environment from home. The size and type of setting can make a difference and there is specific evidence that moving into a reception class at four years is stressful. Gill Barratt's classic study of children starting school in a reception class highlighted some feelings experienced by these new young entrants. Through looking at photographs and in discussion children described feeling scared, fearful of getting things 'wrong' and not knowing what to do. Most of these feelings can be linked to not feeling in control. Barrett's work showed that, partly because of the way the pupil role is understood by young children, usually based on what they have heard from parents, other children and through television, some adopt a passive attitude, are reluctant to take risks in their learning and are anxious about their inadequacies being revealed (16).

Both of these studies show young children facing tremendous demands, both emotional and intellectual. The fear of being wrong is a major inhibitor. Barrett suggested that too often in mainstream schools there was still emphasis placed on children needing to do things correctly and that children do need to feel that it is safe and acceptable not to know something. Lately there have been genuine moves by schools to recognise the needs of their youngest children. Many settings and schools are now working closely together to ensure a gentle and phased transition into a reception class and from reception into Year 1. Settings and schools are increasingly beginning to tailormake a transition to meet each child's needs, rather than expecting every child to fit in to one size of provision. Despite this, too often staffing ratios in reception classes remain inadequate. It is essential that, when children are newcomers to a setting, they are able to have easy access to an adult who will introduce them to the multiplicity of new experiences gently and informally and interpret new requirements for them. The close involvement of parents in this process allows children to feel emotionally supported while they learn.

The practitioner also knows that a child's self-esteem can be fragile. Self-esteem is not constant for any of us. As adults we can have a very positive view of ourselves in one circumstance only to have it knocked down in another. Given a new manager who makes unreasonable demands at work, an important project which proves to be unsuccessful or a failed relationship in our personal lives, our self-esteem can dip. A mature person with a sound self-concept should be able to cope with this over time and indeed to seek out self-affirming situations in which she can succeed.

A young child does not have this ability. Her self-esteem is totally dependent on the people who matter to her and the situations that they provide. A young child will only really value herself fully if she knows that she has the unconditional love of a parent or carer. This knowledge is absolutely critical, and if for some reason it hasn't been acquired during the early years at home then the nursery teacher has a heavy responsibility to demonstrate that love and care.

Proper caring for a child means knowing about her, including how she thinks and what interests her. In order to feel comfortable and 'at home' in a nursery, a child needs to know that she is known and that her behaviour is understood. The first principle of the Early Years Foundation Stage emphasises that every child is unique, with her own particular personality and characteristics. Practitioners therefore need to have ways of tuning in to what lies behind children's thoughts, comments and actions. Chapter 2 deals with the importance of closely listening to children.

Another way in is for practitioners to understand about what Piaget termed young children's 'schemes of thought'. Piaget claimed that children's patterns of thought are evident from babyhood in their early physical and sensory actions. These schemes are strengthened as children repeat their actions; through interactions with others they begin to make connections in their thoughts and so recognise cause and effect. Children's schemes or 'schema' are dealt with extensively in other literature (17, 18, 19).

Some children have one schema while others seem to have a number. Although around 36 schemes have been identified, the staff at the Pen Green Centre of Excellence for Under Fives identified the most common ones. These are those linked to straight lines (trajectory); circles (rotation); joining things (connection); covering things (enveloping); and moving things from one place to another (transporting) (20). Young children will all demonstrate abiding interests in these patterns of movement through what they do and how they behave. We will see this unfold particularly clearly when children play with open-ended materials. In a beautifully illustrated booklet published by Community Playthings, open-ended is defined as 'not having a fixed answer; unrestricted; allowing for future change' (21). When using these materials children create their own scenarios and are in charge of their learning. The booklet further suggests that these powers are at risk when children are fed a diet of ready-made entertainment, a heavy emphasis on use of commercial equipment and access to electronic activities. If we believe that young children learn initially through first-hand sensory experiences 'a wealth of open-ended play – with simple materials – can set children on the road to being confident individuals with a lively interest in life' (22).

Case study 🗁

Daisy at 15 months was introduced to heuristic play (providing her with an array of natural materials and containers which Daisy has time to explore and investigate freely). Her key person observed her on three separate occasions engaged in the following:

- wrapping her teddy up, placing him in a bag and carrying the bag around with her

Continued

Continued

- collecting fir cones and placing them in boxes, taking great care to replace the lid of each box
- attaching dolly pegs in a circle to the lid of a circular wooden container
- covering small play characters with shawls and blankets which were placed nearby
- repeatedly attempting to attach a necklace around her neck.

Comment

Sue, Daisy's key person, felt that she had some secure evidence to suggest that Daisy had an enveloping schema. She supported this by providing more drapes and bags and moving a large cardboard box into the area which Daisy used as a 'hidey hole'.

In order to keep in tune with children, practitioners need to listen and observe closely and then often take an imaginative leap into the child's mind to make sense of their meanings. While this has always been good practice the Early Years Foundation Stage now makes it a requirement that all provision we make for babies and young children is based on our close observations of what they do on a day-to-day basis (23).

Although the child must be sure that she is loved at all times, part of the process of caring is also to help shape her behaviour (see also Chapter 6). A problem can arise where the expectations for behaviour differ from home to the setting. It may be that the basis for praise at home is 'to stand up for yourself and hit them back', or 'you make sure that you are the best in the class'. These are powerful messages for young children from people who are very important to them; all the practitioners can do is to try to modify these messages by presenting an alternative view and trying to provide the conditions in the nursery to demonstrate them. Hopefully, then, over a period of time a child learns to use language instead of fists to maintain her rights and to understand that every single person in the nursery community can be 'best' at something. Again a confident, bright, creative four-year-old whose parents have encouraged her non-contingent thinking and activity may find it difficult to conform in any group setting; she will certainly find life extremely hard in a nursery which puts very heavy emphasis on a narrow definition of correct behaviour. She risks being herself and receiving constant reprimand for her responses, or complying with requirements and feeling herself to be in an alien and unreasonable environment in which she has no opportunity to show her strengths. In this situation self-belief will ebb away unless a watchful practitioner understands the behaviour that has been encouraged at home and is prepared to be flexible with the requirements in the setting.

Having a positive esteem for oneself is dependent on having a clear view of who you are; this is often difficult for children from minority groups. Tina Bruce points out that too often people from minorities are stereotyped into an identity with which they are not comfortable (24).

Case study 🗂

Kofi was black and an adopted child. His younger two brothers were white as were his parents. Kofi was only aware of being the much loved oldest child in the family – his colour was incidental although he was proud of it. He was the only black child when he started at the nursery. When one or two children at the nursery started to call him 'black boy', Kofi was taken aback. He started to wash obsessively at home. After a week he asked his dad if he could have medicine to change colour. When the parents informed the nursery of their concerns the teachers realised that all the children needed help to see different aspects of their identities. Kofi, with others, was recognised as an important member of his family and the nursery community. Children were encouraged to describe each other in terms of their physical appearance and made a display of their differences and common features.

Comment

Kofi's teachers were initially not prepared for the reactions of the children to a child of a different colour. They felt strongly that the comment 'black boy' was simply descriptive and was not discriminatory. However, the incident made them more aware of the need to avoid stereotyping, and they were careful to avoid any possibility of discrimination when a child with cerebral palsy was admitted to the nursery shortly afterwards.

Moving a child who does not appear to be thriving during the early years at school is not to be considered lightly, although, this was eventually seen as the right decision for James. Andrew Pollard, in his social study of five children starting school, describes James who stayed at the local state primary school for the first two years of his school career, after which his parents transferred him to an independent school. James found the move to infant school difficult and his self-esteem suffered. James was not accepted by other children although he badly wanted friends; overall he could not adapt to the robust climate of school life. His teachers supported him, but perceived him as cautious and 'nervy'. There was a clash of culture between the school and the parents who were strongly supportive of James, had high academic aspirations for him and provided home tuition for him. It was apparent that James could not meet the requirements of both school and home. When he started to be influenced by the other children at the end of the reception year, the parents became alarmed and described his new behaviour as 'rude' and 'cheeky'. Pollard suggests that this little boy's unhappiness sprang from the poor home/school communications. The parents had always aspired for James to move to an independent school where more formal teaching methods were seen to be in keeping with what they wanted for their son. Most importantly, James subsequently flourished in his new school, in his learning and social life (25).

So, optimal conditions to promote children's self-esteem include care and respect for their ways of thinking and appreciation of difference, which enables children coming from different backgrounds and cultures to experience feeling good about themselves. Self-esteem is only likely to be fostered in situations where all aspects of all children are esteemed, including their gender, race, ability, culture and language.

SELF-KNOWLEDGE

When people are acknowledged and respected, this contributes to the regard they have for themselves. However, this must also go hand in hand with them getting to know themselves. As young children develop they start to learn about themselves and what they can do; they begin to recognise those things that they find easy and where they need help and support.

Initially, however, children have limited self-insight and they look to others to provide information. At first, young children are dependent on the adults around them to gain a view of their strengths and weaknesses. Nevertheless, although guidance should be given and boundaries for behaviour established, ultimately, as Pat Gura suggests, the main aim must be to help children develop a sense of control over their lives and build their own aspirations (26).

The way in which an early years programme is organised reflects the practitioners' beliefs about the degree of responsibility to give children and the importance of helping them to get to know themselves. Studies have shown that children can spend their time in either controlling or informational environments. In a controlling environment the emphasis is very much on the adults being in charge, and requiring children to comply. An informational environment will encourage children to take responsibility for themselves by learning to plan their work, decide what resources to use and then have a part in assessing what has been achieved (27).

In a setting where adults control, children can only respond. An informational environment will allow children to make and learn from mistakes, discover the best way of doing things and learn how to make decisions. Evidence from two longitudinal studies in the USA and Europe highlights the benefits and costs of the different learning environments. Children were studied over time having experienced one of the following three different curricular programmes:

- a skills-based programme controlled by adults
- a free choice programme
- a High Scope programme which incorporates opportunities for children to plan–do–review.

In both instances the children who were in the High Scope programmes were shown to develop more satisfying social and personal lives (28).

As always the educator's actions are a powerful influence on the way in which the child develops. Questions which allow children to give open-ended answers and which spring from genuine interest in all that they do will encourage individuals to think about their achievements.

The ways in which adults respond to children will also have a powerful effect on each child's developing knowledge about him- or herself. For example, the skilled practitioner sensitively balances giving positive affirmation to her children, while establishing clear messages about acceptable behaviours. Pam Lafferty, the director of High/Scope UK, usefully distinguishes between 'praise' and 'encouragement'. Lafferty suggests that praise comes from 'outside' the child and is an external judgement of approval, while 'encouragement' is about motivating the child within and creating the ongoing desire to learn (29). Drawing on studies of work with different age groups (30, 31) the following types of responses are suggested which can either hinder or help children.

Responses which hinder children's self-knowledge:

1. *Evaluating through praise* – where adults always take the responsibility for judging what a child has done, believing that this is their job; this restricts the child from forming her own view. Nursery settings are usually defined by constant use of praise and encouragement – comments such as 'that's wonderful', 'I'm really pleased with you' are commonly heard; however, praise can encourage conformity when it leads children to become dependent on others rather than themselves. Gura suggests that constant use of praise can be high on warmth but low in regard to information offered – this is particularly the case when the praise is general. Moreover, overdoses of lavish praise do become devalued even by young children. Robert, age five, told me confidentially, 'It doesn't matter really what you paint because she [his teacher] always says it's really very lovely'. Young children deserve more than a comforting and benign environment. Nevertheless the use of praise is very effective when used with discretion. It is particularly helpful to encourage those children who are not well motivated, to help set the limits of behaviour and for young children who are learning to socialise and become one of a group. The Unit for Parenting Studies at Leicester University encourages parents and carers to give their children 'five praises a day' to improve their behaviour and self-image and to redress the attention that so often is given to misbehaviour (32).

   Use of praise is particularly helpful when children are being introduced to an early years setting, but in a climate of information it should be seen as a means to an end. Praise that is focused can help children to become aware of their achievements, for example 'using those elastic bands to fix the two boxes together is really clever, Dean'.

2. *Evaluating with criticism* – negative comments are inevitably going to leave children feeling inadequate and that they have failed. Importantly, if a child is criticised this usually shuts down her thinking. Early years teachers are very aware of this and negative responses are rarely used in early years settings.

Responses which help children's self-knowledge:

1. *Using silence* – often in a busy nursery, and particularly when adults feel under the pressure of time, young children are not given sufficient time to reflect and collect their thoughts. However, if when asking a question, an adult pauses to allow a child time to respond, the chances are that, as with older children, the time allowed for thinking means that the response given is of greater quality. It also demonstrates the adult's faith that the child will be able to respond, which in turn fosters the child's confidence. Young children will learn to recognise that they are not expected to come up with quick answers and that it is more important to have time to explore what they really feel.

2. *Clarifying* – young children often find it difficult to put their thoughts into words. Sometimes, in their eagerness they rush to communicate and then tail away as they struggle to recall the sense of their message. Adults can actively accept children's contributions by paraphrasing or summarising what they have said. Although the teacher may use different words she will make sure that she maintains the child's intention and meaning. 'I know what you are saying, David. Your idea is ...' In this way a teacher shows that she has both received and understood what the child has said.

3. *Asking for information* – if practitioners show genuine interest in children's views of what they have done, this helps children to become confident in making judgements.

4. *Providing information* – if young children are helped to see how their paintings and constructions have developed over a period of time they will start to understand that achievements and progress are linked to growing up. A child will take pleasure in recalling her limitations as a baby and contrasting them with what she is doing now.

SELF-ESTEEM, SELF-KNOWLEDGE AND LINKS WITH LEARNING

It is generally accepted that a child who has sound self-esteem is well placed to learn. The Early Years Foundation Stage stresses that practitioners make a critical contribution to children's learning by creating the climate and conditions that encourage their involvement. The prime way of doing this is by building their self-esteem and confidence (33). Positive self-esteem, though, is not sufficient in itself; self-knowledge is important in order for people to develop not only an optimistic view of themselves but also one which is realistic. However, in order to learn, young children must believe that they are able to do so. If this belief is not secured during the early years of life it is unlikely to blossom later. In a study to accelerate learning in science with pupils of secondary age, about half made impressive progress, the others did not. One of the main reasons for this difference was that the latter group of children were afraid of failing in thinking tasks and so gave up the mental challenges required (34).

Some children on admission to an early years setting do not regard themselves as learners. Their thoughts and views may have been disregarded by adults; caring and protective parents may not have trusted children to try out things for themselves and so learn from mistakes. These children will have learned to accept that they are not important or competent to do things for themselves. By comparison, other children on admission shine as eager and capable learners. Their early experiences have included opportunities to try things out and discuss the outcomes with adults. They have been gently helped to frame their ideas in words and their increasing command of language has helped them to feel 'in control' of events.

Figure 1.2 Feeling in control

Carol Dweck suggests that the view that children (or adults for that matter) adopt for themselves significantly affects the way they lead their lives. This is demonstrated when children show either helpless or mastery patterns of behaviour when confronted with obstacles in learning (35). Children who follow a mastery approach are confident and have a positive view of themselves. They seek new, challenging experiences and believe that they can succeed even in the face of difficulties. Other children are unsure of themselves; because their self-esteem is not secure they constantly look for approval from others. These children show helpless behaviour in that they 'give up' easily, and when things go wrong they believe that it is their own fault because 'they are no good'.

While the 'mastery learners' forge ahead in learning, often on their own initiative, the 'helpless children' need constant reassurance and support from parents and teachers (see also Chapter 5). Although Dweck's work was with older children, similar patterns of behaviour are evident with three- and four-year-olds as they begin to recognise who they are and what they can do.

Practitioners now have firm support from the Early Years Foundation Stage to provide well-planned, play-based activities which give children scope to be creative and imaginative and have a sense of being in control. In terms of building confidence in learning, play is invaluable; Vygotsky describes this so well when he asserts that in play it is as if a child is a head taller than himself (36). This description sums up a masterly approach to play where children make their own judgements, take initiatives and seek resources and information when they require it. However, despite the national recommendations, both in schools and other early years settings there remains a degree of uncertainty about how play methodology aids learning and the practicalities of planning and provision.

As part of their training programme to implement the Early Years Foundation Stage, local authorities are supporting practitioners to provide for play which is appropriate for 0–5-year-olds. In the interests of continuity of learning, Year 1 teachers and assistants need access to similar support.

Case study 📁

Pascale and Jeremy were the same age, three years 11 months, and they had started nursery at the same time during the previous term. Pascale sat at a table drawing. She was clutching the pencil in a pincer grip and her movements were repetitive. Try though I might I could not gain eye contact with her or get her to respond in any way. On mentioning this to the teacher, she said that she was not surprised. When Pascale was admitted to the nursery, her name was Cheri. A month later, her mother requested that the name be changed to Amanda. On returning to the nursery that term the staff were further informed that Amanda was no longer to have that name but was to be called Pascale. The little girl was not sure who she was. Her teacher reported that every day Pascale refused to move from the drawing table and join in any other activities in the nursery.

On passing through to the next classroom I met Jeremy who was with a fairly large group of children listening to a story about a little boy who was walking along a very long road. Jeremy, having grasped the conventions of being a pupil in a group, raised his hand to make a comment. When invited to do so he politely asked if the road in the story went on and on into infinity! The teacher, somewhat taken aback, said that it might do but suggested that Jeremy explain what the word meant. 'Well', said Jeremy, confidently raising his voice, so that all in the group might hear, 'if it goes on into infinity, it might never, ever end!'

Continued

Continued

Comment

Despite being of a similar age and having had a similar amount of time in the nursery, these two children were poles apart. Pascale, alias Cheri alias Amanda, was not even able to recognise herself in her name and showed helpless behaviour in her refusal to accept new challenges. Jeremy's high regard for himself as a learner was evident in his active participation in the story. He was able to question and make links in his learning using a fascinating new word he had acquired. Jeremy showed all the elements of a master player using the teacher as a resource for further learning.

Before they arrived at the nursery, home experiences had already had a potent effect on Pascale's and Jeremy's views of themselves as learners. The staff were faced with different challenges for these two children. Pascale needed the security and consistency provided by a predictable programme and the attention and care of one adult in whom she could learn to trust. Close and sensitive links with Pascale's mother would hopefully enable her to recognise Pascale's needs and try to meet them at home. Jeremy's inner resources for learning were already firmly in place. The nursery's task here was to ensure that staff respected Jeremy's contributions, provided additional stimulus to motivate him, and extended his skills and knowledge based on what he understood already.

The psychologist Carl Rogers says that children need two conditions in order to be creative learners. These are psychological safety and psychological freedom (37). Pascale's future progress depended initially on the first condition being met. Rogers suggested that psychological safety is dependent on: having total trust in a child and accepting all that the child does; encouraging the child to become self-aware; trying to see the world from the child's perspective and so getting to understand how she feels. It is only when Pascale feels safe that she will make any progress towards mastery learning. Jeremy shows that he has already benefited from positive support at home; this now needs to be sustained in the nursery; at the same time Jeremy needs the psychological freedom to try out new things and ideas.

Practical suggestions

Observe

- Observe how babies signal their needs through crying, wriggling with discomfort, responding to attention.
- Observe a child's emerging schema, demonstrated through her patterns of play, e.g. lining up small animals in a row, covering objects, wrapping herself in a blanket.
- Observe individual children and note those who adopt mastery and helpless patterns of behaviour.

Continued

Continued

Get to know your children
- Consider your group/class and note how much you know about each individual child: their personal characteristics (likes, dislikes, interests, talents and learning dispositions). Ask yourself 'What is this child like and how do I know'?
- Fix a clipboard and pencil in all the areas of provision. Encourage all staff to note significant comments, questions and actions from different children as they work in these areas. At the end of the day, the key person can: collect these observations in regard to his/her children; reflect on any noted behaviour that is significant; decide on any implications for next steps.
- Plan a regular time at the end of each day/week when you meet as a staff and share any other information about children that you have gathered.

Create a climate to promote self-esteem
- Consider how your spoken and body language can affect small children, e.g. pursed lips, tensed body, toe tapping and abrupt tone of voice communicate irritability; a genuine smile, relaxed body posture, eye contact, gentle touch and warm voice communicate approachability and friendliness; a tight smile and rigid body posture communicate a mixed message and can confuse.
- Demonstrate that you are interested in, and have time for, each child, e.g. bend down to their level when speaking and listening to them; give them time to talk and try not to interrupt to cut across their thinking.
- Make each new baby and child feel special, e.g. ensure that babies are held in ways that they prefer and are soothed by tapes of rhymes and music that are familiar to them; ask each new child to bring in a photograph of herself and her family. This can be displayed on a large board and used as a topic of conversation.
- If funds allow or parents will contribute, arrange for each new child to have their photograph taken and enlarged. Attach the photograph to a card and cut to form a jigsaw. Older children will enjoy working in small groups and sorting out their own photograph and those of their friends.
- Pronounce children's names correctly – if this is difficult, be honest with parents and ask for their help.
- Remember and refer to important details in the child's life, e.g. How is your new kitten, Isaac? Did you enjoy the fair, Angelo?
- Provide mirrors in different parts of your environment to enable children to view themselves when working at different activities.
- Have artefacts and scenarios that reflect children's circumstances, e.g. books where the main characters look like them, dolls which resemble their colour and characteristics, domestic play scenarios which depict familiar contexts, posters and jigsaws which make people like them and their families appear important.

Help children to talk about themselves
- Ask children to do a painting/drawing of themselves and take time to listen to them talking about their picture.

Continued

Continued

- Ask children about their likes and dislikes about the food they eat, the clothes they wear and their favourite activities at home and in the nursery; these views can be scribed and displayed together with each child's self-portrait or made into individual books.

Provide for those children who are less secure
- Position coat pegs with the child's personal clothing so that children can see them during the day.
- Encourage children to bring a familiar toy to the nursery, in order to maintain a link with home.
- Support a child to separate from his parent/carer; suggest that he carries with him a personal memento that he can refer to during the session, e.g. a photograph of the parent or a personal item such as a scarf which carries a familiar perfume.
- Ensure that an adult is available to less secure children particularly at vulnerable times of the day, e.g. the start and the end of the session, at transition times, and when children are outside.
- Make it possible for these children to be physically near to an adult during group activities.

Help children to recognise what they have learned
- Publicise children's achievements, e.g. 'Liam is really good at doing up his buttons – would you like to show everyone, Liam?'
- Encourage children to teach others, e.g. showing a friend how to use the mouse on the computer; how to hang their painting to dry.
- Build into your session relaxed and informal recall sessions when older children demonstrate and discuss with others what they have experienced, e.g. six children with a key person when each child talks about and shows any outcomes of her most recent activity. It is important that each child feels free to opt out or to make a minimal response. As children grow accustomed to the session they can be encouraged to comment on other children's contributions.

Professional practice questions

1. How do my daily routines make it possible for me to get to know and treat my key children as individuals?
2. How does my environment demonstrate to children that they are welcome in the setting?
3. How far does my planning and provision reflect a balance between a 'controlling' and 'informational 'environment?
4. How are my children helped to consider critically what they achieve?
5. How do I help all my children to adopt mastery patterns of behaviour?

The following references in the *Early Years Foundation Stage* link to this chapter:

Statutory Framework and Guidance: pp. 12, 37
Practice Guidance: Appendix 2, Areas of Learning and Development
Self-confidence and Self-esteem (pp. 28–9)
Principles into Practice Cards: 3.2 Supporting Every Child, 3.3 The Learning
Environment, (The Emotional Environment) 4.2 Active Learning (Mental and
Physical Involvement)
The CD-ROM *in depth* offers further guidance on the above principles and
commitments.

The following Early Years Professional Standards link to this chapter:
1, 2, 3, 4, 8, 10, 14, 22, 25, 26, 27, 28.

REFERENCES

1. Siren Films (2008) *Attachment and Holistic Development. The first year.* DVD and User Notes, Siren Films Ltd.
2. Siren Films (2002) *Exploratory Play* DVD and User Notes, Siren Films Ltd.
3. Meggitt, C. (2006) *Child Development: An Ilustrated Guide.* London: Heinemann.
4. Holahan, C.K. and Sears, R.R. (1999) The gifted group in later maturity, in D. Goleman, *Working with Emotional Intelligence.* London: Bloomsbury, p. 71.
5. Katz, L.G. (1995) *Talks with Teachers of Young Children.* Norwood, NJ: Ablex.
6. Department for Education and Skills (DfES) (2007) *Practice Guidance for the Early Years Foundation Stage,* Appendix 2. London: DfES Publications p. 22.
7. Roberts, R. (1995) *Self-esteem and Successful Early Learning.* London: Hodder & Stoughton, p. 8.
8. Selleck, D. (2006) Key person in the Early Years Foundation Stage, *Early Education,* Autumn.
9. Waite, T. (1993) *Taken on Trust.* London: Hodder & Stoughton, p. 297.
10. Robinson, M. (2003) *From Birth to One: The Year of Opportunity.* Buckingham: Open University Press, p. 128.
11. Siraj-Blatchford, I. (2006) Diversity, inclusion and learning in the early years, in G. Pugh and B. Duffy (eds) *Contemporary Issues in the Early Years.* Fourth edition. London: Sage, p. 115.
12. White, M. (1996) What's so silly about self-esteem? *TES,* 26 April, p. 3.
13. Thomas, S. (2008) *Nurturing Babies and Children under Four.* London: Heinemann.
14. Tizard, B. and Hughes, M. (2002) *Young Children Learning.* Second edition. Oxford: Blackwell.
15. Fabian, H. (2002) Empowering children for transitions, in H. Fabian and A-W. Dunlop (eds) *Transitions in the Early Years.* London: Routledge and Falmer, p. 123.
16. Barratt, G. (1986) *Starting School: An Evaluation of the Experience.* Norwich: AMMA, University of East Anglia.
17. Athey, G. (1990) *Extending Children's Thinking.* London: Paul Chapman.
18. Nutbrown, C. (2005) *Threads of Thinking.* Third edition. London: Sage.
19. Bruce, T. (2005) *Early Childhood Education.* Third edition. London: HodderArnold.
20. Pen Green Staff (1995) *A Scheme Booklet for Parents and Carers.* Corby, Northamptonshire: Pen Green Centre for Under-Fives and their Families.

21. Community Playthings (2008) *I made a unicorn.* Robertsbridge, East Sussex: Community Playthings, www.community playthings.co.uk, p. 3.
22. Community Playthings (2008) op.cit. (note 21) p. 20.
23. Department for Education and Skills (DfES) (2007) Early Years Foundation Stage: Statutory Framework. London: DfES Publications, p. 16.
24. Bruce, T. (2005*) Early Childhood Education.* Third edition. London: HodderArnold.
25. Pollard, A. and Filer, A. (1996) *The Social World of Children's Learning.* London: Cassell, pp. 225–44.
26. Gura, R. (1996) What I want for Cinderella: self-esteem and self-assessment, *Early Education*, no. 19, Summer.
27. Deci, E.L. and Ryan, R.M. (1985) Intrinsic motivation and self-determination, in *Human Behaviour.* New York: Plenum Press.
28. Sylva, K. (1998) The early years curriculum: evidence based proposals. Paper prepared for NAEIAC Conference on Early Years Education.
29. Lafferty, P. (2007) A desire to learn or a desire to please, *Eye,* Vol. 9, No. 4, August, p. 8.
30. Costa, A.L. (1991) *The School as Home for the Mind.* Australia: Hawker Brownlow Education, pp. 53–66.
31. Gura, P., op. cit. (note 26).
32. Gaunt, C. (2008) Give them 'five a day' in praise, parents advised, in *Nursery World,* 20 November, p. 6.
33. Department for Education and Skills (DfES) (2007) Early Years Foundation Stage: CD-ROM *in-depth,* 4.2 Active Learning, p. 2. London: DfES Publications.
34. Gold, K. (1999) Making order out of chaos, *The Guardian Education,* 11 May, p. 2.
35. Dweck, C. (2006) *Mindset: The New Psychology of Success.* New York: Random House.
36. Vygotsky, L.S. (1978) *Mind and Society: The Development of Higher Psychological Processes.* Cambridge, MA: Harvard University Press.
37. Rogers, G. (1961) *On Becoming a Person.* Boston, MA: Houghton Mifflin.

2

Living and Learning with Others

Summary of contents

- Babies are attracted to others from birth and grow up in a social world which initially consists of the immediate family.
- Every child needs a key person to form a special relationship with them and provide them with a point of contact when they move to an early years setting.
- Young children learn to relate to a wider group of adults and children when they move from the security of home into a nursery setting. As they grow in confidence children relate to other children. Their friendships are dependent on them acquiring and practising complex social skills.
- The Early Years Foundation Stage is a time for practitioners to monitor and develop children's burgeoning social competence.

'Being good with people' has always been recognised as a strength in people's work and personal lives. Perhaps this is even more crucial in today's world when the pace of life does not easily allow time for personal contacts. Professor Philip Zimbardo of Stanford University told the British Psychological Society that we are entering a new ice age of non-communication. The use of computers, faxes and mobile phones and the disappearance of shop assistants and bank tellers with whom to 'pass the time of day' are contributing to what he calls a worldwide 'epidemic of shyness'. An increase of 40–60 per cent of this condition is reported in almost every country. Zimbardo's theory is that there is now less personal contact and small talk that holds communities together (1).

This malaise is certainly not evident in early years settings. Children are open and friendly. They chatter as they work and play. Disputes that flare up are usually settled amicably. Perhaps the most noticeable aspect to any newcomer visiting a nursery is its sociability. However this social environment is not achieved easily. We know that young children are, as with everything, brimming with potential but lacking in life experience; interpersonal skills only develop over time. Around the age of two young children start to respond with caring gestures to a person who is upset or hurt and begin to take some part in role play with others (2). Considerable social learning is required in learning to become part of a group and this aspect forms a major part of the Early Years Foundation Stage.

WHY DO SOCIAL RELATIONSHIPS MATTER?

When we consider the basic attributes for young children to acquire, social skills must be a priority. Our children live in a democratic society and in order to survive they must learn to rub along with others. We may know of adults who are able and attractive but for some reason they are not able to relate easily – they are uneasy with people and consequently people find them difficult. This can be a serious disability in life. Practitioners know that they have an important task to ensure that children are equipped to live with and relate easily to others.

A good experience of transition can enhance a young child's well-being and learning and a poor experience can cause damage. Having a friend is now found to be a strong factor in supporting a positive transition to a new setting. Children who move into a reception class or Year 1 alone can feel unsure, isolated, nervous, anxious and afraid. A friend (even a temporary one) can offer companionship, physical closeness, shared past experiences and reassurance. Howes showed that children who made transitions in daycare with friends found it easier than those who came alone (3). Judy Dunn also found that when children had moved with friends into new settings, they remembered that the friends had helped them to feel happy (4). There are wider claims that positive relationships with those around you and sustaining friendships is an important factor in gaining the desirable state of being happy (5).

THE PLACE OF SOCIAL SKILLS IN EARLY PERSONAL DEVELOPMENT

To ensure their healthy growth and development, babies and very young children need to feel securely attached and become socially competent.

Attachment

The Early Years Foundation Stage recognises the fundamental importance of attachment, which is dealt with later in the book (see Chapter 3). For the purposes of this chapter, we recognise that a secure initial attachment underpins any further relationships. Significant people who are special, and who forge a primary link with the young child, gently introduce him to the wider world; the special person encourages the child to branch out, meet new people and learn to trust others. This is beautifully illustrated in the DVD *Life at Two*, where at 26 months, Ava's very secure relationship with her mum helps her to adjust to her key person in the nursery (6). Maria Robinson suggests that the child who is loved, encouraged, respected and comforted is able to learn about the world in a context of emotional safety and about themselves as fundamentally loveable (7).

Social competence

Babies are primed to be social and to communicate. Within a very short period of time babies are 'reading' eye contacts, facial and body gestures and the tone of voice of those significant people who care for them. But we can't help but notice that some babies and toddlers are particularly keen to interact. My experience suggests that these are the small individuals who have already had their early attempts at conversations valued; they quickly learn that the sounds they make are of interest to adults and they want more of this affirming experience. The adult's task is to tune in to the baby's intentions and efforts and maintain this social dialogue. This applies even if the baby does not share a common spoken language with the practitioner as babies are able to tune in rapidly to other languages and will be reassured by warm gestures, expressions and tone of voice (8).

In order to communicate, babies, young children, and indeed all of us need to have someone to communicate with. Piaget (an educational giant in his time) encouraged us to believe that the very young child was a little scientist – the role of the practitioner was predominantly to provide interesting and stimulating resources and then observe the child as he freely interacts with them. This belief led to marginalising the adult's work. Further study has emphasised that all of us, children and adults, grow up and learn more with others. As a result, practitioners have an important responsibility to pave the way for young children to reach out and communicate with a widening circle.

Social relationships with peers develop very early out of the family. Babies will respond to other babies. Eleanor Goldschmeid and Dorothy Selleck have shown in their studies that children from a few weeks old are able to use sound, gazes and touches (later they exchange objects) to develop loyalties and attachments to other children in their group (9). From this very early start, other children continue to be important. Toddlers already show considerable interest in what people do. They tune in to how adults react to different situations and use these reactions as a point of reference for their own behaviour. All parents and caregivers will have experienced a toddler's delight when she is praised for an activity or their knowing look when the adult says 'no'. By three years, friendships start to become of interest although at this stage they are transitory. The development of relationships has always been a fundamental part of early childhood education. Young children are recognised not just as individuals but as part of their family. Practitioners recognise that the development of close links between the home and the setting is above all else in the interests of the child (see Chapter 10). Depending on their family experiences, children will also have learned a great deal already about getting on with people. They may be used to warm loving relationships within the family and have had many and varied chances to meet a wide circle of different adults and children. Other children may have been sheltered from social contacts, been reared in a culture of privacy, or live in geographically isolated areas with no other young families nearby. Parents are usually keen for their children to spread their social wings; for most parents, an important reason for sending their child to a nursery is to help them to mix with other people which they recognise as a key factor in living a happy and successful life.

Whatever social experiences young children have had prior to coming to an early years setting, it is likely that many relationships will have been established since babyhood and will have developed with the support of parents. The process of moving into a new environment and facing often a completely unknown group of children and adults is a challenge for any child. For those who have experienced only a small social circle of contacts at home the experience can be daunting. The vast majority of children now have some early experience in a nursery setting, but for the few who make a direct transition from home to a reception class in a mainstream school, this is probably the most challenging move for a child during her school career. In Pollard's study of five children who started school very shortly after their fourth birthday, the children's parents provided constant emotional, practical and intellectual support in the early days of school. Pollard emphasises the vital role that parents and carers play as the reference point and interpreter for their children as they move into a wider social context (10).

Relating to adults

Babies and toddlers are very concerned with themselves and they do need attention given to their particular needs. Most children will have received this at home as part of a loving upbringing. Parents and other close family members and friends will have listened, responded and demonstrated interest in all that the child does. Within this secure and interested environment children thrive. On moving to a group setting the child's first need is to develop a link with new adults whose task it is to provide a similar framework of security. When they first separate from their parents, children must be able to feel confident in the care of the people who are temporarily taking the place of their parents.

Children need to make this relationship with at least one adult in the setting who they know is there for them. This is no longer left to chance as it is now required for every baby and child in a setting to have a key person. The importance of a key person for babies and young children is described clearly by Rosie Roberts. She suggests that a key person and significant people at home often do the same things. They help the very young child manage through the day; they think about him; they get to know him well; they sometimes worry about him; they get to know each other; they talk about the child (11).

Confident and sociable children who are already socially experienced may rapidly 'branch out' to relate to other children. The Early Years Foundation Stage points out that creating a climate of good relationships will encourage children to relate to each other and suggest that early friendships can emerge in children as young as two years (12). Other children, however, continue to have a greater need for adult attention throughout their early years.

It may be that for various reasons, some children have been denied the time of an adult at home. Other children who initially may require a great deal of the practitioner's attention and time may be those who are used to having a great deal of attention – possibly an only or first child. Some children need the practitioner more at specific times when they are vulnerable – this can happen when a new baby arrives or if there is illness or turbulence in the family. In all these cases it is important for the practitioner to be aware of and to respond to individual needs and give the message that he or she is consistently there for the child.

Good communication is at the heart of any successful relationship; Petrie suggests that 'Whether it involves children, babies or adults, interpersonal communication is a two-way process. Listening to children shows our respect for them and builds their self-esteem' (13). In this context, it is a matter of the adult tuning in to all that young children are trying to convey. This involves using professional skills and developing attitudes which are at the heart of good practice. However, a study initiated by the Coram Family highlighted that this practice is far from universal. The 'Listening to Young Children Project and Training Framework' (14) began because of concerns, expressed particularly in national reports, that young children were not being given a voice. The project concluded that this was largely to do with a belief that children under eight years were too inexperienced to have a view or make a useful contribution about matters that concerned them. The Training Framework suggests ways in which children can be encouraged to communicate both verbally and through the visual and expressive arts.

DEVELOPING UNDERSTANDINGS AND SKILLS OF FRIENDSHIP

Making friends is very important to young children; they approach other children openly, often asking 'Will you be my friend?' They also show great distress if they are refused friendship. Common and heart-rending cries from some young children are 'Peter won't play with me' or 'Zareen says that she is not my friend'. One small-scale study demonstrated that when a number of children in a kindergarten left for their new school, both the group transferring and the group left behind showed signs of negative behaviour and mild distress.

Although the researcher admitted that the agitation demonstrated by the leaving group may have been due to the anticipated transfer, the group of children remaining appeared to have missed their 'friends' after they had gone (15).

Studies suggest that the first six or seven years of development are critical for the development of social skills. By four years a child should easily be able to deal with several peer relationships. If a child fails during this time to learn to relate to other children, this can lead to great unhappiness. Nurseries and schools, as we have seen, are social communities. If a child is condemned to attend school daily without having the support of friends she is unlikely to learn well; studies show that lack of friends can ultimately lead children to refuse to attend school (16).

Some children have difficulties with friendships, particularly if they are shy or not inclined to co-operate (17). Other reasons may be less obvious and the fact that most young children in the settings do make friends easily and quickly sometimes makes us overlook the complexities involved in establishing relationships. These complexities include developing certain understandings which are explored below.

Becoming aware of others' viewpoints

Piaget tested young children in a formal situation and consequently found that most individuals under four were not able to appreciate any other view than their own. However, as Margaret Donaldson has shown, when they respond in everyday situations that make sense to them, children show a higher level of understanding (18). The most familiar context for children is the home. Judy Dunn's work with young families in their homes shows that even babies in their first year are sensitive to those who are close to them. Toddlers less than two years old show some understanding of how older siblings will react when teased or annoyed (19.) They observe and are able to 'tune in' to quarrels between members of their family. Their own behaviour is sympathetic and supportive to the member of the family who is upset, but they are also able to recognise and join in with a shared joke. By the age of three, children in one of her studies were able to recognise, anticipate and respond to the feelings of their baby brothers or sisters (20). (See also Chapters 3 and 6.)

These studies offer powerful evidence of how, even before they can talk, very young children take a real interest in and begin to understand how other people behave. Although they are not able to appreciate another's perspective in an intellectual task, they already work from a sharp social intelligence. However, during these first three years of life, this understanding of people's behaviour is largely influenced by the child recognising feelings that they have themselves. In the best circumstances young children will have been able to observe family interactions and have been encouraged to take an active part in them. They are then able to take their social learning into a group setting.

Case study 📁

Jodie brought into the nursery her new teddy, which she had received for her fourth birthday. She proudly showed it to the other children but became very upset when Gary, a new three-year-old, grabbed it from her and sat on it. The other children pushed Gary away and returned the bear to Jodie. Later she was observed going to Gary and offering for him to borrow the bear. Jodie explained to her teacher that Gary was only little and she knew that he really wanted a bear like hers.

Comment

Jodie's generous response showed her ability to recognise, empathise and respond positively to Gary's envy and longing for a similar toy.

Figure 2.1 Children come to understand what is involved in being a friend and maintaining that friendship

Understandings about friendships

Young nursery-age children regard their current playmates as their friends. When a three-year-old says 'I'm your friend now', it's likely to mean that 'I am playing with you now'. By four, a friendship is becoming more stable, based on shared experiences over a period of time. At this age children look for each other in the nursery and may spend considerable amounts of time together. It is at this stage that 'friendship' has a much more sociable meaning although a long-lasting relationship is rare until a child is around seven or eight.

These social understandings are linked to a child's level of maturation. Generally speaking, the more practice that young children have in making and playing with friends the more experiences they will have of both rejection and acceptance. In this way they come to understand what is involved in being a friend and maintaining that friendship. However, it is not always simply a matter of providing the experience, as there are powerful factors, which affect relationships. Young children are differently equipped to make friends and have friendship preferences.

Ramsey suggests that young children's social behaviour can be grouped into four different categories (21):

- **Popular** children are usually very capable and more intellectually, socially and emotionally mature than their peers. It is also a sad but evident truth that popular children are often more physically attractive and this is particularly noticeable with little girls (22).
- **Rejected** children may show aggressive or withdrawn behaviour. They may angrily retaliate to others or avoid other children.
- **Neglected** children appear to take little part in the social life of the group and are often quite content with their own company.
- **Controversial** children are described as having a major impact on the social group, socially and intellectually talented but often in trouble for aggressive behaviour and rule breaking. Although these children are often group leaders, they are regarded with caution by some of their peers.

It can be helpful to recognise these behaviours, although Ramsey recognises that they are crude descriptors and many children may be socially well adjusted but not fit into these categories at all. When looking at friendship preferences research indicates that, for whatever reason, girls find it a little easier to make friends than boys. Children also tend to select friends who are like them. Thus the popularity of an individual child may be affected by the child being in a group with others of the same ethnic origin, or with those of a similar level of maturity or ability. Moreover, while little girls will play with either boys or girls, boys prefer to be with other boys.

Rubin's study of nursery-age children suggests that there are intricate social skills involved in making friends. These include the ability to gain entry to group activities, to be approving and supportive of one's peers, to manage conflicts appropriately and to exercise sensitivity and tact. The most popular children were seen to be particularly accomplished in using these skills (23).

The more experiences young children have of relationships and contacts with others in their play, the more they gain from it. Rubin's work and his reference to other studies show that the children who make friends easily show generous behaviour; they involve others in their play, praise them, show affection and care. These socially experienced children also learn that, in order to maintain a friendship, they need to recognise when others are upset and do something about it. They start to learn the skills of reconciling arguments and negotiating roles.

It is very noticeable when young children find it difficult to relate and establish friendships and it is important to distinguish between 'aloneness' as a matter of choice rather than necessity. 'Neglected' four-year-olds may have all the social skills to communicate and play with others, but may prefer to spend time alone. Practitioners quickly learn the difference between that autonomous and self-sufficient behaviour and behaviour demonstrated by the child who is longing but unable to relate to others. The 'rejected' children are the ones who become socially isolated, although this is not their choice.

Scarlett's study of nursery children suggests that socially isolated children spend a considerable amount of time 'on the sideline' observing others at play but without the strategies for joining in. When they do become involved, they are necessarily inexperienced players and they need direction from other children. This can mean that they are devalued in the group and they are very often the individuals who end up in role-play being the dog or the baby (24). When these children do try to make friends, their overtures to others are often either too timid or over-effusive and other children 'back off'. Vivien Paley vividly describes her concern about the social exclusion that operated in her class when some children announced to others 'you can't play' (25).

THE FAMILY AS A SOCIAL CONTEXT FOR LEARNING

Piaget's view of the child making sense of the world through her own investigation emphasised the importance of the environment rather than other people. Since then his views have been modified to take account of the importance of social contacts. We all need other people to help us learn and young children need adults and other children. Thus, a child's ability to form good relationships not only enhances her personal development but helps her to progress intellectually. Despite the quantity of daycare, most children still spend the bulk of their time at home, particularly those who are under two years, and during this time they learn a great deal from daily social interactions. One of the great strengths of family relationships is that they are founded on mutual interests and shared past experiences. Tizard and Hughes' classic study vividly describes the rich and easy conversations that can take place between parents and young children as a result of daily routines and social contacts (26). Any practitioner who has visited young children in their homes is aware of most children being comfortable and confident on known territory and with people who know them. One of the most challenging tasks for the practitioner home visiting for the first time is to develop a relationship with the child, given that she knows little about him. She will take care to be a gentle presence, only following a lead from the child, observing his interests and willingness to be approached. She carefully notes the parent's ways of holding, soothing and interacting with her child. This information is invaluable to pass on to the child's prospective key person, although ideally the key person should home visit as part of her role.

LEARNING WITH ADULTS IN THE EARLY YEARS SETTING

This task of really getting inside children's minds and understanding them can only be properly achieved though observing their actions and conversing with them. Since the last edition of this book there have been noticeable developments in these practices. Increasingly, practitioners recognise that observation is the basis for planning for young children's future development. Where this work is taken seriously, time is set aside to observe children at play and note their social behaviour. Young children's social development is going to be most noticeable in situations where they make decisions in self-chosen play experiences. A good rule of thumb is to follow advice from the National Assessment Agency for no more than 20 per cent of evidence for each scale in the Early Years Foundation Stage Profile to be drawn from observations of adult-focused or adult-led activity (27). This advice refers to children in the reception class. Younger children essentially need time for choice although they can benefit from social experiences focused and led by practitioners who know their key children really well and can build on play the children enjoy already.

Access to communication is every young child's entitlement and of course involves much more than talk. We know that long before young babies can communicate verbally, they listen to and respond to intonations in adults' voices. Tina Bruce and Jenny Spratt suggest that babies and children note and use:

> the sounds and subtle messages of non-verbal communications, to do with pauses, the music of anger, lovingly, affectionately muttered sounds, surprise, fear, protective shouts, a sudden look, meeting someone's gaze, or avoiding eye contact, pulling someone to look and share a focus, pointing (28).

Daily routines of meal times and nappy changing offer wonderful opportunities for informal social conversations with babies and toddlers. For those very young children who are new to English it is particularly reassuring if they can hear practitioners use a few words of their home language, but above all practitioners will take their cues from the baby and respond to their sounds, expressions and gestures. The overall experience should be relaxed and enjoyable for both parties.

By the age of two children start to use language to make sense of social boundaries such as telling others not to do things. Most three- and four-year-olds who are settled and secure in their setting are hungry to talk and by listening to them we gain insights into their interests and ideas. But adults also need to contribute in order to develop and sustain a conversation. Too often in the past dialogues with young children have been dominated by practitioners, using management talk, linked with routines such as clearing up, organisation of snack time and washing hands, with children not encouraged to have a voice (29, 30). Increasingly, practitioners recognise that a successful conversation with a child or small group of children needs to be reciprocal and based on the child's interest. And it is dependent on using similar interactions that we would have when chatting with an adult. Early Education training materials designed to support young children's thinking (see Chapter 3) suggest some useful common conversational ploys which include:

- tuning in – listening carefully to what the child is saying or conveying through gesture and expression
- showing genuine interest – giving eye contact, affirming, smiling, nodding
- respecting a child's own decisions and viewpoint
- inviting a child to elaborate on an idea – 'I really want to know more about this …'
- gently recapping or clarifying what has been said – 'so what you are saying is …'
- speculating on what might happen – 'I wonder …'
- offering an alternative viewpoint – 'maybe he wasn't the baddie …'
- sharing your own experience – 'I was scared of that bit as well …'
- asking open questions (but sparingly to avoid the impression of interrogation).

The training materials emphasise that adults who engage young children in worthwhile talk have established warm trusting relationships with them. 'They are able to enter the child's world, recognise his/her interests, dilemmas and concerns and have a conversation which encourages further thinking' (31).

Case study 📁

Leila in her first term in a reception class decided to make a box for her teddy to use as a hidey-hole. Margaret, a teaching assistant, observed her cutting out squares of thin cardboard to make the different faces of the box. Simon approached and commented that Leila would not be able to make a box like that because the pieces wouldn't stick together. Leila ignored him but became upset when she was clearly not succeeding with her construction. Margaret suggested that the three of them think of an alternative approach. Simon said that he had seen boxes stacked flat in the supermarket and the sides had been folded. He suggested that folding was a good idea. Margaret collected a box and together they looked at its construction. Leila was delighted to find that she could produce a box through a combination of folding and cutting. 'We're friends aren't we', she said. 'That's what friends do – they help each other.'

Comment

Margaret observed carefully and only intervened when Leila was upset. When she helped, it was to work alongside Leila and Simon as an equal partner. Her main role was to support both children on the basis of what she had observed. Leila's comment at the end shows how her experience of being helped confirmed in a practical way her view of what constituted friendship.

The potent role of the adults is further exemplified in the Italian pre-schools in Reggio Emilia. Warm, supportive relationships underpin all of the work with children but the scaffolding of learning is never underestimated. This scaffolding is likened to a game of ping-pong where the educator helps the child to clarify and articulate her ideas; she also picks up one child's idea and offers it for consideration within the group; other children throw back their responses. The educator also encourages conversations that help children to reflect, exchange and co-ordinate points of view; she acts as the 'memory' of the group by making tape recordings and taking photographs of the children's discussions and activities. The continuing relationship between the practitioner and child is recognised as so significant that in these schools children stay with the same teacher for three years (32).

This way of working is not limited to the Italian schools. In the best nursery settings in the UK, practitioners develop easy social relationships with children and with consummate skill use this as a means of helping children learn more.

LEARNING WITH OTHER CHILDREN

For years we have accepted the need for children to be with other children, to play together and learn how to live with others. In addition we now recognise how important children's relationships with one another are in assisting their thinking. Lev Vygotsksy strongly supported social learning; he claimed that mental activity begins with social contacts and exchanges between people. Eventually these exchanges are taken on board; a child will use conversations as a basis for her own thinking. Vygotsky suggested that what the child does in co-operation with others she eventually learns to do alone (33).

Azmitia's work also highlighted the value of shared thinking. She observed five-year-olds working in pairs and produced the following conclusions. Having a partner can increase the amount of time children work on a task. The presence of a partner can prevent children from giving up in a difficult situation and it can also provide added enjoyment to the activity. Moreover, when children work together this can often increase their total work strategies as different children bring different skills to a task. Finally, when less mature or less experienced children are paired with an older or more able partner, the 'novice' learns a great deal from observing her partner and through benefiting from 'expert' guidance (34).

Children new to a setting with English as an additional language can be helped greatly by another child (35).

Case study 📁

Antoni, three years old, had recently arrived in England and started at a nursery class attached to a primary school. He appeared very confused and his key person, Marie, despite trying different approaches, found it difficult to communicate with him. Although there were no adults in the school who spoke Polish there was one Polish boy in Year 1 who had adapted very well to school life. Marie introduced Brunon to Antoni and asked him if he would be a buddy to the younger boy. Brunon was delighted to be asked and to have the chance of conversing with another in his mother tongue. Brunon initially visited Antoni in the nursery daily for half an hour. He read stories with him and played with construction which was proving to be Antoni's favourite activity. Brunon also stayed near Antoni at lunch times – often eating with him and encouraging him to play outside. During these times Antoni proved to be a different child – vivacious, chatty and interested. By the end of half term the little boy was mixing with others, understood most of the routine of the day and used a few words of English. At that stage Brunon reduced his visits to one day a week.

Comment

Brunon played a very important role in helping Antoni settle into nursery life. Although he did not usurp Marie's role as a key person, initially Antoni trusted Brunon to interpret the nursery conventions for him and to represent his thoughts and views. Antoni's parents spoke very little English and it was Brunon who told Marie about Antoni's interest in animals and how he longed for a dog of his own. Marie built on this through showing Brunon photographs of her dog and later, bringing the dog to the nursery. Brunon also taught Marie several Polish words which were a great help in establishing early spoken conversations with Antoni.

However, not all young children socialise naturally and for some, as we have seen, social skills are difficult to acquire. In order for children to work collaboratively they have to learn the skills of turn taking and sharing. Sally Thomas suggests that young children are gently introduced to these skills through a progression: first helping the child to 'wait a minute' with adult support and then with a resource such as an egg timer, then taking turns in a structured game and finally in a freely chosen activity. The aim should be for the child by 5 years to share confidently but always with the proviso that maturation levels and circumstances may differ (36). The environment will also be influential. Elizabeth Jarman's useful toolkit encourages practitioners to look critically at how well their environments are designed to support children to communicate with one another (37).

In the Reggio Emilia schools practical ways of fostering social knowledge are encouraged deliberately through their project work and the way in which the building is planned. Dressing-up areas are situated in a central area; classrooms are connected by phones, passageways and windows; both dining areas and cloakrooms are designed to encourage children to get together; the daily menu for lunch is a vivid display of close-up colour photos of the food to be served that day, encouraging children to comment on the shape of the pasta or the colour of the vegetable.

Furthermore, these Italian pre-schools believe passionately in the effectiveness of learning in small groups; the staff consider that this is the most favourable type of organisation for an education which is based on relationships.

Figure 2.2 What a child learns to do in co-operation with others he eventually learns to do alone

These small groups are not set up as a convenient way of managing learning but as the best way. Staff assert that contact between children can provide opportunities for negotiation and communication that can be at least equal to that achieved when an adult is working with a child, and sometimes greater. When children are with children the contacts are equal; although children can learn a great deal with an adult there can be the relationship of authority and dependence, which can detract from a child's confidence. When children form their own groups they choose to work with others who share their interests or schemes of thinking (see also Chapter 5). Cath Arnold found that children played in this way in her family group at the Pen Green Centre; she also noted that when disputes arose, this was often because these interests or schemas conflicted (38). My own observations of four-year-olds revealed some particularly concentrated work from pairs of boys who shared the same schema.

Case study 📂

Mark and Ben, three years six months, used large brushes and buckets of water to paint patterns on stone paving slabs. They painted long, straight lines and matched them for length. Mark noticed nearby pine trees and commented that their lines were like 'lying down trees'. Ben said that they could make their trees stand up and he rushed off for some drawing paper and pencils. The boys drew their trees, and compared them as horizontal lines and as vertical lines when they held the paper up. Mark drew two short vertical lines on a separate piece of paper which he described as baby trees which are still lying down.

Comment

The boys shared a strong interest in up and down (vertical schema). They rubbed ideas off against one another and Ben discovered how to transfer one means of representation to another.

MONITORING THE DEVELOPMENT OF SOCIAL SKILLS

Children's social development is dramatic during the first six years of life. The very experience of being alongside other adults and peers means that all children 'pick up' some of the conventions of living and learning in a group. Depending on their starting point, for some individuals this is a hard and slow lesson, while others leap ahead with their interpersonal skills and show an ability to lead and influence others. Most practitioners are broadly aware on a day-to-day basis of their children's different levels of sociability. Others dig more deeply; they closely observe and reflect on the child's play and activity in order to acquire a properly informed and more detailed picture. The Social Play Continuum developed by Pat Broadhead (39) provides a useful tool for observing and assessing children's social play. It highlights four domains of play – associative, social, highly social and co-operative. The emphasis in the observations is on the children's activity and use of language, with a stress on continuity and progress as play moves across the four domains. Some helpful signals of progression are identified, one being when children's actions and language become reciprocal. Another sign is the impacts of altercations on play; for example, in the earlier domains the adult is often called on to resolve a dispute which inevitably halts the momentum of the play; when children play more co-operatively, they tend to resolve their own disputes rather than call on an adult to intervene.

The Social Play Continuum not only provides a good structure for observations, but also encourages practitioners to assess the level of play in a particular area of provision and to reflect what action might help children to move into a higher social domain.

GROWING TO BE A GOOD CITIZEN

Although the term 'citizenship' is not included in the Early Years Foundation Stage Guidance it is very applicable in the early years. If children can learn to be at ease with others and start to develop a social responsibility for them, then clearly this will affect their personal well-being, but will also better prepare them to contribute in a larger social world. Consideration for others must be learnt early on and good interpersonal skills are one of the most valuable of all factors when we look at what contributes to success in life. On a broader canvas it matters as well. Every day we are confronted with examples of inhumanity: random killings, intransigent racism, callous indifference to the plight of poor people and the casual sacrifice of human lives for minor material gain. Surely, by helping our young children develop a greater awareness and concern for others and skills to relate to them, we can hope that, in some way, we are contributing to the future state of human relations.

Practical suggestions

Observe developing social relationships
- Observe how babies make contact with others, through gazing, imitating and responding to interactions particularly from their key person.
- Observe how toddlers reach out to other children, initially by playing alongside them, handing out and receiving objects.
- Observe how children aged 3–5 years approach others to make friends.

Learn more about children's relationships
- Note the patterns of young children's friendships to find out who are the most popular and those children who have difficulties in making relationships.
- Note children in role play and identify the leaders, followers and those on the sidelines. Note friendship patterns in various activities; which children are constantly together; which children share similar interests (schema); and how they share this in their construction/drawing/painting/movement/stories.

Strengthen your relationships with children
- Consider what messages you send to babies and children through non-verbal communication. Think what signals you convey at the start and end of the day, when you hold a baby when you feed her and when you prepare a toddler for a rest time.

Support children's friendships
- Place babies lying and seated alongside one another and offer treasure baskets for them to 'share'.

Continued

Continued

- Model caring and sharing skills in role play, e.g. comforting a sad doll, sharing a cake with teddy.
- Give new children a 'friend' on their arrival in the nursery. Emphasise the importance of this role and encourage the 'friend' to take real responsibility for showing the new child the nursery routines.
- Provide a large stuffed animal and place it in a quiet corner of the nursery. The animal is introduced as a friend to anyone who is feeling lonely.
- Give children 'access strategies' to enable them to join a group: encourage hesitant children to join in with an activity by imitating what other children are doing. By doing this the child is often accepted as part of the group.

Help children to appreciate the effect of external events on friendships
- Support those children whose friends move away with their families. Encourage two friends to each make a gift by which they can remember one another, e.g. a special shell or stone which they found in the nursery garden or a photograph in a frame.
- Help children to accept that although they will feel lonely if they are parted from their friend (on account of holidays or illness), this is an opportunity to try out new friendships.
- Encourage a child to keep a scrapbook of nursery activities while a friend is in hospital. This can be given as a present.
- Encourage children to think of their friends whilst they are on holiday and to send them a postcard.

Provide specific support for those children who lack friendship skills
- Work with small groups of children and use puppets and miniature dolls to enact scenarios and provoke discussion. Help children to develop their understandings about relationships. Use events and comments that occur in the nursery as a starting point, e.g. taking turns, being kind and offering to play with a new child, ensuring that no one is lonely.

Provide activities and opportunities which encourage children to share and take turns
- Purchase wheeled toys which are for two children to ride. Help children to agree that each should have a set number of turns jumping down from the climbing frame. Have a large illustrated rota for cookery to allow each child to see when it is her turn.
- Provide 'treasure boxes' which contain props and dressing-up clothes to suggest different types of role play.
- Provide for small-scale play, e.g. identify a designated and preferably secluded area.
- Provide a selection of attractively decorated boxes which contain small-scale people, animals and vehicles. Include ready-made floor layouts or a sheet and felt tip pens for children to create their own floor map.

Professional practice questions

1. How well do we communicate with babies and very young children during daily routines?
2. How does my room arrangement encourage babies to be with others, children to talk together, to share and co-operate?
3. Have I sufficient apparatus to enable children to have reasonable opportunities to share and take turns?
4. How well does the layout of my outside area and the resources promote children's social skills?
5. How well do I tune in to children's thoughts and concerns through: listening to what they say, noticing their actions, reflecting on their meanings?
6. How do I extend my relationships with children to share thinking with them?
7. What model of social behaviour do I provide for my children when I interact with them, their parents and other adults?
8. How closely do I monitor children's social development and use the information gained to improve it?

The following references in the *Early Years Foundation Stage* link to this chapter:

Statutory Framework and Guidance: p. 12
Practice Guidance: Appendix 2, Areas of Learning and Development Making Relationships (pp. 30–2)
Principles into Practice Cards: 2.1 *Respecting each Other (Friendships)*, 2.3 *Supporting Learning*, 2.4 *Key Person (Secure Attachment)*
The CD-Rom *in depth* offers further guidance on the above principles and commitments.

The following Early Years Professional Standards link to this chapter:
1, 3, 7, 12, 17, 25, 26, 28.

REFERENCES 📖

1. Zimbardo, R. (1997) quoted in the *Guardian,* 22 July, p. 8.
2. David, T., Gooch, K., Powell, S., and Abbott, L. (2003) *Birth to Three Matters: A Review of the Literature.* London: DfES, p. 58.
3. Howes, C. (1987) Peer interaction of young children, in *Birth to Three Matters: A Review of the Literature* op. cit. (note 2), p. 66.
4. Dunn, J. (1993) *Young Children's Close Relationships. Beyond Attachment.* Newbury Park, CA: Sage.
5. BBC 2 (2006) The Science of Happiness, in BBC series *The Happiness Formula.* 30 April.

6. Siren Films (2006) *Life at Two: Attachments, Key People and Development.* Siren Films Ltd, www.sirenfilms.co.uk
7. Robinson, M. (2003) *From Birth to One: The Year of Opportunity.* Buckingham: Open University Press.
8. Department for Children, Schools and Families (DCSF) (2007) *Supporting Children Learning English as an Additional Language.* London: DCSF, www.dcfs.gov.uk
9. Goldschmeid, E. and Selleck, D. (1996) *A Framework to Support Children in their Earliest Years.* London: DfES.
10. Pollard, A. and Filer, A. (1996) *The Social World of Children's Learning.* London: Cassell.
11. Roberts, R. (2002) *Self-Esteem and Early Learning,* Second edition. London: Paul Chapman Publishing.
12. Department for Education and Skills (DfES) (2007) *The Early Years Foundation Stage, Positive Relationships, Effective Practice: Respecting Each Other* CD-ROM. London: DfES.
13. Petrie, P. (1997) *Communicating with Children and Adults: Interpersonal Skills for Early Years and Play Work,* Second edition. London: Arnold, p. 25.
14. Coram Family Sure Start (2004) *Listening to Young Children: A Training Framework.* Buckingham: OUP.
15. Field, T. (1984) quoted in R.K. Smith and H. Cowie (1991) *Understanding Children's Development.* Oxford: Blackwell, p. 102.
16. Parker, J. and Asher, S. (1987) Peer relations and later personal adjustment: are low accepted children at risk? *Psychological Bulletin,* Vol. 102, pp. 358–89.
17. Department for Education and Skills (DfES) (2007) *The Early Years Foundation Stage: Principles into Practice 2.1 Respecting Each Other.* London: DfES.
18. Donaldson, M. (1978) *Children's Minds.* London: Fontana.
19. Dunn, J. and Kendrick, C. (1982) *Siblings: Love, Envy and Understanding.* Cambridge, MA: Harvard University Press.
20. Dunn, J. and Munn, P. (1985) Becoming a family member: family conflict and the development of social understanding in the second year, *Child Development,* Vol. 56, pp. 480–92.
21. Ramsey, P.C. (1991) *Making Friends in School.* New York and London: Teachers College Press.
22. Vaughan, B.E. and Langois, J.H. (1983) Physical attractiveness as a correlate of peer status and social competence in pre-school children, *Developmental Psychology,* Vol. 191, pp. 561–7.
23. Rubin, Z. (1983) The skills of friendship, in M. Donaldson (ed.) *Early Childhood Development and Education.* Oxford: Blackwell.
24. Scarlett, W.G. (1983) Social isolation from age-mates among nursery school children, in Donaldson op. cit. (note 18).
25. Paley, V.G. (1992) *You Can't Say You Can't Play.* Cambridge, MA: Harvard University Press.
26. Tizard, B. and Hughes, M. (2002) *Young Children Learning,* Second edition. Oxford: Blackwell.
27. Qualifications and Curriculum Authority (QCA) (2008) *The Early Years Foundation Stage Profile Handbook.* www.naa.org.uk
28. Bruce, T. and Spratt, J.(2008) *Essentials of Literacy from 0–7.* London: Sage, p. 16.
29. Woods, D., McMahan, L. and Cranstoun, L. (1980) *Working with Under-Fives.* London: Grant McIntyre.
30. Sylva, K., Roy, C. and Painter M. (1980) *Child Watching at Playgroup and Nursery School.* London: Grant McIntyre.
31. Dowling, M. (2005) *Supporting Young Children's Sustained, Shared Thinking: An Exploration.* Early Education, www.early-education.org.uk

32. Gandini, L. (1993) Fundamentals of the Reggio Emilia approach to early childhood education, *Young Children,* November, pp. 4–8.
33. Vygotsky, L.S. (1962) School instruction and mental development, in Donaldson op. cit. (note 18).
34. Azmitia, M. (1988) Peer interaction and problem solving: when are two heads better than one? *Child Development,* Vol. 59, pp. 87–96.
35. Department for Children, Schools and Families (DCSF) (2007) op. cit. (note 8), p. 10.
36. Thomas, S. (2008) *Nurturing Babies and Children Under Four.* London: Heinemann, p. 34.
37. Jarman, E. (2007) *Communication Friendly Spaces.* London: The Basic Skills Agency, www.basic-skills.co.uk.
38. Arnold, C. (1990) quoted in T. Bruce (1997) *Early Childhood Education.* London: Hodder & Stoughton, p. 81.
39. Broadhead, P. (2004) *Early Years Play and Learning: Developing Social Skills and Co-operation.* London: RoutledgeFalmer.

Becoming Independent

Summary of contents

- Babies are born with the powerful urge to be independent but early experiences strongly influence their later ability to take responsibility for themselves.
- A young child's independence is reflected in his readiness to separate from home and move into a group environment. It is also evident in his development of physical and practical self-help skills.
- Young children can be helped to have a stake in their learning through: making choices and decisions; asking questions; and making connections through engaging in sustained, shared thinking.

Independence is an essential life skill and one that needs to be nurtured from the earliest age. There is general awareness in early childhood settings that young children should be encouraged to become independent; however, the term is often understood to mean different things. For example, some practitioners consider that the main aim should be to support children to be able to be apart from their families for periods of time or become self-sufficient in personal care such as toileting, washing and dressing; others believe that the priority is to develop children who can think for themselves. In fact all aspects of independence are important in order for young children to take steps to become self-standing individuals.

THE DRIVE FOR INDEPENDENCE STARTS EARLY IN LIFE

Although very young babies are necessarily dependent on their care-givers for their physical needs, as Winnicott stresses, babies are 'going concerns' whose growth and development are 'inevitable and unstoppable' (1). It quickly becomes noticeable that babies do exercise choices in what they play with, what they like to eat and when they sleep. These decisions about their physical needs and their subsequent levels of independence are significantly affected by the style of care-giving. Winnicott suggests that when adults feel responsible for shaping and forming children without being aware of these processes of developing auton-omy, they make life difficult both for themselves and for the small people with whom they are living. Winnicott's views are borne out when we see adults either restricting children's development or pressurising them into achieving develop-mental milestones too early. Two-year-old Elise was fiercely protected at home. She was never allowed to try to climb stairs or steps and only allowed to walk out-side on a rein with an adult. These restrictions continued until Elise was four years old. By this time her movements were poorly co-ordinated and tentative. At the other extreme some parents are very keen to accelerate their children's inde-pendence. Sitting up, walking and becoming dry at night become milestones that are immensely important to achieve early. Both of these shaping approaches stem from loving parents who genuinely want the best for their children. Elise's par-ents, however, failed to trust her to learn through trial and error; on the other hand, parents who do not understand that independence only grows from a time of dependence and push their children towards maturity before they are ready, risk them experiencing failure and losing confidence. In both cases this can lead young children to become over-dependent. Jenny Lindon states that 'We need to resist over-loading young children with stimulation and to avoid the "build bet-ter baby" type products that have emerged, especially in the United States'. Lindon suggests that babies and toddlers need time to use their physical abilities and apply their ideas. 'The clear preference of very young children for "do it again" is ideal for their learning' (2).

Settings are increasingly aware that, given scope, babies and toddlers are capa-ble of making decisions for themselves. For example, a baby will choose which items to select in a treasure basket. Mobile babies may select a new area of the room to explore or, according to their sleep patterns, may move in and out of sleep nests or use sleep mats as they choose. Opportunities for these choices demonstrate the respect that staff give to such young children, and also of their belief that even at this age babies are capable of deciding what is best for them.

SOCIAL AND EMOTIONAL INDEPENDENCE

As children develop from birth they move from home to a different learning environment. Each transition is a major event for a baby or child and during the early years it is likely that children experience more 'handovers' than they ever will in later stages of their lives. Moreover, every baby and child will encounter a transition differently.

'Some children and their parents will find transition times stressful while oth-ers will enjoy the experience' (3). This statement from the Early Years Foundation Stage highlights the need to tailormake the experience to fit each child and family rather than expect them to fit in to a standard arrangement. However, all babies and children are likely to go through common stages in transition, which Manchester Education Partnership usefully identify as Trying to Let Go, Being Uncertain and Taking Hold (4). These will be explored in turn.

Trying to Let Go is a stage when young children can feel confused and over-whelmed as they leave a secure and familiar context for new horizons. For a baby or toddler making a first move away from home this is a huge step as they are pitched into a welter of new sensory experiences – different sights, sounds and smells. The greatest change of course for the very young child is the move away from her parent to a stranger (albeit her key person). The role of the key person is explored further in Chapter 4, but her primary responsibility here is to support the young child's move into the wider world through forming a sim-ilar (but not identical) attachment to the one which the child has already with her parent or primary carer. We know now that a successful initial attachment helps the child to make easy steps from being dependent on a close family member to a widening social contact; a child who has made a successful initial attachment within the family is more likely to bond happily with another sig-nificant person. Nevertheless very young children under two can experience high levels of stress when they move into a group setting. A Cambridge study of babies (11–20 months) during the first nine days of daycare, who were start-ing nursery full time after being cared for at home, showed doubled levels of the stress hormone cortisol. Even five months later, these levels were still sig-nificantly high (5). Although the authors of the report emphasised that there was no evidence of long-term effects of high cortisol levels it alerts as to how very young children can be psychologically challenged. If we are surrounded by strange people and unknown events, we are really in survival mode, unsure, suspicious, disempowered and so unable to start to 'feel our feet'. This disem-powerment can apply equally to babies and older children during the early days of separation although responses can vary. In a study of four-year-old children moving into reception classes (6), parents recounted their children's different responses. For example, one child was hesitant about lining up with others in the playground; another self-reliant child complained to his mum about her accompanying him into school. Although it is usually desirable for parents ini-tially to spend some time in the setting with their children, this last comment highlights the need for rules to accommodate individual needs. Consideration of the child's previous experience in being separated from home and observa-tions of her levels of confidence and adaptability in the new reception class should always play a part when deciding when it is appropriate for parents to leave their child. The teachers in the reception class study made great efforts to help children into school. This was easy when admitting small groups initially on a staggered basis. One or two upsets were reported as later groups of children were admitted into a larger class group.

When a child starts in an early years setting, ideally any family should feel that the staff are doing all possible to accommodate their needs. Initial time spent with the family may well avoid anxieties and problems arising at a later stage. In order for a new child to feel comfortable about leaving her mum or dad she must be at ease in her new setting. Such rituals as finding coat pegs, learning how to hang up a coat, moving into a room with other children and saying goodbye take time. Some small individuals will respond to these new procedures easily and rapidly; they are very ready for this new experience. Others are unsure and each new step is a burden; in this circumstance any moves to try to jolly the child into separating from her parent or carer is misguided; the child is not yet ready to make this tremendous move on her own and patience, sensitivity and more time are needed.

Being Uncertain Even when a young child is able to separate from her parent she may still feel apprehensive about the new experiences on offer, particularly when she encounters something new to contend with. Babies and children can face transitions on a daily basis when they are moved from one provision to another. Even within a children's centre where all provisions are under one roof a toddler may arrive early for a breakfast club, move onto core provision in a different room, into the hall for lunch and onto daycare in the afternoon. At the end of the day the toddler may join a wider age group in a different room for teatime and a story. Each one of these transitions can require the toddler to mix with different adults and children, recognise and adjust to different expectations and routines, and adapt to a new environment. To avoid these considerable and confusing challenges staff need to work closely together to provide common and constant approaches which allow a child to feel on familiar ground wherever she is during the day.

Older children can face similar challenges (see Chapter 4). There is also no clear evidence to show that pressure for children to attend school early is worthwhile. Indeed, Caroline Sharp's paper relating to school starting ages for children across the world indicates that a late start to school appears to have no adverse effect on children's progress (7).

Travelling through the Early Years Foundation Stage involves babies and young children moving into different groups or classes. Each move is a rite of passage and potentially a celebration of children's progress and achievement. Any rite of passage involves change and disequilibrium. It can cause us to be excited and full of anticipation but can equally stir up feelings of anxiety, trepidation, uncertainty and fear. These negative feelings can very effectively diminish self-esteem (see Chapter 1) and can mean that a child doesn't feel in control. Uncertainties occur when children encounter difference. While any transition will provide new challenges, these can easily prove to be overwhelming. Initially a child needs to recognise and feel reassured by elements of the familiar.

Practitioners should expect to spend more time with the child who is still insecure in a new setting and is emotionally dependent on one adult. Although we know that young children need to be helped to make a gentle and comfortable initial transition, there are instances when children do not have enough adult support once their parent has left them. An early study of transition from home to pre-school found that the total adult time given to all new children was less than 10 per cent (8). Thirty five years later, my own study of pre-school settings showed that, although never neglectful, in some cases practitioners were not being sufficiently proactive; new children were more likely to be left to their own devices unless there were noticeable signs of distress. At this point a child was always comforted and often encouraged to stay with an adult for the rest of the session. However, that is often too late; experienced and good quality early years practitioners are very aware that young children can appear to be coping with situations but are in fact finding situations very stressful. During the initial days in the setting children should be observed closely by their key person who will understand that transition is a process rather than a one-off event (9). It is helpful if each child knows that at all times there is one adult in particular who is there for them and this is now assured through the requirement for a key person. In this way children are reassured that they are never on their own; this reassurance prevents the bottling up of anxiety which can then lead to problems at a later stage. Over time and given initial help, children delight in learning that they can cope for themselves in many new situations.

Many children receive a great jolt in their early years learning journey when they move from the reception year at the end of the Early Years Foundation Stage into a different culture in Year 1 (see Chapter 4). Increasingly, staff recognise that it is important to minimise change during this experience. Reception and Year 1 teachers try to look at the transition from the child's perspective and consider useful questions such as: what do our children see, experience and encounter that is the same and that is different when they move from reception into Year 1? (10).

Taking Hold Helping children to feel secure and to be comfortable with others are basic requirements for any sound transition. But only when a child shows that they want to branch out and investigate on their own or with others can we be sure that the transition has been successful. This might include:

- a baby who crawls away from her key person, but turns back just to check that the adult is still there
- a two-year-old who plays happily alongside other children, observing and mimicking their actions
- a four-year-old who enters a classroom and wanders over to join a group of other children in the construction area.

These observations indicate that young children are starting to feel that they belong. The baby trusts her key person to remain in sight and support her adventures. Infants and children are beginning to feel part of a group.

Children become more sure of their new identity as members of the setting as they become familiar with the pattern of the day. This helps them to feel in control of what they experience; they are able to predict what will happen next rather than being simply passive recipients to what is happening. Young children will demonstrate their growing familiarity with the setting by placing events into a sequenced framework. When a child recounts her 'script', this tells us a story about her understanding of what she is experiencing during the day.

Case study 📁

I visited a reception class three days after children had started school. I wanted to find out how much of an understanding children had about school life in this short space of time. I approached Gavin and asked him, 'What do you do in this school?' He paused for a moment and then told me 'Well, we paint and draw and go outside to play. Sometimes we have a story and we must try to sit and cross our legs'. After another pause, Gavin continued, 'That's not all. We have lunch and then we go to the hall. I like that. We have to take off our clothes and put them together, 'cos they will get lost. Then our mummies come to take us home'. Over the other side of the class I approached Joe with the same question. Joe avoided looking at me. He simply hung his head and muttered, 'I dunno, I dunno'.

Comment

After only three days in school Gavin has already got a wonderfully clear grasp of some main school events. His detailed script and understanding of what is required and why shows that he is rapidly feeling himself to be a member of the class community. Joe, on the other hand, is lost. He is unable to talk to me about his life at school because at this stage he has no clear understanding. Things happen during the course of the day over which he feels he has no control. For Joe, school life is still a buzzing confusion; he needs considerable support from a caring adult who will help interpret events for him.

PHYSICAL AND FUNCTIONAL INDEPENDENCE

Healthy babies and toddlers strive to develop skills that enable them to become less physically dependent upon adults. A one-year-old may start to use a feeding cup and want to feed herself. Toddlers insist on trying to dress and feed themselves, they start to control their toileting habits and they want to move to explore new territories. Three- and four-year-olds progress and refine these skills. They learn the sequence of dressing themselves and develop their fine motor skills to enable them to deal with zips and buttons on clothes. They learn to go to the lavatory unaided. Their co-ordination improves and they are able to pour a drink for themselves and carry a plate of fruit to the table. As they gain confidence they practise their physical skills using apparatus both inside and outside. The child who is physically able to climb by himself to the top of the climbing frame has achieved a considerable milestone in independence.

Loving parents recognise that each developmental step towards physical independence is a significant achievement for their child. They proudly recount to friends and family each new example of what their child has managed to do for herself. Despite this, some parents are not always aware of their role in encouraging self-sufficiency. Although their child often surprises them they are understandably not sure of what to expect. They know that at two and three years

Figure 3.1   Physical independence is very important

Figure 3.2   Some parents promote their child's autonomy

children do not write or draw representational pictures and so it may not occur to them to give a child a pencil or crayon in order to practise making marks. Moreover, time is often the enemy. Naturally, young children's manual dexterity will not allow them to do things swiftly. Fumbling small fingers struggle with buttons when dressing and turning on the tap. In the bustle of daily life it is much easier to do things for the child than to wait for what seems endless time to allow her to try for herself. Parents and carers are also rightfully protective of their children. This sometimes leads them to be over-anxious about their physical safety. Elise, as we saw earlier, was protected from potential hazards inside and outside the home. Her parents could not bear to think of her tumbling down a step, or even falling in the garden.

In other families young children's autonomy is not only celebrated but carefully promoted. Toddlers are encouraged to feed themselves early on, even though the initial results are messy. Parents show their child how to put their vest on and do not worry if socks are first put on inside out. They provide equipment for drawing, painting and sticking and simply let their child experiment. They allow their children to take some small physical risks in learning to climb and balance on equipment in a playground, while standing by alert to prevent any real danger. Moreover, some parents help their young children to become practical and useful members of the family; they are shown how to take responsibility for small tasks such as watering the plants, laying the table and helping to wipe up pans in the kitchen. They may help to fetch and carry things for a new baby.

As a consequence of their different home experiences, when children start at a nursery setting their physical independence will differ vastly. Some three-year-olds will have had little opportunity to practise physical skills for themselves and may find co-ordination difficult. They have learned to be dependent; their initial drive and confidence to try for themselves has lessened and they expect others to try for them. Other children of the same age are agile and physically confident. They can cope with their personal needs and are very keen to apply their physical skills in the new experiences offered in the nursery. They are keen to extend their functional skills in the nursery and take messages or a piece of apparatus to another room or help to mix the paints. Some children are particularly adept at doing these things and become known for their reliability.

Practitioners realise that those children who are already physically independent are likely to adapt more easily to life in the setting. Children who are more dependent need time and encouragement. They also need to know that although they will be helped, it is expected that they will become physically self-reliant. Usually, once they recognise this, the vast majority of children grow in confidence and will fulfil expectations by the end of the reception year to 'dress and undress independently and manage their own personal hygiene' (11).

Case study 📂

Andrew appeared to adapt reasonably well to the nursery except for periods of out-door play. Whenever these times were voluntary for children, Andrew opted to stay indoors, even in very warm weather. On the one daily occasion when all children were expected to have time outside, Andrew did all he could to hide, or pretended that he had lost his shoes. His key worker Sue noticed this at an early stage and made a particular effort to stay and chat with Andrew during outside sessions. It eventually became clear that Andrew was afraid that if he played outside he would not be able to locate the lavatories (which were situated inside the building). Sue reassured him that if in need, he should simply let her know and she would return inside with him. This worked successfully; after one week when Sue accompanied Andrew to the lavatory, he told her that 'he knew the way now to have a wee' and didn't need her.

Comment

Sue's early observations of Andrew's behaviour resulted in her spending time with him to forge a relationship and gently find out the cause of his concern. Her practical support allowed Andrew to cope with outdoor play and also to practise finding his way round the new nursery building. Once Andrew became familiar with the location of the lavatories he was keen to demonstrate his independence.

A degree of physical and functional independence assists young children to feel more in control of their own lives and gives them self-respect. It is also extremely helpful to busy parents and practitioners if children are able to cope with their own physical needs. However these skills are not acquired out of thin air; they need to be taught gently and systematically with plenty of encouragement. Sally Thomas refers to a helpful technique known as backward chaining (12). This is a form of scaffolding where the adult initially offers close support and gradually withdraws it as a child becomes competent to cope for himself. Adam, nearly three years old, was keen to learn to dress himself. His key person demonstrated and talked through each step, including folding each item of clothing in turn when undressing in order to retrieve each item easily and the sequence in which to dress. Gradually this scaffolded support was lessened as Adam became more competent and his achievements were celebrated. Schools have traditionally always stressed the desirability of new children having physical self-help skills and most emphasise this in school brochures for new parents. However, it does not just rest there. If we consider independence in a broader sense it should include children's development as independent learners.

INTELLECTUAL INDEPENDENCE

Most practitioners would agree that it is helpful for both children and adults if children are trained to tidy away resources after playing with them, or to take messages. There remains less certainty about the extent of intellectual independence that should be encouraged. And yet, this wider issue of intellectual independence is possibly more crucial to children's futures.

This view was officially supported by the government, probably most famously in the Plowden Report in 1967 when Lady Plowden recommended that 'children should be agents in their own learning' (13). During the 1990s, the Plowden Report was largely discredited as being utopian. However, the belief that young children should be supported to and act for themselves is now strongly represented in the Early Years Foundation Stage (14), and for children at Key Stage 1 it is included in the non-statutory guidance for citizenship (15). A report from the Joseph Rowntree foundation stresses how important it is to involve young children in making decisions about all aspects of their lives. It makes the important point that often our youngest citizens are ignored. They have very different needs and interests to older children and yet many consultations effectively exclude anyone under eight years of age (16).

Anyone who has been employed in or visited a setting where young children are working autonomously, making decisions about what they are doing with whom and where, cannot fail to be impressed with the control that these children have over the activity in their lives. It is clear that when children are encouraged and expected to use their minds they show themselves to be very capable. It is now generally accepted that babies and young children are already powerful and persistent thinkers. Although they lack experience of the world, they compensate for this to a large extent by their inner drive to make sense of all that they experience. Given the opportunity they will self-direct themselves.

Case study 📁

Carl, three years and four months old, had taken great care to build a construction of blocks which he proudly described as his house. He told his teacher that he wanted to show it to his mum. Rosemary, his teacher, explained gently that this would not be possible, as today his neighbour would be collecting him from the nursery at the end of the session. Carl persisted that he wanted his mum to see his work. Rosemary suggested that Carl thought carefully about how this might be possible. After a pause, Carl declared that he would draw his construction. He spent 20 minutes on his drawing ensuring that the representation was completely accurate. Rosemary provided him with ribbon and helped Carl to present his drawing as a scroll.

Comment

Instead of providing Carl with a solution to his problem, Carl's teacher made it possible for him to make his own decision. The amount of time spent on the drawing and the quality of the work reflected Carl's investment in his self-directed learning.

As with any new learning, though, children have to be introduced to the skills of independence and given the opportunity to practise and apply them. Some of the most important attributes of independent learning include children being able to use the environment for themselves, to make choices and decisions, and to develop their own thoughts and ideas. An early years setting places high priority on helping children to develop these attributes.

USING THE ENVIRONMENT INDEPENDENTLY

If children are to become self-sufficient learners they must recognise that they can use space and resources for themselves without having to constantly refer to adults. Space is essential to enable children to be physically independent. A setting which is organised as a workshop can increase opportunities for children to use their initiative. The practitioner who takes the view from Reggio Emilia that the environment is the third teacher plans the setting to promote independence and will take great care with the management and layout of physical space. This applies to all age groups. Babies who are learning to crawl should have comfortable floor space to move around freely but they also need boundaries to feel safe and help them to concentrate. Very young children can easily be overwhelmed by a bombardment of sensory stimulation and an overly busy space is more likely to bewilder rather than excite a toddler.

The quality of children's self-chosen play is hugely influenced by the quality and range of continuous provision – the resources that are made available on a daily basis. Practitioners understand that the resources are there for the child to use in her own way to represent her thoughts and ideas. Commonly, room spaces are organised in areas of learning. If so, we should understand that children will not play neatly in each of the six areas. They must be aware of what is available for them and feel free to mix and combine materials and resources. Different philosophies of early childhood are reflected through the environments they provide to enhance independence. The Montessori philosophy emphasises self-reliance and decision-making; consequently most Montessori nurseries will encourage children to select apparatus for themselves rather than have it readily available on tables. The High Scope programme particularly stresses the importance of the physical arrangement of a room and the need for resources to be accessible to children. The programme requires that resources in each area are logically organised and clearly labelled. Steiner settings put great store on children developing their ideas through using open-ended natural materials.

Having prepared the environment, children need to be supported and trusted to use it. A toddler may be encouraged to use a handrail to support her in being mobile. Older children arriving new to a class or group need to be carefully introduced to what is available for them and where it is located. Sometimes it is helpful to model ways of using equipment in the spirit of suggestion. In order to use space and resources for themselves new children need to understand the sorts of experiences and activities they can have, what they are allowed to use and how they return materials after use. Tidying up is part of children learning to be responsible and even toddlers will enjoy putting away blocks after playing with them. It can be a contentious issue though and should not dominate a session; tidying up works best if adults have reasonable expectations of what should be achieved, work with the children, make it fun, allow good time and offer lots of encouragement for effort. Importantly any induction should concentrate on helping children recognise that the environment is there for them to use.

MAKING CHOICES AND DECISIONS

Active learners are not dependent on just doing what others tell them but bring their own ideas and initiative to situations. Given guidance and opportunity, young children are very capable of making choices and decisions about what and how they learn, when they learn it and with whom. The Early Years Foundation Stage suggests that an active learner goes far beyond physical activity, but rather involves children being mentally active as they form their own ideas in response to experiences (17).

Not all children find it easy initially to make decisions. For example, at first some new entrants may be overwhelmed by the amount of choice in the activities available to them in an early years setting. At this stage it is helpful to make suggestions as to what they might start to do and to watch if there are signs of children being at a loss as to what to do next. As they become comfortable and at ease in the nursery they will respond to gentle encouragement to try different options.

Different experiences should include possibilities for choice. Heuristic play providing a rich array of natural and open-ended materials invites a toddler to move around and decide on something particular to explore and investigate. Older children need to be able to select what materials or tools to use. Before children are able to describe materials, make considered choices or consider similarities and differences, they need to have had many and varied opportunities to observe and handle materials and listen to descriptive language (18). Practitioners will observe individual children at play and provide these opportunities in a way that meets specific needs. Initially, young children will act on impulse taking the first thing available or opting to use everything. This is a necessary stage; over time children can be encouraged to reflect on their choice and so become more intentional and selective.

Organisation in the setting should make it possible for children to make decisions about with whom they wish to play (see Chapter 2) and also to determine what they do with their time. Some young children have their lives at home heavily programmed by adults; they are subjected to a relentless timetable of outings, shopping and planned activities such as swimming, dancing and music lessons; in these cases the gift of time is particularly precious. Others, of course, are provided with large chunks of time for themselves, but the only choice available to them is which DVD or television channel to view. Again, a carefully planned programme in a setting should allow scope for the child's enterprise but also provide a place for adult guidance and, when appropriate, adult involvement and intervention. As Tina Bruce suggests, 'At times the adult leads and at times the child. Each takes note of and responds to the other's actions and words' (19). Children who are given choices and real opportunities to take responsibility for their actions are more likely to understand that adults are there as a resource to support their enterprise. Their confidence as decision makers is strengthened as they begin to understand how they can have a stake in their own lives. By the end of the reception year, many children make choices and decisions about their learning and also about aspects of their personal lives, such as healthy eating and taking exercise.

FOSTERING INDEPENDENT THINKERS

The most ambitious aim in fostering young children's independence is to support and extend their thinking.

Why is children's thinking so important?

The growing interest in young children's thinking derives from:

- strong support from research evidence
- imperatives in National Frameworks
- increased insights from practitioners in their day-to day-work
- listening to the voice of children.

Support from research evidence

During the last 25 years studies have recognised that thinking starts very early; very young babies are primed to think in their unceasing efforts to make sense of the world. We do not have to teach babies to think because they are born with mental abilities that fully function, which allows them to make sense of experiences and anticipate future events (20). Studies also show that babies and young children strengthen their thinking through warm social contacts with people who are close to them. Sue Gerhardt, in her wonderful book *Why Love Matters*, suggests that being lovingly held is the greatest spur to development. Her work points up the importance of babies forming close attachments both with immediate family members and then with a key person in daycare, nursery and in a reception class. These significant people are able to 'read' a young child's behaviour and provide a 'tailormade' response to individual needs (21).

Support for children's thinking is showing some long-term benefits. Previous findings from two major research projects, EPPE (Effective Provision of Pre-School Education), and REPEY (Researching Effective Pedagogy in the Early Years), stated that one of the ways in which we could identify high quality early years practice was where children were helped to improve their thinking skills. In the most effective early years settings staff provided opportunities to sustain and challenge children's thinking and to model this for children to share their thoughts with other children (22, 23). Since then the EPPE project has followed the same children from pre-school into Year 5. The study found that these older children had continued to benefit from attending good quality and effective early years provision and this was reflected in their achievements in mathematics and reading. This was particularly noticeable for the most vulnerable groups of young children who have had a poor start to life. EPPE also recognises the strong influence of home and stresses that the greatest impact on children's progress is likely to be improving the quality of learning (which includes encouraging children's thinking) in both the home and early years setting (24). In the light of these findings, messages from the interim report from the Cambridge Primary Review are concerning. This large-scale independent enquiry suggests that for primary age children too much emphasis is being placed on knowledge-based learning rather than understanding and enquiry and recommends an overhaul of the primary national curriculum (25).

Imperatives in National Frameworks

The Early Years Foundation Stage in England and the Foundation Phase Framework in Wales became mandatory in September 2008 and give clear statements about the need to have regard to and offer support for young children's thinking. Both Frameworks emphasise the importance of inclusion and the need to provide learning opportunities which are personalised for each child. Inevitably this means that practitioners must identify a child's interests and thoughts which will be at the heart of all they plan and provide.

The guidance document in the Early Years Foundation Stage shows how to achieve these expectations by paying attention to children's creativity and critical thinking (26). This commitment makes clear that if children have opportunities to play around with ideas in different situations they start to make connections. Over time this allows them to alter and deepen their understandings. Early educators have a responsibility to provide scope to help babies and children grow ideas, forge links in their learning and so make genuine intellectual progress. The Welsh Assembly Foundation Phase Framework for Children's Learning includes developing their thinking as part of a non-statutory Skills Framework which applies across all of the areas of learning (27).

Increased insights from practitioners in their day-to-day work

These research findings and requirements in national frameworks which point up the significance of young children thinking really reinforce what so many practitioners have intuitively long known to be true. In recent years those who work directly with young children have been required to give priority to planning and 'delivering' the curriculum. In their hearts practitioners recognise that in these endeavours to *provide* for children they may be in danger of missing what children are interested in and where they are investing their energies.

Practitioners also recognise that, unless we understand ways in which children express their ideas and thoughts, we may be in danger of under-estimating their potential for learning. Commonly we look at children's mark making as an indicator of their achievement. However, a child may have poorly developed fine motor skills, he may have little pencil control and his drawings, paintings and models may be immature. In this case the representations may not reflect the child's complex and original ideas which perhaps are revealed in self-chosen role play or when he is engaged in constructing outside.

Practitioners also know first-hand from experience, that where young children are good thinkers this is a pre-cursor to later achievement. In order to write clearly and imaginatively and solve problems by using and applying mathematics at Key Stage 1, children must first become clear and inventive thinkers. If young children learn to reflect on their actions and recognise the link between cause and effect they learn to regulate their behaviour and are less likely to act impulsively – surely a lesson for life. Above all, children who are encouraged and become able to think for themselves are likely to become eager and autonomous learners.

Listening to the voice of children

Finally, if given the opportunity young children will share with us their intimate thoughts, for example about growing up in today's society. The interim findings of the Primary Review revealed through interviews with children that some as young as four years think deeply about issues in the world that confront us all (28). They try to make sense about the worrying turmoil in their family lives, the effects of climate change, crime, violence and the tragedy of wars that they witness daily on the media. They are concerned about the distress caused to their parents who separate and anxious about their own safety and their futures. High quality practitioners recognise how critical it is to encourage children to share and discuss their thoughts and concerns with us in the interests of their well-being and their learning. Emotional issues take up a great deal of space in our working memories (see Chapter 4). If young children spend time dwelling on their worries, they are not in a frame of mind to make a good transition in a group setting or to learn effectively.

What is going on?

Thinking causes a mental imbalance or disequilibrium. We can be going about our daily affairs cheerfully when we come up against something new that causes us to pause. It doesn't quite fit in with what we know already. This challenges our current understanding and we have to mentally adjust and then accommodate to the new idea.

A baby is playing with a rattle when suddenly he drops it and it falls to the ground. Someone returns it to the baby; he repeats his action and the rattle is returned again. The baby relishes this new game and tests it out again and again before he starts to make a tentative connection between cause and effect, what he does and what happens as a result. Babies and toddlers show their thinking when they remember such familiar routines, games and rhymes. Each time these enjoyable experiences are repeated they support and strengthen early connections.

We cannot force new thinking. It can take considerable time for a young child to give up current understanding and move on to adjust to a new idea. Sometimes they are just not developmentally ready to make the leap in their thinking, for example a child who insists that shopkeepers give you money, not change.

Children's thinking develops as they are exposed to the ways of the world, they note how things work and what people say and do. They are alert to the conduct of adults and other children and reflect this social intelligence in their own behaviour.

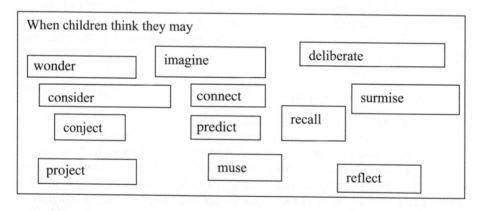

These descriptors make us realise that we cannot directly teach young children to think independently. There is no package of structured materials that will achieve this. We can only provide supportive conditions to encourage thinking. Kahil Gibran in his book *The Prophet* describes this so well; he gives a profound and perceptive definition of a wise teacher who 'does not bid you enter the house of his wisdom, but rather leads you (the child) to the threshold of your (the child's) own mind' (29). Practitioners might consider how far their provision provokes young children to engage in the above types of mental activity.

How do we recognise young children's thinking?

It is relatively easy to gain insights into the thinking of older children; they will lay their interests and views before us in their writing and in discussions.

We can ask them questions about their concerns and difficulties and expect to receive some responses. Younger children's thoughts are less visible, and we need considerable skills to spot and understand them. The following are important signals.

Levels of involvement: We now recognise that when children are deeply absorbed in what they are doing this assumes that there is mental activity going on. We can usefully spot a child's body language and facial expression as well as the time he spends persisting at that activity. If we note her behaviour carefully we may move closer to gain insights into what she is interested in.

Preoccupations or schemes of thinking: Young children develop deep interests from a very early age. Babies and toddlers can become absorbed by patterns of movement. Cathy Nutbrown describes them as 'Threads of Thought' which captures so well the fragile nature of the baby's mental activity (30). These early 'threads' are linked to young children's fascination with aspects of space and movement, such as inside, outside, near and far, up and down, over and under. They are strengthened when young children have opportunities for similar experiences where they can repeat their actions again and again as they work through their interest.

Case study 🗀

Carol worked with a group of children ranging from two to four years who were accommodated in one room in a children's centre. She set up richly resourced role-play environments, particularly to challenge the older children's ideas, including a shoe shop, a pirate ship and a builder's yard outside. However, Carol became frustrated and demoralised when too frequently three of the youngest children invaded the role play and created 'chaos'. They collected up many of the resources and carted them off to other areas; in turn, dough and small-scale vehicles were brought into the role play. The older children were sometimes resentfully forced to abandon their play in the ensuing disorder. Carol sought advice and soon learned that the two-year-olds were simply playing appropriately. They all shared a preoccupation with transporting things from one place to another. The difficulty was overcome when Carol ensured that these children had other transporting experiences. For example, she introduced them to sturdy wheelbarrows outside and with the children she gathered piles of fir cones and leaves which could be moved around.

Comment

When Carol learnt that the two-year-olds were demonstrating their schema in transporting she recognised that she needed to respect the needs of both groups of children, and so allow them scope for their thinking. This was difficult as the setting only had one room but she made full use of the outside area.

Representations: Children will relish rich curriculum experiences and then represent their understandings and ideas in many different ways, for example, through dance, role play, constructing, painting and drawing. Every child will have a preferred way to characterise or record what he has gained from the experience; a broad range of media and resources will allow children good scope to demonstrate their thinking.

Talk: Given a receptive audience, young children are keen to share their ideas and thoughts in conversations. The High Scope programme encourages children to review their activities and to learn over time to become reflective and self-critical.

In the process of recalling what they've done, children attach language to their actions. This makes them more conscious of their actions and more able to refer to them and draw upon them for later use. Talking about, recalling and representing their actions helps children evaluate and learn from their experiences. When planning and doing are followed by recall, children can build on what they've done and learned and remember it for the next time they plan an activity (31).

Many children (like adults) are inhibited to share talk in large groups. Being with many other children in a semi-formal situation can be stressful; even when given gentle encouragement to participate, these children's responses are often limited and compliant as they try to tune in to what they are expected to say and try to marshal their thoughts into language. Children are most likely to reveal their ideas when they believe that they are working away from adults. Given an illusion of privacy, particularly when playing in dens, they relax and chat easily as they set up their own scenarios. In these circumstances they argue, negotiate, sort out roles and freely share their beliefs and views. The National Strategies programme *Every Child a Talker* offers lead practitioners useful guidance to support young children to converse with others (32).

Young children spend a great deal of time trying to figure things out in a fascinating and puzzling world. In an encouraging and familiar climate they are persistently curious and questioning as they search for explanations. Sometimes their questions appear bizarre and irrelevant to the matter in hand but there is always a link back to their own logic. When playing outside, five-year-old Ana suddenly asked her key person, Sue, if there were restaurants under the ground. Later, Sue discovered that Ana's granddad had recently died and Ana was understandably trying with difficulty to make sense of his burial.

In 1992, Dr Karin Murris developed a way of helping young children to think their way through big issues through using picture books and asking questions. She describes this activity as philosophical enquiry and this way of working is now widespread in reception and Year 1 classes. Murris believes that young children are able to play around and engage with ideas in a way that is more difficult for older children (33). In providing the conditions for philosophical enquiry it is important that: children set the agenda for discussion through their questions and responses to the story; each child's contribution is fully respected; the adult remains strictly neutral and avoids steering the discussion.

In order to access the treasures of young children's thoughts, we must be prepared to observe their behaviour, note their actions, listen to them closely and then take an inspired leap into their minds.

What conditions best support young children's thoughts and ideas?

I have adapted some circumstances described by Tina Bruce which help children's thoughts to take root and flourish (34):

- When they are in a familiar setting with adults they trust. If children do not make a really secure transition to a setting they will not have the confidence or emotional vigour to develop their own ideas.
- When they are exposed to a wide range of thought-provoking experiences. If children are intrigued by what they encounter they are likely to invest their mental energies into investigating further.
- When they are supported to make their own decisions and select resources and materials for themselves. In situations where they take responsibility for their learning children learn to plan, negotiate, consider and reflect on their actions.
- When they have time to pause, re-visit and re-consider, make connections and practise and apply what they know.
- When they are free to make mistakes and are encouraged to see these as a valuable way of learning.
- When they are encouraged to share their ideas with others.

Two educational thinkers, Robert Sternberg and Lev Vygotsky, offer further guidance to support children's thinking. Sternberg argues that children (and all of us) need to learn to plan, monitor, reflect and transfer in developing powers of thinking. They also need opportunities to use these skills and strategies through problem solving, making choices and decisions. Vygotsky stresses the role of language in thinking and making meaning from experience. Both Sternberg and Vygotsky emphasise that children will only be able to think well in familiar situations when they make use of their previous experience and knowledge (35, 36).

The above conditions for independent thinking are most likely to be found when children have opportunities to freely choose their experiences. Where this happens children: concentrate on their interests rather than what is decided for them; make choices and decisions about what they are going to do, how and where they are going to do it and who they will work with; are free to make mistakes and come to see them as a valuable way of learning; practise and apply what they know and start to explore new possibilities (37).

Case study 🗁

Richard had made a fire engine using junk materials. He proudly showed his nursery nurse and the seven other children during small group review time. 'I nearly didn't make it so good though', Richard admitted. 'I stuck the wheels with glue but they fell off.' In response to a question from Lynda, his nursery nurse, Richard thought that he had made a good mistake. 'My good mistake helped me to fix the wheels right – and look they can turn.' (The wheels were attached with split pins.)

Comment

Richard recognised that his first solution to provide wheels for his construction was not going to work. During his activity he had seen another child use split pins to attach two pieces of card. This gave him an idea for attaching his wheels. Richard persevered with a different approach which proved to be successful. He understood that his first mistake had been useful. He had learned that one approach to attach wheels was less successful than another. Richard would use this lesson in a future activity.

Practical suggestions

Listen and observe
- Observe signs to show that a baby/toddler has made a strong second attachment and a secure transition to a setting, e.g. content with a handover to the key person, shows interest in surroundings and new experiences, happy to greet mum or dad at the end of the session and not overly distressed.
- Observe when babies/toddlers convey a preference, e.g. when exploring treasure baskets, in heuristic play or when selecting books, and use these resources when you play with them.
- Observe experiences that children have that encourage them most to be independent.

Support social and emotional independence
- Make it clear to each child new to a setting that he is known through referring to some aspect of his life that you shared with him during a home visit, e.g. discussing his dog, his favourite toys, or sharing some photographs of his family and home.
- Ensure that a key person pays particular attention to each new child until it is evident that she has made a sound transition to the setting, e.g. the key person should be alert to occasions when a child does not understand instructions, cannot remember where to find things, cannot remember routines, is confused and tense when making a transition from one activity to another, when clearing away or going outside.   *Continued*

Continued

- If children are to stay full time or for extended daycare, encourage parents or carers to join them for breakfast/lunch/tea sessions during the early stages of transition.

Support children in separating from their parents (see also Chapter 8)
- Be alert to when a parent needs to leave the nursery and be physically present when this happens.
- Agree with the parent a procedure for saying goodbye such as waving from the window or taking the child's teddy shopping with her.
- Talk through with the child the daily routines that will take place until 'mummy' returns.

Promote physical and functional independence
- Provide easy-grip feeding cutlery to encourage older babies to feed themselves and an environment that allows babies to move easily and comfortably to different areas.
- Play games that need buttons, zips and buckles to be fastened.
- Encourage children to take responsibility for their own possessions, e.g. clipping wellington boots together with a named wooden peg.
- Provide older children with areas of responsibility, e.g. keeping the book area tidy, checking that all the jigsaws are intact, checking the painting aprons for repairs.
- Encourage less confident children to take messages; as a safeguard provide a written version for the child's pocket which she can produce if she wishes.
- Help children to be tidy, e.g. sew large curtain rings onto painting aprons to make it easy to hang aprons onto pegs, provide a dustpan and brush for clearing up dry sand, provide a floor cloth or short-handled mop for coping with spillages.
- Provide pictorial notices which help children to remember self-help skills, e.g. a picture of two large hands displayed with the caption 'Please wash your hands'.
- Check how well the storage of your resources makes it possible for children to access them easily. Provide easily fitting lids on containers and low shelves with sufficient space for each piece of apparatus. Space for individual jigsaws can be marked out and symbols/colours used to match each puzzle to the space allocated.
- Check that children know where things are. Play a game in the group 'Can you find where it lives?' Prepare a drawstring bag containing various objects, e.g. pencils, blocks, counters, scissors. Ask children in turn to withdraw an item from the bag and return it to its home.

Promote intellectual independence
- Build in choice and decision-making in experiences.

Continued

Continued

- *Painting*: provide a range of paper of different shapes, sizes and colours. Make the paper easily accessible by having it available on a low table in the painting area.
- *Collage*: provide a range of materials and adhesives to allow toddlers simply to explore and older children to compare the different properties.
- *Storytime*: provide two alternatives for a story and ask children to state their preference.
- *Snacks*: provide alternative options of fruit or crackers; allow children to pour the amount of milk or squash they wish to drink rather than be expected to consume a standard measure.
- *Displays*: consult children about whose work is going to be displayed on walls (ensure, through gentle encouragement, that all children's work is eventually presented).
- *Outings*: provide alternative suggestions for a walk and ask children to select.
- *Planting bulbs*: ask children to browse through bulb catalogues in order to select their favourite colour bulbs.
- *Celebrations*: consult children about what food to have for a summer picnic or Christmas party.
- Support children to choose how they use their time:
  - make clear what resources are available by having the room/outside area clearly organised and displayed
  - introduce children gradually to each part of the room in turn, and the resources that are available to be used
  - encourage older children to record their decision of where they decide to play by sharing this with an adult who acts as a scribe for them or by asking them to attach their name card to a picture/photograph of their chosen activity.
- Recognise independent thinkers:
  - be alert to when babies and children appear to be making a connection in their learning, e.g. through their repeated behavior or a question/comment
  - note the experiences and environments which encourage young children to grow and develop thoughts and ideas, e.g. small-scale play, exploring nature outside, simple science investigations
  - ensure a daily programme which protects uninterrupted time for children to try out and share new ideas and mull things over
  - provide spaces in your setting or class which are specifically designed for quiet reflection, e.g. a baby in a pram underneath a tree.
- Offer older children:

Continued

Continued
  - spaces and varied open-ended resources which encourage den making displays of models, drawings and paintings that are particularly completed and engage children in discussion about what might be added next
  - prompts to develop a structure for independent thinking, e.g. provide an attractive pictorial chart with the following headings: What do I want to do? Who do I want to do it with? What do I need in order to do it? How well did we do it?
  - encourage opportunities for open and reflective discussion, e.g. children to ask questions, make suggestions about features in a picture or aspects of a story that are unresolved or that puzzle them.

Professional practice questions

1. What scope do babies have to handle and control items when lying on their backs or their tummies ?
2. How well do the storage space and labelling make clear to children where to access and return resources?
3. How many of the following things have I done today that children could have tackled just as well:
   - dressing and undressing themselves
   - sending and delivering messages
   - preparing materials, e.g. making playdough, mixing paints, combining ingredients for cookery
   - tidying away equipment?
4. What decisions and choices are my children encouraged to make about:
   - the experiences they have
   - the materials/apparatus they use
   - how they use their time
   - who they work with
   - when they go to the lavatory
   - when they have a mid-morning snack
   - playing inside or outside?
5. What opportunities have my children to:
   - make and share judgements about their representations
   - respond to what others think or do and have others respond to their ideas
   - have their views respected ?
6. How well does my continuous provision allow children to use resources in ways which enrich and deepen their ideas?

The following references in the *Early Years Foundation Stage* link to this chapter:

Statutory Framework and Guidance: pp. 12, 37
Practice Guidance: Appendix 2, Areas of Learning and Development
Self-care (pp. 35–6), *Language for Thinking* (pp. 47–9), *Exploration and Investigation* (pp. 77–8), *Being Creative* (pp. 106–7), *Developing Imagination and Imaginative Play* (pp. 112–14)
Principles into Practice Cards: 1.3 *Keeping Safe* (Making choices), 2.4 *Key Person*, 3.2 *Supporting Every Child* (The Learning Journey), 3.4 *The Wider Context* (Transitions and Continuity), 4.1 *Play and Exploration*, 4.2 *Active Learning* (Decision Making), 4.3 *Creativity and Critical Thinking*.
The CD-ROM *in depth* offers further guidance on the above principles and commitments.

The following Early Years Professional Standards link to this chapter: 1, 3, 4, 16, 17, 22, 27.

REFERENCES 📖

1. Winnicott, D.W. (1964) *The Child, the Family and the Outside World*. Harmondsworth: Penguin.
2. Lindon, J. (2003) Good practice in working with babies, toddlers and very young children, *Birth to Three Matters: A Framework to Support Children in their Earliest Years*. London: DfES.
3. Department for Education and Skills (DfES) (2007) *The Early Years Foundation Stage: Principles into Practice Cards, 3.4 The Wider Context*. London: DfES Publications.
4. Manchester Education Partnership/Sure Start (2004) *Effective Transitions in the Early Years*, Manchester City Council, Manchester Education Partnership, 3rd Floor, Fujitsu Tower, Wenlock Way, West Gorton, Manchester M12 5DR.
5. Ward, L. (2005) Hidden stress of the nursery age: childcare study, *Guardian News*, 19 September, p. 3.
6. Ghaye, A. and Pascal, C. (1988) Four-year-old children in reception classrooms: participant perceptions and practice, *Educational Studies*, Vol. 14, no. 2, pp. 187–208.
7. Sharp, C. (2002) 'School Starting Age: European Policy and Recent Research'. Paper presented at the LGA Seminar *When Should Our Children Start School?* NFER/Local Government Association.
8. Batchford, P., Battle S. and Mays, J. (1974) *The First Transition: Home to Pre-School*. Slough: NFER/Nelson.
9. Department for Education and Skills (DfES) (2007) *The Early Years Foundation Stage: Principles into Practice Cards, 4.3 Supporting Every Child*. London: DfES Publications.
10. Qualifications and Curriculum Authority (QCA) (2005) *Continuing the Learning Journey*, QCA online order ref: QCA/05/1590. www.naa.org.uk/naa17856.
11. Department for Education and Skills (DfES) (2007) *The Early Years Foundation Stage Appendix 2: Areas of Learning and Development*. London: DfES Publications, pp. 35–6.
12. Thomas, S. (2008) *Nurturing Babies and Children Under Four*. London: Heinemann, p. 11.

13. Department of Education and Science (DES) (1967) *Children and their Primary School,* Report of the Central Advisory Council for Education. London: HMSO, para. 529. p. 2.
14. Department for Education and Skills (DfES) (2007) *The Early Years Foundation Stage: Principles into Practice Cards, 4.2 Active Learning.* London: DfES Publications.
15. QCA (2002) *Non-Statutory Guidance for Citizenship at KS1.* London: QCA/DFEE.
16. Willow, C., Marchant, R., Kirby, P., and Neale, B. (2004) *Young Children's Citizenship: Ideas into Practice.* York: Joseph Rowntree Foundation.
17. Department for Education and Skills (DfES) (2007) *The Early Years Foundation Stage,* CD Rom *in depth, 4.2 Active Learning.* London: DfES Publications.
18. Dowling, M. (1995) *Starting School at Four: A Shared Endeavour.* London: Paul Chapman.
19. Bruce, T. (1987) *Early Childhood Education.* London: Hodder & Stoughton, p. 23.
20. Gopnik, A., Melzoff, A. and Kuhl (1999) *How Babies Think: the Science of Childhood.* London: Weidenfeld and Nicolson.
21. Gerhardt, S. (2004) *Why Love Matters.* London: Brunner-Routledge.
22. Sylva, K., Melhuish, E.C., Sammons, P., Siraj-Blatchford, I. and Taggart, B. (2004) The Effective Provision of Pre-School Education (EPPE) Project: *Technical Paper 12 – The Final Report: Effective Pre-School Education.* London: DfES/Institute of Education, University of London.
23. Siraj-Blatchford, I., Sylva, K., Muttock, S., Giden, R. and Bell, D. (2002) *Researching Effective Pedagogy in the Early Years (REPEY),* DfES Research Report 356.
24. Sammons, P., Sylva, K. et al. (2007) EPPE (3–11) *Influences on Children's Attainment and Progress in Key Stage 2: Cognitive Outcomes in Year 5,* Research Brief No: RB8, 28 February.
25. Cambridge Primary Review (2009) *Interim Findings of the Cambridge Primary Review,* Esmée Fairbairn Foundation/University of Cambridge, Faculty of Education.
26. Department for Education and Skills (DfES) (2007) *The Early Years Foundation Stage: Principles into Practice Cards, 4.3 Creativity and critical thinking.* London: DfES Publications.
27. Department for Education, Lifelong Learning and Skills (2007) *Foundation Phase, Framework for Children's Learning,* Welsh Assembly Government.
28. Esmée Fairbairn Foundation/Faculty of Education, University of Cambridge (2007) *The Primary Review: Community Findings.* www.primaryreview.org.uk.
29. Gibran, K. (1926) *The Prophet.* London: Heinemann, p. 67.
30. Nutbrown, C. (2006) *Threads of Thinking.* Third edition. London: Sage Publications.
31. Hohmann, M., Banet, B. and Weikart, D.P. (1979) *Young Children in Action.* Ypsilanti, MI: High/Scope Press, p. 88.
32. The National Strategies Early Years (2008) *Every Child a Talker: Guidance for English Language Lead Practitioners.* DCSF.
33. Murris, K. (1992) *Teaching Philosophy with Picture Books.* London: infonet.
34. Bruce, T. (2004) *Cultivating Creativity in Babies, Toddlers and Young Children.* London: Hodder & Stoughton, p. 71.
35. Sternberg, R.J. (1985) *Beyond IQ: A Triarchic Theory of Human Intelligence.* Cambridge: Cambridge University Press.
36. Vygotsky, L.S. (1978) *Mind in Society: The Development of Higher Psychological Processes.* Cambridge MA: Harvard University Press.
37. Dowling, M. (2008) *Young Children Thinking through their Self-chosen Activity,* Training Materials (DVD and Training Guidance), Early Education, www.early-education.org.uk.

4

Emotional Well-Being

Summary of contents

- People's emotional lives are increasingly seen as critical to their success in life.
- Young children's emotional development is emphasised in national frameworks and is closely tied to other areas of development.
- The link between feelings and brain development is important. Young minds are strengthened through warm and loving relationships, demonstrated through close attachments with key persons.
- To achieve emotional health, children need to experience and express a range of emotions in their own way through a broad range of experiences. They need to be able to communicate negative emotions, particularly during times of stress.
- Children's understanding about their feelings are heavily dependent on the support they receive from their families.
- Early Years settings can be important in aiding children's emotional well-being.

Feelings affect everything we do and this is a clear message echoed throughout the Early Years Foundation Stage. Despite this, strong concerns for children's well-being have been expressed recently; some of these are linked to the current thrust on raising standards and pushing young children into a 'hurry along' curriculum rather than allowing them to enjoy an unpressurised childhood. Our education system is increasingly seen as a means of satisfying the demands of industry and commerce; these being mainly interpreted in terms of academic achievement. And yet the Good Childhood Enquiry reported that one in ten 5–16-year-olds has severe mental problems often linked to not having a stable family or friends (1). Surely this points to the importance of working with parents and fostering children's relationships early in life. The report recommends that, throughout their schooling, children's personal, social and emotional development should be given the same priority as their cognitive development.

Nevertheless, in other fields of corporate life and medicine there is clear acknowledgement of the significance of the emotions for people's well-being and learning. The many forms of alternative medicine take account of people's feelings and how they are linked to physical health. Holistic remedies such as yoga and aromatherapy are used increasingly as part of treatment for cancer patients. Therapists are discovering that introducing their clients to simple techniques of thought adjustment can have as much impact on the power to curb anger and aggression and cope with depression as many years of analysis. New hospital rooms are now being designed to enable patients to have the comfort and support of their families staying with them. On modern management courses we hear that 'feminine' stereotype qualities which include sensitivity and intuition are requirements for effective leaders regardless of the gender of the leader.

Daniel Goleman summarises the view from the business world:

> The rules for work are changing. We're being judged by a new yardstick: not just by how smart we are, or by our training and expertise, but also by how well we handle ourselves and each other. This yardstick is increasingly applied in choosing who will be hired and who will not, who will be let go and who retained, who passed over and who promoted (2).

Practitioners have always recognised the importance of young children's emotional lives in relation to their overall development. They warm to messages in the national framework which urge them to recognise and support children's feelings (3). However, many staff, particularly in reception classes, now believe that the downward pressure on attainment has forced them into practices which they know intuitively are counter-productive for children. Nursery practitioners are pressured into teaching early phonics to children through rote learning. Reception teachers are urged to document children's progress in detail and ensure that the children achieve a good standard across all of the Early Learning Goals despite two of the goals for writing being pitched too high to allow the majority of children to succeed at this level. School leaders, in turn pushed by local authority officers, require teachers to set literacy and numeracy targets for children which can mean a focus on outcomes rather than on the process of learning. Staff in some private and voluntary settings still feel intimidated by the prospect of inspection where they believe that inspectors are mainly interested in children learning to read, write and calculate; this leads them to try to accelerate younger children's attainment in early literacy and numeracy at the expense of attention being given to the other areas of learning. Sometimes these fears and practices happen as a consequence of misunderstandings of requirements. Nevertheless it is a hard and worrying fact that many practitioners continue to feel compelled to act in a way which does not recognise or value how children might feel.

Common sense and our own experiences tell us that we cannot function properly if we are unhappy, upset or angry. Our behaviour and thinking is heavily influenced by our feelings. Emotional development in young children is rapid and profound. Their feelings affect their self-esteem, the way in which they relate to others and their grasp of right and wrong. In order to equip them for living now and later, early years practitioners need to understand how children's emotional life unfolds and what is required to care for it.

EMOTIONAL INTELLIGENCE

We may be puzzled as to why a friend or family member who is academically very able fails to make a success of his career or his family life. After all, it appears that he has so much going for him. Or maybe another person who has modest intellectual qualities seems to accomplish so much in her personal and professional life. One clue may be to do with the emotional abilities these people have rather than their rational or academic competencies.

There is increasing recognition that emotional abilities have been underrated in the role that they play in helping to ensure a successful and fulfilling life. Regardless of intellectual capacities, some people are blessed with emotional stamina which helps them to withstand the stresses and difficulties in life and to have insights into and empathy with others. Others who lack this stamina and are emotionally fragile are likely to find problems in dealing with their own and others' feelings. Both rational and emotional abilities are now seen as being equally influential in determining how people enjoy and what they achieve in life.

This recognition is increasingly documented. Howard Gardner's well-known work on multiple intelligences includes reference to intrapersonal and interpersonal abilities. The first refers (albeit implicitly) to knowing about one's own feelings and the second to tuning in to the feelings of others (4). Both abilities involve emotions as a means of regulating behaviour. If young children are helped to develop these abilities this will strengthen their sense of self and their relationships with a range of other people. Nowicki and Duke's study supported this. They found that children who were aware of their own feelings and sensitive to others were, not surprisingly, more emotionally stable, more popular and achieved more in school than those with similar intellectual ability but less emotional ability (5). Goleman in his work on emotional intelligence lists a number of studies that highlight both the worrying consequences when people are not emotionally competent and also the great benefits when they are. He also refers to brain studies which suggest that a person's emotional state of mind is closely linked to her ability to think more effectively (6, 7). This informed awareness tunes in well with beliefs of practitioners that, when working with young children, they are educating more than an intellect. However, the link between children's emotions and other aspects of their learning has only recently been emphasised. Past work on children's learning paid little attention to the affective aspects of development. Piaget only mentioned it as a factor which energised intellectual activity (8). Although Vygotsky stressed the importance of social relationships, he largely ignored the fact that emotions are part and parcel of those interactions (9). In 1994 Sarah Meadows described work on emotions as the 'Cinderella' of cognitive development (10). Although there is need for more work in this area, encouragingly studies now increasingly recognise emotions as integral to learning.

Ferre Laevers' project 'Experiential Education' (EXE) identifies the degree of a child's emotional well-being as one of two key factors to be considered when judging the means of a child learning effectively and the quality of an educational setting. His definition of emotional well-being is broad:

> the degree to which children do feel at ease, can be spontaneous and are satisfied in their physical needs, feel the need for tenderness and affection, the need for safety and clarity, the need for social recognition, the need to feel competent and the need for meaning in life and moral value (11).

Some of these factors are explored elsewhere in this book (see Chapters 1, 2, 5 and 6); here we concentrate on the importance of regard to feelings. Laevers' work is strongly echoed in the current important action research project 'Accounting Early for Life-Long Learning'. Pascal and Bertram claim that emotional well-being is one of four factors seen in children who have potential to be effective learners (12).

References to children's emotional well-being are now evident in early years frameworks in England, Wales, Northern Ireland and Scotland (13, 14, 15, 16). In England the guidance document *Social and Emotional Aspects of Development* (SEAD) highlights emotional development as one of the three building blocks of future success in life (17). In the New Zealand Early Childhood Curriculum document *Te Whariki*, there is a section on well-being which states that two of the entitlements for children are: 'an expectation that the early childhood education setting is an enjoyable place to be; a place where they have fun; and to develop a trust that their emotional needs will be responded to' (18).

HOW FEELINGS INFLUENCE EARLY LEARNING

Although emotions can foster or inhibit learning for children of all ages, the link between feelings and early brain development is particularly critical at the very start of life.

Attachments

Research indicates that where children start their lives having at least one person with whom they have a strong bond or attachment they can develop a resistance to stress in their lives (19). This bond provides a form of protection both for the early years and in their future lives and it is a basic requirement for children to establish wider social attachments as they grow up. If a baby is physically and emotionally close to one person initially (most usually his birth mother), this makes later separation from her more tolerable rather than less. From birth, every day that this significant person can be with the baby, to discover him, help him to know her, meet his needs, give him pleasure and take pleasure in him will contribute to a fund of confidence and inner peace. Even a brief few weeks of this relationship will offer the baby a good start. As parents spend time with their new baby they get to know her signals: a hungry or tired cry or sign of discomfort; a prolonged gaze as the baby starts to focus; body movements which suggest the baby's need to play and communicate.

Figure 4.1 Ruby bonds with her dad

Responsive and loving adults are crucial to all aspects of infant development. And you cannot overdose young infants with attention. Every time a baby receives a response to something she appears to need, the better. Penelope Leach draws attention to historical evidence of the possible consequences of the strict rationing of attention. After the Second World War, thousands of orphaned and refugee babies were kept in institutions where their physical care was excellent, but wholly impersonal. Many of these babies failed to thrive – worse, some died without, seemingly, any physical reason for this. In 1990, the same dreadful situation became apparent in the packed orphanages in Romania. Quite early on, researchers concluded that these babies and small children suffered from lack of maternal care – later this was amended, recognising that it was not so much the lack of a link with their natural parent, but the deprivation of responsive and loving care. Leach, Stein and Sylva stressed that this lack of attachment can of course occur within the family, for example, where a potentially loving parent becomes clinically depressed and is unable to sustain a loving bond with the child (20).

Very young babies rapidly tune in to a close relationship with their mother or main carer. The baby is already familiar with her mother's voice and starts to recognise her face and smell. When held by her mum or dad a baby's heartbeat calms immediately. The deepest part of the brain is concerned with feelings and its development is fundamental to all other aspects of development. From a safe and secure base the young baby will start to explore her environment and become open to new experiences. A young brain grows through sensory experiences, taste, touch, hearing, seeing and smell. If experiences are repeated often enough, connections between brain cells are strengthened. When babies are provided with familiar and consistent routines this helps them to start to make sense of what is happening to them – they begin to build up a predictable mental structure in their lives. Daily routines such as feeding, nappy changing and bath time allow babies and their carers to enjoy loving exchanges.

Young babies cannot handle their feelings and are dependent on their carer to interpret their signals of distress – a hungry cry or wriggle of discomfort. Over time, if the baby's signals are recognised and responded to he begins to trust that his mum or carer is always there to 'make things better'. The most effective provision is based on 'contingent care' which is a bespoke response to the baby's actual needs rather than what the carer thinks he might need (21). Given this optimal start the baby is helped to be calm and to start to manage his behaviour. For example, a toddler, who has been loved, respected and listened to, starts to show care and concern for others.

Importantly, babies' brains also thrive on companionship. Colwyn Trevarthen suggests what this looks like for a child and this description applies equally to a baby:

> Children do need affection and support and protection and so on but they need a lot more than that. They need company which is interested and curious and affectionate ... Children are very good at private research. They can do it very well, but they don't do it if they are discouraged, if they feel unwanted or lonely then they don't explore (22).

Although mum or dad are likely to be the most significant carers, a baby may form a bond with other close family members – a sibling or grandparent in particular. However, important attachments will only be made with a small group of people who know the child well. A young child's need for an attachment is also ongoing throughout and beyond the early years phase. For those who have established a secure close relationship as babies the roots of security are already established; however at times, for example when facing change or stresses, the child will need to be reassured that his special person is still there for him.

THE KEY PERSON

When babies and small children move into a group setting and come to separate from their parents, the essential need is to appoint a key person with whom the child can make a similar (but not identical) attachment. It is now mandatory in England for all children in the Early Years Foundation Stage to have a key person. This section examines the role and looks at implications for the key person when working with children of different ages.

What is a key person?

The young child's need for intimate interaction through close attachment continues when he moves to a childminder or into a group setting and this is where the key person plays a critical role. As we have seen, very young children thrive on familiarity and predictability and these involve ensuring a continuity of attention through a staff member developing a personal relationship with that child. Whether the term 'key worker' or 'key person' is used, the role is based on relationships. The key person forms a special association with both the young child and his parents. When this approach is well established it offers benefits to all concerned, as clearly described by Peter Elfer and colleagues and summarised here:

- Babies and young children will experience a close, affectionate and reliable relationship and are helped to feel unique and special.
- Parents have a link with someone who is fully committed to their child and this can offer them 'peace of mind'.
- The key person feels that she is really important to the child and family which offers great job satisfaction.
- The manager or head recognises some important requirements for quality provision are met: that children are settled and well cared for, parents feel comfortable with the provision, and staff are involved and committed to their work (23).

The quality of the key person relationship has a direct bearing on a very young child's learning. The chemical cortisol, present in all of us, surges in conditions of stress and can close down functions. When the child is loved and cherished he is relaxed and in the right state of mind to learn. When these conditions are not present, levels of cortisol rise. Penelope Leach offers a cautious warning about the effects of full daycare for very young children under two years when they are in the care of inexperienced and poorly trained staff – in these circumstances staff may care for each child's physical needs but not be aware of the need for close and intimate interactions to foster each child's unique qualities. This approach of treating all children equally can lead to a flatness of affect which is insufficient to support a developing personality (24). A key person approach ensures consistency for a young child and this is particularly important in a large, free-flowing nursery setting or Foundation Stage Unit. In a reception class usually staffed by a teacher and assistant, it is easier to establish similar interactions and expectations and a key person role may be shared. Nevertheless careful thought needs to be given to the organisation of playtimes and lunchtimes when reception children may encounter other adults. At these times new children can be particularly vulnerable and during these early days where possible should be supported by a key person being there for them.

More detailed guidance on the key person may be found in the *Social and Emotional Aspects of Development: Guidance for Practitioners Working in the Early Years Foundation Stage* (25).

EXPERIENCING AND EXPRESSING EMOTION

Children's experiences and expressions of feelings develop tremendously during the early years of life. Most of a child's basic emotions are in place by the time she is two years old but the process starts long before then. Trevarthen suggests that

> every infant is born with the receptive awareness and expressive body needed to communicate fully with others. They can feel and express curiosity, intention, doubt and anxiety, love and pride in admired accomplishment, shame and jealousy at being misinterpreted. Their manifest need is for expressive contact with sympathetic joy-seeking, generous company (26).

Young children also quickly develop their unique means of expressing their feelings and then use them deliberately to suit the occasion (27).

Case study 🗁

Maggie's emotions change frequently and rapidly. She can be furious one moment when her block construction collapses, but jump for joy the next moment when her childminder announces they are going out to the shops. By contrast, Kirsty's feelings are more long lasting and even. She rarely shows excitement, but plays equably by herself for most of the time. When Kirsty is upset or angry it is difficult to cheer her up. Her angry feelings (or mood) remain with her, sometimes for a whole day.

Comment

Linda, the child minder, was aware that these two three-year-old girls had different emotional styles which required a different approach. Maggie was often easier to deal with, although unpredictable. Kirsty's feelings were less easy to 'read'.

In certain situations young children may cope with their feelings in ways which are puzzling to adults. On experiencing the death of a loved relative or a close family friend, children will show their grieving through withdrawal, anger or denial. Paula Alexander, a parent at the Pen Green Centre of Excellence, describes how her three-year-old son went back to bed-wetting at home after being told that his father had died:

> At nursery he kept taking things to the sandpit, burying them and digging them up to bring them back to life again. Then he'd say out of the blue 'My daddy's dead'. You have to pay close attention to what they are trying to express. The nursery did a lot of work with him through play.

Adults are usually very prepared to cope with a child's grief in the short term but may not recognise that the impact of bereavement is not always immediate. In the same article, Dr Richard Woolfson, a child psychologist, suggests that while adults feel the need to recover from their grief,

> there is no urgency in children. You tell them the news and their immediate reaction is to go and play, but it all takes time to work through. One minute a three-year-old will say 'Granny's dead' and the next minute will ask you not to forget to set a place at the table for her (28).

It is important for adults not to have any preconceptions about how children will react to grief. However, there is likely to be a time, once children have absorbed the news, when they will want to talk about their loss and, like Mrs Alexander's small son, to recreate their understanding through play. Early years practitioners can play a vital role in responding to each child's needs at a time when the child's family members are likely to be distressed and vulnerable themselves.

Despite important differences in expressive style, most young children are full of raw emotion and feel acutely. The power of their emotion is heightened as their feelings are not tempered by experience. Most things are happening for the first time; as a consequence children can be desolate in their distress, pent up with fury and over-brimming with joy. They are receptive to all experiences that are offered to them. The effect of this responsiveness for those children who live turbulent lives is that they may live their lives on an emotional rollercoaster. In situations like this children can be ruled by their emotions. This is particularly noticeable with those young children who find it hard to express themselves in spoken language. It is difficult for an adult to be fluent and articulate when she is angry or distressed – how much more so for a two- or three-year-old when emotions overwhelm them.

Young children's feelings, positive and negative, will initially be best reflected through their actions. They will dance for the sheer pleasure of twirling their bodies in space; they will make marks, daub colours, stick materials, make patterns, build and construct imaginary scenarios to depict pleasures and turmoils which initially they are unable to talk about. Provision of a broad programme allows all children to find appropriate ways to represent what they are feeling. A narrow programme which only allows them to use limited materials or which places undue emphasis on representing experiences through only written symbols, is not inclusive. It is only the children who have already benefited from rich active and sensory experiences who will start to make sense of written numbers and letters; at this stage they will enjoy being helped to count and spot the letters of their name in signs and books and to practise writing them. A nursery programme should actively help all children to make this transition to using symbols. However, children's readiness cannot be pre-empted. Requiring all children to do things for which only some are ready will result in only some of them making any sense of what they are doing.

Figure 4.2 Most things are happening for the first time

THE EFFECT OF TRANSITION ON CHILDREN'S FEELINGS

A young child on familiar territory at home or in a nursery is likely to feel secure and to be confident and competent. Any move means that a child is emotionally challenged. The initial effect on young children's confidence and independence of moving from a known setting has already been explored (see Chapters 1 and 3). We have seen that children experience many complex and often conflicting feelings. Excitement and anticipation of the move are tempered by anxiety, distress and confusion about the unknown. In these circumstances children's emotional well-being is not secure; this affects their ability to learn.

Negative feelings can have an effect on children's working memory. This is stressed in research from Western Australia where working memory is described as a measure of the number of things that one can cope with at one time (29). Adults all have the capacity to keep a number of ideas and skills in their minds at one time. Once these ideas and skills become familiar they become less onerous; in effect, skills which were initially learned individually and laboriously can fuse together and become automatic. Young children who are new to all learning find everything a challenge and there is so much more to remember. For example, a child who is learning to use the painting easel has to learn how to hold her paintbrush, how to apply paint and return the brush to the paint pot, what to do with the painting once it is completed, where to wash her hands and hang her apron. With practice much of this becomes routine and leaves her free to concentrate on the painting itself. However, if a child new to a nursery is worried about getting dirty or is jealous about a younger brother or sister having attention while she is away from home, these feelings can 'block' a working memory; she is literally in turmoil as a result of feeling uprooted and anxious about being abandoned. As a result, a child can become unsure, confused and forgetful about things in which she was previously competent.

Although children will initially show their feelings through what they do, their spoken language is important for them to learn to deal with emotions. In order to cope with such momentous experiences involved when moving from reception to Year 1, children need to talk to express their feelings and also to make sense of what is happening to them. An Oxfordshire project on transition encouraged reception children to say how they felt about the prospective move. Children expressed their worries about facing the big playground, not knowing where to go, fears about being bullied and having to write. Staff were able to pick up on these messages and improve their transition procedures accordingly (30). Other children in the project were very positive and relished the prospect of challenges, doing homework and being with their friends. This reinforces the view that children will respond differently to a transition (see Chapter 3).

The recent influx of immigrant families into this country has meant that their children have been forced to make massive adjustments very rapidly, being faced for a start with a new country, new neighbours and an unfamiliar language. On top of this, family circumstances can mean that both parents need to find work quickly and children are expected to adapt to a strange setting or school.

Case study

Irma, three-and-a-half years old, was a new arrival at the children's centre. She had recently moved from Lithuania with her young parents. Both mum and dad worked shifts at a local hotel and were accommodated in a mobile home which they shared with another Lithuanian couple. Only Irma's dad could speak a few words of English, and all conversations at home were in their mother tongue.

Irma's dad stayed to settle Irma in at the centre for the first day but after that was forced to return to work. Irma attended extended hours but because mum and dad started work very early an elderly Lithuanian lady brought her to the breakfast club and one of her parents collected her in the evening.

During the first four days at the centre Irma appeared stunned. She made no protest when left in the morning, but she refused to take off her coat and sat by the

Continued

Continued

wall hugging a scruffy toy rabbit called Dong. No gentle persuasion could get her to participate in any of the nursery experiences.

There was no dual language assistant who spoke Lithuanian and so Irma's key person, Gay, approached Irma's dad and asked for help to learn a very basic vocabulary. He returned the next day with a list of words and Gay practised them with him.

On Monday morning Gay approached Irma holding another toy rabbit. She pulled two large carrots out of her pocket. Gay smiled encouragingly, and using her newly acquired language she said very haltingly 'Hello Irma, this is Paulo and he wants a rabbit friend. Would you and Dong like to take care of Paulo? Here are some carrots for breakfast'. Gay repeated her message again and suddenly Irma shot out her arms to hold Paulo. Gay withdrew and observed. Irma cuddled the two rabbits tightly; she picked up a carrot and offered it to each one in turn crooning quietly.

Commentary

Irma's resistance to settling in to the centre was unsurprising given the massive changes involved in moving to a new country. Gay recognised that Irma would only be approached through something familiar. Irma's dad really appreciated Gay's readiness to talk with his daughter in Lithuanian and proved a useful resource. Gay also observed Irma's attachment to the rabbit and recognised that this might be a way to link with her.

Following the initial breakthrough, a day later Irma moved with the rabbits into the book corner where she shared some picture books with them. A week later, on entering the centre she took off her coat and looked to Gay to show her where to hang it.

THE INFLUENCE OF THE FAMILY

Young children's understandings and use of their feelings will be heavily influenced by the significant people around them, initially their parents. An important part of knowing about ourselves is to be able to recognise the different feelings that we have and that other people experience. Elfer suggests that this empathetic behaviour is dependent on the child having experienced a good attachment where his own feelings have been understood (31). Judy Dunn also reminds us that once children can talk they will show their understandings of others minds, for instance in the language they use with younger children or adults (32). By stark contrast, there is evidence of how less fortunate children learn different lessons. Daniel Goleman provides case studies of the dire emotional effects on small children who have been repeatedly physically abused (33). The most noticeable result is that these children who have suffered so much completely lack care and concern for others. At two and three years of age they typically ignore any distress shown by other children; often their responses may be violent. All they are doing is mirroring the behaviour that they have received themselves.

In families where feelings are not only expressed but are openly discussed, a young child is helped to recognise and accept his emotions and those of others. In these circumstances children are also more likely to talk freely about what they feel. These intimate contacts between parents and child involve shared experiences and loving attention over a period of time. Some parents do not provide this as a result of the busy lives they lead. Charles Handy points out how those adults who are in full-time and pressurised employment are starting to realise that their work is beginning to interfere with the relationships that they have with those closest to them (34). At the other extreme are parents who, because they are unemployed, have time, but the effects of overcrowded and poor housing and all the other attendant problems of poverty drain them of resources and patience to offer their small children. While the setting would never claim to be able to replace these family interactions, it can play a crucial role in working with parents and sharing the task of helping children understand what they feel (see Chapter 10).

Case study

Karu was an attractive five-year-old, an only child, very articulate and already a competent early reader and skilled at construction. Nevertheless, he rarely talked in school and appeared to use his energies in disrupting activities for other children. He would deliberately tip over containers of apparatus while the teacher was talking, or pinch another child while she was answering the teacher. He refused to sit with other children and often tore up his drawings and early writing before his teacher could see it. By his second term in school Karu had no friends as the rest of the children disapproved of his antisocial activities.

Karu's parents admitted to having their own personal difficulties, but said that they saw very little of Karu at home as he spent most of his time watching TV in his bedroom. His father said that the one regular point of contact was at bedtime when he read Karu a story. On these occasions Karu gripped his father's hand very tightly.

Ann, his teacher, decided to try to spend more time with Karu in order to establish a closer bond. She suggested to Karu that he might meet her for a chat or a story in the library at lunchtime. (Karu had recently asked to stay in at lunchtime rather than go out into the playground where he was increasingly isolated.) Ann made these sessions chatty and welcoming. She always took a cup of tea with her and offered Karu a biscuit. Occasionally she would bring in photos of her home and her cat and tell Karu about things in her own life at weekends. At first Karu said little, but then he opened up. He expressed his terror of his father leaving home and of never being able to see him again (in fact this never happened as the parents sorted out their marital problems). Karu told Ann he felt very

Continued

Continued

angry when he was made to come to school. He thought that his parents were deliberately leaving him there knowing that school made him sad. Initially Karu's behaviour was unchanged, but after two weeks of meeting daily with Ann he came to sit close beside her at group time. He gripped her skirt looking directly at her face. Ann bent down and said quietly, 'I won't leave you, Karu – I am always here'. After that point Karu's progress was slow but steady. He continued to talk with Ann and sometimes talked about happy times with his parents. Eventually he made a friend (a shy newcomer to the school). By the end of term Karu was happy to go into the playground with his friend; he was becoming a sociable and equable member of the class and was able to listen and participate as one of a group.

Comment

Because of his huge anxiety about losing his father, Karu was unable to use his mind to learn from the nursery programme. His anger and resentments were not expressed verbally but were shown in his behaviour towards others. Ann's daily link with Karu helped to meet his hunger for love and security. His improved progress and behaviour was a consequence of being able to talk through his feelings and to trust his teacher.

Children's emotional understandings are dependent not only on the degree of family support but also on what sex they happen to be. Different messages about emotions can be given to boys and girls. In one small study, mothers talked more often to their 18-month-old daughters about feelings than they did to their sons at this age. By the time they were two years old these little girls were seen as more likely to be interested in and articulate about feelings than the boys (35). Other studies offer further evidence. When parents make up stories for their small children they use more emotion words for their daughters than their sons; when mothers play with their children they show a wider range of emotions to girls than to boys. Leslie Brody and Judith Hall who summarised these studies suggest that as a result of the experiences they have, and because girls become more competent at an early age with language than do boys, this results in the girls being able to use words to explore feelings. By contrast boys are not helped so well to verbalise and so tend to be confrontational with their feelings and become less tuned in to their own and others' emotions (36). These early experiences and consequent emotional differences can very often continue into adulthood and be seen in relationships. Goleman suggests that women are well prepared to cope with the emotional aspects of a relationship; conversely, men are more inclined to minimise emotions and are less aware of the importance of discussing and expressing feelings as a way of sustaining a partnership. He argues that this emotional imbalance between the sexes is a significant factor in the break-up of marriages (37).

Given the importance that most of us attach to a stable and loving relationship in our lives, perhaps early years provision should aim to redress these differences in the emotional lessons that children learn.

YOUNG CHILDREN'S DEVELOPING UNDERSTANDING OF FEELINGS

Young children need to have experienced a myriad of emotions before they begin to understand them. Using puppets with children, Denham found that those who showed both positive and negative feelings in their play were more likely to recognise and comprehend what others were feeling in different situations (38). Moreover, using puppets again, Denham suggests that children are beginning to recognise that in a given situation people may feel differently. For example, many children could understand that a puppet could be sad about going to nursery, while they would be happy (39). This ties in with earlier studies which indicate that young children are able to appreciate another viewpoint and are not only focused on themselves (40).

It is much more difficult though for children to recognise that emotions can be mixed. When six-year-olds were asked to predict the feelings of a person who eventually found his lost dog but it was injured, they typically said that the owner would feel totally happy or sad, but not a mixture of both. Children at ten years acknowledged that it was possible to feel both emotions at the same time (41). Furthermore, although they may show complex feelings, they cannot predict them. However, it seems that social convention plays a part; from a young age children can be influenced to show feelings which are socially acceptable but are not genuine. In one study, four-year-old girls responded to social pressures by smiling when the researcher presented them with a disappointing toy, although when they examined their toy alone they showed their disappointment. (Interestingly, boys did not attempt to mask their feelings in the same way.)

Questioned later, when they were able to swap their disappointing gift for a more exciting one, the little girls admitted to being disappointed, but thought that this would not have been recognised because of their polite words of thanks. These children made no reference to their smiling faces or the control of their real emotions and despite their behaviour were unaware of how their displayed emotion could beguile observers (42). As children grow older they begin to understand that the feelings that they show to others may not be the same as their true feelings.

This lesson is a necessary one as part of becoming socialised. Nevertheless, where young children are pressurised or coerced into constantly masking their true feelings and substituting socially acceptable responses, this could lead to them misunderstanding the function of emotions in life.

Case study 📁

Emily settled at her pre-school, seemingly without difficulty. However, she was overly polite in her responses to adults. When greeted in the morning by the nursery assistant, Emily would respond to advances with, 'I'm extremely well, thank you very much'. She would thank individual staff when they supplied paper on the easel and after she had listened to a story. Emily made no advances towards other children – when they took apparatus from her and refused to allow her a turn on their wheeled toys outside she appeared to be at a loss. One day Danny took her beloved teddy from her. Emily did not protest but was later found in the cloakroom curled up in a ball. When the nursery assistant tried to talk through that matter with her, Emily repeatedly chanted, 'I'm very well, thank you', and refused to acknowledge her loss.

Comment

Emily had been heavily conditioned into controlling her feelings and being polite. The effect of this was that some of her behaviour was inappropriate and was regarded as bizarre by other children. When Emily experienced the loss of her teddy she was unable to give vent to her feelings, although her body language demonstrated her great distress.

   The nursery worked closely with Emily's parents in order to help Emily to understand more about her feelings and to feel able to express them. She left the nursery after one year, still effusively and indiscriminately thanking adults but more able to express feelings of anger and frustration where appropriate.

SEIZING OPPORTUNITIES FOR EMOTIONAL LEARNING

We see and hear a great deal about how those adults with emotional problems can track them back to some difficulties in childhood. Goleman suggests that because early childhood is one of the very critical times for nurturing emotional growth, if this opportunity is missed or the nurturing becomes abuse it becomes progressively harder to compensate for this at a later date. If practitioners are to aim to prevent these problems in adulthood they must take advantage of the receptive nature of young children and positively help them to achieve emotional health. This means looking at a climate in the early years setting which helps children to feel, think and talk about feelings. They will think carefully about how to organise this climate. One major challenge is to help children to gradually rein in their impulses. Goleman quotes an interesting long-term study carried out in the 1960s at Stamford University. A group of four-year-olds were offered a marshmallow as a treat. If they were willing to wait for the adult to run an errand they would be allowed two marshmallows when he returned. Goleman reports that some children were unable to wait and grabbed one marshmallow almost immediately after the researcher had left the room. Other children though were able to wait for 15 to 20 minutes for the adult to return. Some found this discipline really difficult:

to sustain themselves in their struggle they covered their eyes so they would-n't have to stare at temptation, or rested their heads in their arms, talked to themselves, sang, played games with their hands and feet, even tried to go to sleep. These plucky pre-schoolers got the two marshmallow reward.

This group of four-year-olds were tracked down at the end of their high school career and the differences between them were starkly clear. The study found that the group who had been prepared to delay their gratification early in life were as young adults more socially competent, self-assertive, personally effective and better able to cope with life's problems (43).

Young children are naturally impulsive and this is particularly so for under threes. Older children can learn to wait, pause and reflect, but it is a very hard lesson for some and slow progress for many. A programme of turn-taking games and activities will help to develop these skills, as will a displayed timeline of routines where children can be encouraged to wait for something special to happen at the end of the session. Above all, if adults regularly share stories and model scenarios which show the benefits of resisting impulse this will influence children over time.

Circle time has become a common means of encouraging children to converse about things that matter to them. In the hands of a sensitive practitioner this can be very effective. However, there are dangers of circle time being accepted as a blanket method for dealing with many personal, social and emotional matters; unfortunately, there are no mechanical teaching methods which automatically give us insights or answers. Circle times with young children can come adrift if they are managed for large groups; if they are not carefully planned and prepared; if they are not conducted by a known and trusted adult; if the adult is not already tuned in to some of the children's needs and concerns; or if they become a dull and predictable routine.

Children, like adults, are more likely to talk about things that affect them with people who show that they are genuinely interested, who are prepared to give time to listen and who reciprocate with some of their experiences. Children's feelings will be stirred by sensory experiences such as listening to music, looking at and touching beautiful things, tasting and smelling. If they can talk about their reactions to these positive experiences, it will alert them to recognise similar feelings on another occasion. In the same way they need to recognise negative emotions. Anger and fury which result in loss of control can be extremely frightening for a three- or four-year-old. Sensitive adults can provide safety and reassurance and encourage children to try to see patterns in their behaviour and reasons for their strong reactions. In this way children will come to accept and regulate their feelings. The Early Years Foundation Stage reminds us that children who are encouraged to feel free to express their ideas and their feelings, such as joy, sadness, frustration and fear, can develop strategies to cope with new, challenging or stressful situations (44).

Adults respond to children's expressed feelings in different ways. While positive feelings are always acknowledged and welcomed, negative emotions are regarded differently in ways that can validate or dismiss them (45). When Stefan showed that he was afraid of being left in the dark his mum tried to reassure him by saying that there was nothing to be afraid of and that he would always be safe when she was nearby. While this response is well intentioned it is giving two messages: that Stefan had. reason to have this feeling, and that he was safe only so long as his mum was around. By validating fears and worries adults can encourage young children to explore and try to understand what they are feeling. They may do this through:

- empathy – trying to understand and identify with the child's fear
- explanation and discussion – encouraging the child to explain the fear and then discussing together how it might be dealt with
- exploration and expression – enabling a child to represent his fear through talking, drawing, painting or through movement and role play
- confronting the fear – taking action by facing a fear together, for example, overcoming a fear of dogs by looking at pictures of them, stroking a furry toy dog, observing the behaviour of a puppy, looking at a dog from a distance and gradually moving closer to it.

Children who are emotionally vulnerable desperately need a calm and safe environment. However, occasionally the nursery that emphasises calm therapy can be in danger of repressing emotions. Children have the right both to witness and to experience different feelings. Living in a calm, bland atmosphere can produce dull people. Children's feelings should also be respected. It is questionable whether adults should attempt to jolly children along when they are bereft at being left in the nursery, or their friend will not play with them. This sorrow and desolation is more devastating than that experienced by an adult in a comparable situation for the simple reason that the child does not have the life experience which tells her that the cause of the distress is only temporary. A simple acknowledgement of sympathy will at least show the child that she is being taken seriously. As always, practitioners themselves play a very important role as models. A strong relationship between adults and children is founded on feeling. In such a setting children understand that the adults care for them, laugh with them, share their tragedies and excitements and also become angry when boundaries of behaviour are broken. So long as the love and care are prevalent, children will flourish and grow given this healthy emotional repertoire.

Practical suggestions

Listen and observe
- Listen and carefully observe any signs of distress in a young baby and learn to identify the reason, e.g. hunger, discomfort, boredom, tiredness.
- Try to catch children's responses during different parts of the day.
- Observe how they cope with the challenges of new activities or a new member of staff.

Continued

Continued

• Observe the body language of those children who cannot easily verbalise their feelings, particularly those with English as an additional language.

Plan clear expectations and support for the role of the key person
Provide a job description based on the following requirements:
Responsibilities
Relationships/Links
• Establish an initial trusting relationship with parents/carers, e.g. through home visits, a pre-arranged initial meeting, introduction to the setting.
• Maintain close, ongoing working links with parents through clear professional boundaries.
• Develop good communication links with parents to exchange information about the child and circumstances which affect him/her, e.g. through face to face contact, daily link book, diaries, photographs, telephone calls (where a family is given two key persons, parents to be aware of the work rota and know which member of staff is working).
• Establish close personal links with each child to ensure that the child feels special, and experiences an affectionate and reliable bond.
• Liaise frequently and regularly with staff, e.g. to exchange information about your key children, provide a voice for the child, over time, to encourage the children to establish relationships with a wider circle of adults.
• Link with other agencies, e.g. in order to provide the family with additional support/expertise, to ensure that the family experience a well managed transition to and from the setting.

Knowledge and understanding
• Clearly understand the need for confidentiality in regard to each family's circumstances.
• Become informed about each child's family background in order to understand more about his/her behaviour and be better equipped to deal with it.
• Develop knowledge of each child's home language, e.g. to use to greet the child and parent each day.
• Develop understanding of child development from birth to age five.
• Tune in to each family when communicating important messages, e.g. early attachment, central role of parents in the child's ongoing development, the expectations for and of parents during their child's time in the setting.
• Become familiar with:
  – the Early Years Foundation Stage and internal documentation, and understand how these might best be used to support the progress and well-being of very young children, e.g. through use of observation sheets, developmental charts
  – internal policies and procedures, e.g. health and safety, child protection, SEN procedures reviews, evaluations
  – daily routines to follow which ensure that children start to recognise a

Continued

Continued

predictable pattern to the day.

Key attributes of the role
- Secure self-esteem
- Emotionally mature and able to cope with complexity
- Willingness to learn from parents
- Comfortable with diversity and respectful attitude towards different family situations
- Strong interpersonal skills, e.g. friendly, open, discrete, patient, tolerant
- Good communication, (verbal and non-verbal) listening and negotiating skills
- Ability to de-centre and empathise with children and their parents
- Genuine interest in each family and the child's developing story
- A reflective approach to practice
- Motivation to develop professionally and so increase expertise and skills.

Recruitment, induction and ongoing support for the key person
- Recruitment procedures to involve staff and parent representation
- Warm welcome from friendly, approachable staff who demonstrate solidarity as a team
- Links to a trained mentor and opportunity to continue to shadow aspects of work
- Provision of a 'buddy' to share the key children and ensure cover when key person is absent (due to sickness, holidays and shifts)
- Access to a staff handbook which provides details of daily routines and procedures
- Access to a library of professional books/articles
- Observation by and feedback from line manager to establish strengths and areas to develop
- Initial training in key aspects of the work, e.g. attachment theory
- Attendance at in-house training, e.g. staff meetings, training days to develop communication and counselling skills.

Provide an environment which enables children to acknowledge and express their feelings
- Affirm a baby's distress by gentle rocking and gently telling him that you know he is hungry or tired.
- Share a toddler's enjoyment of a game, e.g. peek-a-boo and encourage him to repeat it again and again.
- Organise a broad range of experiences which enable children to express their feelings in different ways.
- Provide resources: a punch bag on which to vent angry feelings; a large soft animal or soft woolly scarves for lonely/upset children to cuddle; a large stuffed figure of a granddad sat in an armchair to whom children can

Continued

Continued

confide their worries.

- Have regular displays of adults and children expressing different emotions. Use these in discussions with small groups and encourage children to identify with the feelings and to share their own experiences.
- Introduce a worry bag (a drawstring bag) and display a selection of shells (worry shells) nearby. If a child is worried, he/she can be encouraged to select a shell and take it to an adult to share his/her concern. After the worry has been discussed (and hopefully resolved) the child visibly gets rid of the worry shell by placing it away in the drawstring bag.

Help children to acquire a clear and understandable picture of life in the setting/class
- Make clear the daily sequence of events.
- Provide a pictorial timeline and refer to it throughout the session.
- Have a large clock and make clear the times when certain activities begin and end (with practice, many four-year-olds will learn to use the clock as a reference point).

Help children to develop coping strategies — *ref. mmore*
- Use the language of feelings – suggest labels to describe children's emotions, e.g. bubbly, excited, fizzy, gloomy. Encourage them to use the vocabulary in relation to their own and others' feelings.
- Help self-contained and cautious children to recognise and open themselves to excitement, joy and wonder in the safe knowledge that these feelings are acceptable and can be controlled.
- Provide ways of talking to meet needs, e.g. instead of pushing a child off a bike in anger, suggest that the child requests to have his turn.

Demonstrate that everyone has feelings — *ref. mms?l*
- Talk about how you feel, what makes you angry, excited or worried.
- Use situation stories to help children to understand why people feel differently. → *mirror games* ᵢ

Professional practice questions

1. How well do I read signals of different feelings expressed by babies in my key group?
2. How well have new children come to terms with their feelings on admission to the nursery? How do I know?
3. What have I done today (this week) to help children be more aware of their feelings?
4. How do I help some of my older children to become less impulsive?
5. How do my feelings (impatience, frustration, pleasure, sympathy) affect how I interact with individual children?

Continued

Continued

6. What do I need to know about the children's emotional lives at home that will help me help them to become more effective learners?

7. How well do we support our less experienced colleagues in their key person roles?

The following references in the *Early Years Foundation Stage* link to this chapter:

Statutory Framework and Guidance: pp. 12, 22, 37
Practice Guidance: Appendix 2, Areas of Learning and Development
Self-confidence and Self-esteem (pp. 27–9), *Making Relationships* (pp. 30–1), *Sense of Community*, (p. 38).
Principles into Practice Cards: 1.4 *Health and Well-being (Emotional Well-being),* 2.1 *Respecting Each Other (Understanding Feelings),* 2.3 *Supporting Learning,* 2.4 *The Key Person,* 3.1 *Observation, Assessment and Planning,* 3.2 *Supporting Every Child,* 3.3 *The Learning Environment (The Emotional Environment).*
The CD-ROM *in depth*: offers further guidance on the above principles and commitments.

The following Early Years Professional Standards link to this chapter:
1, 3, 4, 6, 8, 10, 11, 13, 15, 19, 23, 25, 26, 27, 29, 32, 34, 35.

REFERENCES

1. Layard, R. and Dunn, J. (2009) *A Good Childhood: Searching for Values in a Competitive Society*. London: The Children's Society.
2. Goleman, D. (1998) *Working with Emotional Intelligence*. London: Bloomsbury, p. 4.
3. Department for Education and Skills (DfES) (2007) *Principles into Practice Cards: 2.1 Respecting Each Other, 2.3 Supporting Learning, 2.4 The Key Person*. London: DfES.
4. Gardner, H. (1993) *Multiple Intelligences*. New York: Basic Books.
5. Nowicki, S. and Duke, S. (1989) *Helping the Child who Doesn't Fit In*. Atlanta, GA: Peachtree Publishers.
6. Damasio, A. (1994) *Descartes' Error: Emotion, Reason and the Human Brain*, quoted in D. Goleman (1996) *Emotional Intelligence*. London: Bloomsbury, p. 19.
7. Goleman, D. (1998) *Working with Emotional Intelligence*. London: Bloomsbury, p. 239.
8. Piaget, J. and Inhelder, B. (1968) *The Psychology of the Child*. London: Routledge and Kegan Paul.
9. Vygotsky, L. (1978) *Mind in Society*. Cambridge, MA: Harvard University Press.
10. Meadows, S. (1994) *The Child as Thinker*. London: Routledge, p. 356.
11. Laevers, F. (1999) The Experiential Education project: well-being and involvement make the difference, *Early Education*, Vol. 27, Spring.
12. Pascal, C. and Bertram, T. (1998) Accounting Early for Life-Long Learning. Keynote

talk at Early Years Conference, Dorchester, July.
13. Department for Education and Skills (DfES) (2007) op. cit. (note 3).
14. Department for Education, Lifelong Learning and Skills (2007) *Foundation Phase: Framework for Children's Learning.* Welsh Assembly Government. www.wales.gov.uk
15. Northern Ireland Council for the Curriculum Examinations and Assessment (2006) *Understanding the Foundation Stage.* Belfast: Council for the Curriculum, Examinations and Assessment, www.nicurriculum.org.uk/foundationstage.
16. Scottish Government Publication (2008) The Early Years Framework, www.scot-land.gov.uk/early years framework
17. Department for Children, Schools and Families (DCSF) (2008) *Social and Emotional Aspects of Development (SEAD).* London: DCSF.
18. New Zealand Ministry of Education (1996) *Te Whariki: Early Childhood Curriculum.* Wellington: Learning Media.
19. David, T., Gooch, K., Powell, S. and Abbot, L. (2003) *Birth to Three Matters: A Review of the Literature.* London: DfES, p. 46.
20. Leach. P. (1994) *Children First.* London: Michael Joseph, p. 85.
21. Gerhardt, S (2004) *Why Love Matters.* London: Brunner-Routledge.
22. Trevarthen, C. (1988) quoted in P. Elfer, E. Goldschmeid and D. Selleck (2003) *Key Persons in the Nursery.* London: David Fulton, p. 11.
23. Elfer, P., Goldschmied, E. and Selleck, D. (2003) op. cit. (note 22) pp. 18–19.
24. Leach, P., Stein, A. and Sylva, K. (2005) *Families, Children and Child Care Study,* Institute of Children, Families and Social Issues, Birkbeck University of London, 7 Bedford Square, London WC1B 3RA.
25. Department for Children, Schools and Families (DCSF) (2008) *Social and Emotional Aspects of Development. Guidance for Practitioners Working in the Early Years Foundation Stage,* Appendix 1. London: DCSF.
26. Trevarthen, C. (2006) 'Doing' education – to know what others know, *Early Education,* No. 49, Summer, p. 12.
27. Denham, S. (1998) *Emotional Development in Young Children.* New York: Guilford Press.
28. Williams, E. (1997) It's not bad to be sad, *TES Primary,* 12 September, p. 13.
29. Rees, D. and Shortland-Jones, B. (1996) *Reading Developmental Continuum: First Steps Project.* Department of Western Australia, Rigby Heinemann.
30. Oxfordshire County Council (2006) *Transition Foundation Stage to Year One.* Oxfordshire County Council. www.oxfordshire.gov.uk.
31. Elfer, P. (2007) *Life at Two, Attachments, Key People and Development* (user notes). Siren Films Ltd, 5 Charlotte Square, Newcastle upon Tyne, NE1 4XF. www.siren-films.co.uk.
32. Dunn, J. (1999) Mindreading and social relationships, in M. Bennett (ed.) *Developmental Psychology.* London: Taylor and Francis, pp. 55–71.
33. Goleman, D. (1996) *Emotional Intelligence.* London: Bloomsbury.
34. Handy, C. (1994) *The Empty Raincoat.* London: Hutchinson.
35. Dunn, J., Bretherton, I. and Munn, P. (1987) Conversations about feeling states between mothers and their young children, *Developmental Psychology,* Vol. 23, pp. 1–8.
36. Brody, L.R. and Hall, J.A. (1993) Gender and emotion, in M. Lewis and J. Haviland (eds), *Handbook of Emotions.* New York: Guilford Press.
37. Goleman, D. (1996) op. cit. (note 33).
38. Denham, S.A. (1986) Social cognition, social behaviour, and emotion in preschoolers: contextual validation, *Child Development,* Vol. 57, pp. 194–201.
39. Denham, S.A. and Couchard, E.A. (1990) Young pre-schoolers' understanding of emotion, *Child Study Journal,* Vol. 20, pp. 171–92.

40. Borke, H. (1983) Piaget's mountains revisited: changes in the egocentric landscape, in M. Donaldson (ed.) *Early Childhood Development and Education.* Oxford: Blackwell.
41. Harris, R.L. (1983) Children's understanding of the link between situation and emotion, *Journal of Experimental Child Psychology*, Vol. 36, pp. 490–509.
42. Cole, P.M. (1986) Children's spontaneous control of facial expression, *Child Development*, Vol. 57, pp. 1309–21.
43. Goleman, D. (1996) op. cit. (note 33) pp. 60–83.
44. Department for Education and Skills (DfES) (2007) *The Early Years Foundation Stage Practice Guidance*, Appendix 2. London: DfES Publications, p. 22.
45. Sorin, R. (2003) Validating young children's feelings and experiences of fear, *Contemporary Issues in Early Childhood*, Vol. 4, No. 1, pp. 80–6.

5

Dispositions for Learning

Summary of contents

- Dispositions to learn are stable patterns of behaviour, which emerge from babyhood and are affected by feelings and are influenced by family life.
- In order to learn, babies and young children must want to do so.
- On entry to a group setting the child's inclination to learn is strengthened through a secure attachment with a key person who acknowledges and respects the learning and achievements that have already occurred at home.
- Positive dispositions for learning are further strengthened by opportunities to practise them through varied experiences, which take account of children's interests.
- The practitioner plays an important role in identifying, encouraging and extending these interests and through making explicit her own learning traits.

We hear a great deal today about the problem of disaffection in society. Many adults become disaffected with their partners – hence the high rate of family break-up. People in all walks of life grow to be dissatisfied with their employment. Disaffected adolescents are accused of being demotivated towards study, lacking persistence and initiative. There is also a worrying trend of children being excluded from and truanting from primary schools. Yet as the term 'disaffection' implies, at one time there was a positive attitude towards what is now being rejected. All partnerships start on an optimistic note; most people feel positive when starting a new job; at one point in their lives children are strongly disposed to learn and most view starting school as an exciting venture.

This chapter does not intend to attempt to tease out why people become dissatisfied with their lot; there are many books and courses which offer advice and support for living positive and satisfying lives. However, all the literature and counselling courses emphasise that whatever the circumstances, the key to living and learning successfully lies within ourselves – it is to do with our views and attitudes and what we make of what we are given. In the previous chapter we looked at the inextricable link between the emotions and other aspects of our development. We saw how receptive young children are to emotional learning. The same messages apply to attitudes or dispositions. We know that the young brain is very alert – the mechanisms are all present to promote powerful learning. Nevertheless, unless a young child is disposed or inclined to use what she knows, the mechanisms will not function.

WHAT ARE DISPOSITIONS?

Lillian Katz makes a useful distinction between attitudes and dispositions. She states that whereas an attitude consists of a set of beliefs, a disposition demonstrates those beliefs in behaviour. It is possible to have a positive or negative attitude towards something but not be disposed to take any action about it. Katz suggests that young children are not assumed to have attitudes because they are too young to think evaluatively. However, all we are learning about the impressionable young brain indicates that beliefs, attitudes and dispositions are being shaped in infancy. Katz further differentiates between feelings and dispositions. The former are emotional states, while the latter are habits of mind which result in patterns of behaviour (1). As we saw in the previous chapter, feelings can be powerful, but with young children they can be transitory, while dispositions are likely to be more stable and long-lasting. Nevertheless, feelings will significantly affect dispositions.

Case study 📁

Tony was constantly anxious when faced with anything new or a different routine. He looked worried and clearly felt insecure when presented with the opportunity of climbing on a new climbing frame. He was persuaded to climb onto the first rung but was not prepared to persist with the challenge of the new equipment. Tony's anxious feelings had led him to adopt a very cautious disposition.

Katz also points up the difference between predispositions – that is, the genetic gifts that are present at conception – and dispositions which are learned. Moreover, dispositions do not automatically follow on from predispositions. It is easy to believe of a friendly and outgoing baby who is bursting with curiosity that these qualities will remain with her for life. Given supportive experiences and guidance that baby will strengthen her predispositions to socialise and learn; however, if she is not given these opportunities, these early positive traits are in danger of becoming weaker.

Attention is given to attitudes and dispositions in other chapters. For example,

in Chapters 2 and 6 we see how children develop sociable and moral dispositions and in Chapter 8 how attitudes of interest and tolerance towards difference are fostered. This chapter looks particularly at dispositions for learning
and the messages for those who work with young children.

Babies are born with a passion to find out. Gopnik and colleagues suggest that
two-year-olds have a particular drive to make sense of all around them as seen
in their boundless energy to investigate and start to ask questions (2). They lack
experience of the world but their physical, intellectual, social and emotional
antennae are tuned to make sense of it. This is a common endowment given to
all healthy children and it happens without any formal education. However,
the effects of environment influence this heritage. Children's early investigations may be strengthened or restricted and by three and four years of age the
impact of children's early life experiences are already evident. It is easy to see
those individuals who show signs of positive dispositions to learn such as high
levels of motivation and perseverance, as well as those who are more passive or
distractible.

Practitioners now have some common pointers for the dispositions that they
should strengthen in young children. The Early Years Foundation Stage identifies dispositions for learning which include excitement, motivation and interest and practitioners are urged to encourage children to concentrate and
develop autonomy (3). These are closely aligned with Margaret Carr's five
aspects of dispositions namely: taking an interest, being involved, persisting
with difficulty or uncertainty, communicating with others and taking increasing responsibility. Carr usefully suggests that these aspects or domains can be
analysed in three parts:

- being ready – when children see themselves as a learner
- being willing – when they recognize that the environment offers scope for
  learning
- being able – when they have the knowledge, skills and understanding that
  will enable them to be ready and willing (4).

DEVELOPING DISPOSITIONS AT HOME

Once again, dispositions to learn are grown in family life. Children who live in
a well-organised household will observe and become accustomed to daily routines. They will learn to predict the pattern of each day, to organise their personal belongings and to value order. The effect on a small child may, of course,
differ according to the impact and strength of the daily messages, the way in
which parents help the child to make sense of what is happening and the
child's own personality. One child may use these early lessons to develop sys-
tematic and orderly habits of learning. Another may be dominated by and
become dependent upon routine which can lead to her becoming rigid and
inflexible.

Case study 📁

Chloe at 18 months loved to draw. The crayons that she used were stored in a large biscuit tin. Chloe carefully chose her crayon, used it and then replaced it in the tin, saying 'back, back', before selecting another. She clearly enjoyed making marks but also selecting and replacing the tools.

Three-year-old Amy spent most of her time in the nursery tidying books. She smacked children's hands when they came to the book area to browse through books and use them. Directly a book was removed from the shelf Amy replaced it. She was unable to concentrate on a group story if any books were lying around and would dart off to tidy them up. Amy disliked any change in the nursery regime. One sunny morning the nursery teacher announced that children could have their snack outside. Amy refused to go out. When gently encouraged to do so, she shouted, 'I don't like this, we don't do this'.

Comment

Chloe's mother had encouraged her to be independent and to tidy away her toys as part of a game. The toddler was already enjoying the mastery of managing her drawing tools as well as the magic effects of using them. For Amy, tidiness and routine had assumed an undue importance; so great was her need to be in control that it meant that she was unable to relate to other children or to enjoy different curriculum activities.

LEARNING IS NOT COMPULSORY

Although a very young child's learning and progress are influenced both positively and negatively by the care, stimulus, neglect or indifference of his family, ultimately they are hinged to the child's own motivation. The same applies when the child moves to a group setting. His inner drive to learn remains the key factor in his subsequent achievement. This suggests that above all else practitioners need to reflect on how their provision strengthens this drive.

One of the major tasks for any early years practitioner is to identify what learning has occurred before the child starts in a group setting. Fisher (5) likens the 'composition' of each child's learning to a jigsaw puzzle, with individual pieces gradually fitting into place, so casting light on wider and deeper understandings. Following this analogy, the practitioner needs to recognise the pieces of cognition already in place and support each child in adding to their personal cognitive jigsaw. This approach to assessment and teaching respects the child's initiatives and places the practitioner in the position of a tutor. Conversely, if the practitioner ignores previous learning and attempts to 'take over' the construction of the cognitive puzzle, this damages the disposition to learn. The child is confused, the puzzle is no longer under her control and her motivation to know more is diminished.

The key person once again plays a significant role in bonding with each baby and child as rapidly as possible. An attachment grows as the key person carefully observes her new charge and so finds out what he likes and dislikes and what really interests him. The more the key person can identify how each child 'ticks' the greater the chance of her providing for his needs and fuelling his curiosity.

Learning is hard work for anyone; very young children have so much to learn and they must feel energised to do so. Much will be achieved through their own natural curiosity, but babies and young children also need warm support and encouragement from adults who are close to them. This support should stem from a clear understanding of the significant steps in the child's natural development and the signals that these give for future learning. These are usefully outlined by Bruce and Spratt in regard to developing children's essential literacy skills. Some of the steps they include are:

- relating to others – engaging in social interactions such as eye contact, turn taking and imitation
- movement – being aware that a baby's gross and fine motor co-ordination are closely linked to reading and writing later
- making and using symbols – recognising the personal symbols that children make and use through singing, dancing, drawing, painting, constructing and other ways of communicating without words
- conversations – having interactions with children which are based on the tenets of easy and reciprocal verbal and non-verbal exchanges
- listening to sounds in language – encouraging recognition of matching sounds
- rhythm, rhyme, intonation, alliteration – all help children to later learn about syllables in words, understand punctuation, hear patterns in sound and recognise repetition of sounds at the beginning of words. Enjoyable opportunities for this learning are through action rhymes and songs and stories
- well-being – preserving the child's enthusiasm for literacy learning by offering support at the right pace and in the right way for each child (6).

It is now well understood that young children learn more effectively when they are active, having fun and have regular and frequent access to adults. Many children under the age of five find it difficult to sit still even for short periods or to understand new knowledge or concepts when they are taught to a group. Although reception practice is changing radically to meet the requirements of the Early Years Foundation Stage, this is still standard procedure from the time that children enter many reception classes. The best literacy and numeracy sessions are creatively adapted to meet these needs through flexible timings, good staffing ratios and regular use of enjoyable play methods to allow children to practise new skills and ideas. In these sessions children are supported in their learning, and are likely to want to learn more. Without this attention to young children's diverse learning needs, routine and prescriptive programmes may not reach some children and may not challenge others. Confusion and boredom will result in demotivation; in extreme cases the result could be putting children off reading for leisure or delighting in numeracy patterns and problems for life. In short, we could end up with children who are able to read, write and calculate, but who have no desire to use these competencies. Lillian Katz points out that an appropriate pedagogy is one that takes into account the acquisition of knowledge and skills in such a way that the disposition to use them and positive feelings towards them are also strengthened (7).

Even young children can show signs of disaffection towards their schooling. Gill Barratt, in her arresting study of young children starting school in reception classes, shows how they can be turned against school by a curriculum and organisation that do not take account of their interests, what they know already or the ways in which they have learned it. At this age they do not have open to them the options of older children who may try to avoid attending school. At four and five children have little choice as they accompany their parents. However, as Gill Barrett says, they do have the power to withdraw their goodwill (8). Any knowledgeable early years practitioner will recognise the body language of a three- or four-year-old who does not wish to comply with a request or take part in an activity. We may insist on attendance but we cannot require children to learn.

Case study

Kane at four years was excited about starting school. His nursery had served him well for two years, helping him to become confident and independent, but for the last term it had not offered him sufficient challenge, particularly to match his deep interest in numbers. At home Kane's dad played cards with him regularly and Kane was very able to see number patterns and to do simple number calculations. He was visibly bored with the nursery and very keen to go to 'big school'.

Kane learned school routines quickly. He was eager to show his ability in numeracy and was daunted when his responses were sometimes ignored in order for other children to contribute. He had little interest in sorting and matching activities and found the early practical recording of numbers easy and routine. After three weeks Kane's teacher, Sue, was concerned about him. He was restless and inattentive for much of the day and no longer volunteered answers in group times. In contradiction to the picture that Kane's mum had provided of his abilities, he appeared to have no interest in mathematical activities and his baseline assessment score for maths was low. Sue arranged for a Year 6 boy who was interested in maths to work with Kane for 20 minutes a day for a trial period of two weeks. Initially the boy played similar games to the ones that Kane played at home with his dad. This developed into a programme of number problems, mental arithmetic and logic. After one week Kane's behaviour had changed noticeably. He continued to look forward to sessions with his Year 6 friend (which were reduced to weekly occasions) but was now enthusiastic about other activities, particularly construction and design technology. He developed and applied his abilities in numeracy, shape and space and produced some exciting models. Kane was pleased to help other children with their work.

Continued

Continued

Comment

Before Kane was admitted to school, Sue had fortunately taken time with Kane's parents to gain a clear picture of his interests and capabilities. She rapidly noted the mismatch between Kane's reported abilities at home and what he demonstrated in the reception class. She recognised that Kane was not being challenged and her prompt and imaginative action helped to reverse Kane's early disaffection.

NURTURING DISPOSITIONS TO LEARN

Lillian Katz puts forward a number of important points relating to the nurturing of dispositions in any early childhood programme (9). These will be examined in some detail.

1. *Newly acquired knowledge and skills will only be secured in learning if they are used.* Children may be able to do something but not wish to do it. On the other hand, positive attitudes by themselves are not sufficient. It is not very helpful to want to do something for which one is ill equipped.
2. *The way in which something is taught may either strengthen positive attitudes or damage them.* For many years now, early years practitioners have become concerned that the 'paper and pencil culture' evident in primary schools had a negative influence on practice with younger children. However, the Early Years Foundation Stage with its emphasis on active learning and play, is tailormade for babies and young children and conducive to them enjoying learning (10).

Case study 🗁

The staff at Tachbrook Nursery School deliberately develop children's experience of and capacity for sustained, imaginative play; they encourage story play to develop over lengthy periods of time, often a term and sometimes longer.

In a move to deepen children's super-hero play, the headteacher, Tess, shared informally with a small group illustrations and stories of some characters from myths. The Russian story of the witch Baba Yaga Boneylegs particularly captured the children's interest and this was the start of a play theme which lasted for two terms. The play was always situated outside; children were provided with open-ended props, boxes and fabrics, and the freedom to use these as they wished. Different strands to the play included hunting Baba Yaga and other monsters such as the Minotaur and Medusa. Children also explored ideas about power and the usefulness of magic charms and potions. During the play, staff saw children coping with their

Continued

Continued

fears, supporting friends, developing an understanding of cause and effect and ways to represent things through signs and symbols. They internalised the story and, using their own mark-making, were able to narrate the plot onto large sheets of paper.

Comment

The children's high levels of commitment to their play is self-evident, together with the tremendous benefits to their personal development. In particular it helped them delve into their deepest fears and concerns. The 'teaching' which made this possible is subtle and sensitive. Staff provide a daily time for story play and initially set the ground rules. However, importantly, adults do not dominate but 'pump-prime', encourage and help to embellish and lift children's ideas. The headteacher refers to the adult's role being to 'supply nuggets of inspiration to take the play forward' (11).

Clearly it is not possible to make learning fun all of the time but methods of teaching with young children must, above all, ensure that they strengthen positive attitudes towards what is being learned. Those positive attitudes will be needed when the learning becomes difficult.

3. *Dispositions are not easy to regenerate once they are extinguished.* Katz makes the important point that whereas knowledge and skills may be taught successfully in later life, it is more difficult to bring back to life attitudes that have been discouraged. This makes it vital to include in any early years programme a strong and explicit emphasis on nurturing the habits of mind that support learning.

Case study 🗁

Kieran, a much loved only child, attended a kindergarten from age two years. He appeared settled and his parents were very pleased with his apparent progress. From three years onwards, Kieran completed a page a day in his numeracy and English books and learned words to prepare him for entry to a reading scheme. His teacher reported to Kieran's mother that, at times, Kieran was reluctant to 'get down to work', but they had found ways of persuading him by offering lots of praise, including large Mickey Mouse stickers in his book. By age four years Kieran's record showed that he could write two sentences and tackle addition and subtraction equations. He had completed all the books in the first level of a reading scheme.

On transfer to a nursery reception class Kieran was given a choice of activities and was captivated by the construction apparatus. He spent every possible available moment building. He talked about the constructions that he had made but told the teacher that he did not like reading and that he could not write. He appeared to have no interest in numbers and actively avoided any questions to do with calculations.

Continued

Continued

Kieran was keen to come to school but his parents were very dissatisfied with the teacher's comment that after one term he appeared to have made little progress in reading, writing and numeracy. The teacher made great efforts with Kieran and suggested that he needed time to work through his fascination with construction. Despite this, at the end of the year Kieran's parents removed him to a private school, which had a good 'academic' reputation. His parents explained that they felt that their son needed further challenge. At seven years Kieran was refusing to go to school and was attending a therapy clinic at the local child development centre.

Comment

Kieran's parents genuinely believed that their child was having a head start by being taught formal knowledge and skills early in life. Kieran, in turn, had learned that learning to read, write and become numerate involved dull repetition. He quickly learned that the constant praise that was offered in the nursery was not to be valued. Given the option to do more interesting things in school, Kieran was not prepared to use his time and energy doing activities that had become a chore; his reception teacher was unable to repair his damaged motivation to learn to record formally. Kieran's negative dispositions towards learning became stronger as he faced the additional stress of starting at a new school. Within one year, faced with a curriculum that emphasised the very aspects of work that he disliked, his negative attitudes had spread to an aversion to school.

Case study

As a baby and toddler Evan had been readily interested in picture books and later he had happily occupied himself making marks with large crayons on sheets of scrap paper. His mum was delighted in these early signs of interest in literacy and when he was three years old, she sent him to a nursery which stated that early development of reading and writing was a priority. Evan was required to spend some part of each day completing a workbook when he learned to copy his name and other simple words. He learned to recognise flash cards of common words and came home with lists of these words to practise. Positive reports were given of his progress.

Evan made a sound transition to his reception class at four years of age but his teacher reported that he was very reluctant to spend any time engaged in reading and writing activities. He refused to take part in any 'play writing' in role play, claiming that he did not know the words. This attitude persisted throughout the first two terms in school despite his teacher's constant efforts and encouragement. It changed significantly when a new teaching assistant arrived. Despite many demands on her time, she spent 15 minutes a day with Evan, playing word games, sharing writing activities in role play and writing him a special card each day for Evan to take home to 'read'. She introduced Evan to a soft toy panda who 'lived' in a cardboard box. She said that the panda was lonely and suggested that Evan

Continued

Continued

write to him. Evan's numerous written communications with the panda were reciprocated on 'panda headed' notepaper.

By the end of the year Evan was very keen to share books; he often 'wrote' at length using many of the words he had learned previously in the nursery; he particularly enjoyed writing and illustrating cards for the teaching assistant.

Comment

Evan's initial motivation towards literacy was probably 'force-fed' at nursery.

By the end of his nursery career Evan had developed certain reading and writing skills but his enthusiasm was dampened. On starting school, because of his reluctance to enjoy books and seeming lack of confidence to practise and apply what he knew, Evan initially made slow progress in literacy. He required a one-to-one relationship with a sympathetic practitioner to help restore positive attitudes to learning. Without this prompt support Evan might well have lost his urge for learning more about literacy for a much longer period.

4. *Any early childhood curriculum must take into account how desirable dispositions can be strengthened and how negative ones can be weakened.* The receptiveness of young children to all influences means that there is just as much potential to develop unhelpful or even harmful inclinations to learning (passive, inflexible, distractible) as there is to promote the positive. A baby is only likely to be well inclined to learning if there are items readily available which intrigue him and if his key person takes an interest in how he explores them using his senses. Although children mature in learning, four-year-old children are still very concerned with themselves, the people closest to them and the environment in which they live. They continue to gain information through touching, tasting, smelling, listening, observing and through using their bodies. They can concentrate really well when things make sense to them. They need to try things out for themselves, practise what they have learned and be helped to clarify their thoughts through discussion. A play-based programme which pays attention to these characteristics is likely to feed children's urge to want to learn more and to think more.

Conversely, in settings where the new mandatory curriculum for 0–5-year-olds is misunderstood, an early years programme can be more concerned with attainment and focused towards teaching a particular range of concepts and skills which are regarded as essential for children to attain high standards at a later stage in schooling. Typically this includes instructing children to learn rudimentary concepts of colour, letters and shapes often through limited pencil and paper exercises where attainment is recorded. Physical skills of cutting and sticking may be taught but with few opportunities for children to use these for their own purposes. In these circumstances children learn certain things but only on adult terms. Prescriptive activities may set a ceiling on attainment and so some children may not be challenged sufficiently. Bored children are likely to switch off any enthusiasm to learn and many will become distractible and inattentive. Even more disturbing is when children are conditioned to this type of regime; they simply comply with what is being offered. Compliant behaviour, unlike restlessness, will not provide the sharp signals of disaffection. Nevertheless, compliancy is not a mark of active learning. Young children may comply simply in order to please the adult. This becomes an easy route to 'learning'; as a consequence, other more active learning channels diminish when they are not used.

Some babies and children may, of course, arrive at a nursery setting with negative inclinations towards learning. For many different reasons they may not be confident or willing to try new experiences. In these cases the key person needs time to establish a trusting relationship with the child and then gently encourage small steps towards a mastery approach (see Chapter 1). However, it is important to distinguish between a negative disposition and developmentally appropriate behaviour. For example, it is perfectly acceptable for a young three-year-old to 'flit' between activities and to be easily distracted in a small group activity; this same behaviour in a child of five may need to be considered more seriously; by the age of seven the behaviour would seriously inhibit a child's progress.

5. *Positive dispositions for learning should be strengthened as opposed to dispositions for performance.* As children become older their enthusiasm for work can differ. Those who are focused on learning are interested in it for its own sake. They are keen to gain new skills and understandings in order to improve. They are attentive and believe that their efforts in learning will pay off. Other children become more concerned about their performance and how competent others judge them to be. This group depends on comparing their achievements with those of others – test and examination results matter more than satisfaction achieved from learning. Although these patterns are more noticeable in older children, the seeds are sown in early childhood, one example being a tendency to shower extrinsic rewards such as stickers and badges on a child which, over time, become meaningless. Katz rejects this approach but suggests that it is reasonable to assume that if young children are regularly exposed to experiences that are intrinsically interesting and that absorb their energies, this is more likely to support a future disposition for learning. The Early Years Foundation Stage recognises how play is fundamentally motivating for young children and states that 'through play, children learn at their highest level' (12). By the same token, those young children who are exhorted to compete with others and to complete tasks in order to gain adult approval, are not likely to be so disposed towards learning but rather to perform and succeed against others.

6. *There should be some means of assessing children's dispositions in an educational programme.* Although there is an increasing acknowledgement of the important role of dispositions in early education, making sure that they are in place is more difficult. It is quite easy to misconstrue young children's behaviour. Mechanical compliance when completing a task, or a child's attraction towards a novel activity, can be misinterpreted as evidence of genuine concentration and interest. Measuring these aspects of personal development is a very different matter from measuring the acquisition of skills and concepts.

There is a particular danger of using simplistic methods to gather information. For example, young children may be asked to record their attitudes to aspects of daily life in a nursery through highlighting happy or sad faces. Who is to say what factors may influence the recording? The chances are that young children may guess what will please the adult and act accordingly, copy their neighbour, or record their decision impulsively, without having a clear understanding of the issues. Some of the most effective methods of finding out about children's thoughts and feelings, which underlie dispositions, are through listening, conversing with and observing the child in action. Gill Barrett's approach (see Chapter 1), using pictures depicting children's different actions, encouraged children to describe their own thoughts and feelings which they recognised and identified with some of the behaviours shown. Susan Denham used puppets effectively to gain similar information about children's emotions (see Chapter 4).

Figure 5.1 Children can concentrate really well where things make sense to them

Assessment and evaluation of early years practice and children's outcomes have emerged as government initiatives largely as a consequence of public money being used to fund two- to five-year-olds in nursery settings. Major initiatives have been developed to provide a means of quality control and quality improvement. All settings in receipt of grant monies are required to make provision which will enable children to achieve certain goals by the time they leave the Early Years Foundation Stage and move into Year 1. The Early Years Foundation Profile is completed at the end of the reception year and includes a recorded assessment of a child's dispositions to learn.

The Profile, which was originally introduced with little training and regarded by many teachers as a time-consuming and unhelpful summative document, is now being used in increasingly refined ways. This is partly due to useful guidance now available in the *Early Years Foundation Stage Profile Handbook*. For example the handbook emphasises that any assessments should draw at least on 80 per cent of evidence of knowledge of the child, observations and anecdotal significant moments, and no more than 20 per cent of evidence from adult-directed activities. This gives practitioners expressed permission to focus on child-initiated activities where inclinations and attitudes are richly exemplified.

> A self-initiated activity is one wholly decided on by the child and is the result of an intrinsic motivation to explore a project or express an idea. In doing this they may make use of a variety of resources and demonstrate a complex range of knowledge, skills and understandings (13).

This approach is exemplified clearly in the well-established project work in Reggio.

Reception teachers are now comparing scale points that they use to assess children's attainment in order to evaluate their provision. For example, one school found that only 70 per cent of boys gained the scale point 'continue to be interested, excited and motivated to learn' in contrast to 95 per cent of the girls. This raised an enquiry as to why. The teachers reviewed every scale point in the Profile to find differences in attainment of boys and girls. This revealed that the boys who had lower scores in dispositions were particularly distractible and poorly motivated in some sedentary indoor activities. This had had a 'knock on' effect in terms of the boys' development in communication, reading and writing, social and personal development and the desire to learn. These findings led to a review of use of the outdoor area and more active methods of learning.

Margaret Carr's approach to assessment is particularly geared towards children's dispositions and she asks the crucial question, 'How can eager learning be described and encouraged?' (14). Carr responds to her own question through introducing the notion of Learning Stories as a way of assessing dispositions. A Learning Story is a structured narrative which includes the context and relationships with adults and other children, it highlights the activity and includes an interpretation from the author who knows the child well. The story concentrates on the five aspects of dispositions and gives evidence of new or sustained interest, involvement, challenge, communication and responsibility. Carr gives an example of a Learning Story for four-year-old Sean in which Sean perseveres with a difficult task even when he gets 'stuck'. Attached to the story is a photo of Sean using the carpentry drill. The teacher, Annette, writes: 'The bit's too small, Annette, get a bigger one.' We do, drill a hole and then use a drill to put in the screw. 'What screwdriver do we need?' 'The flat one.' Sean chooses the correct one and tries to use it. 'It's stuck.' He kept on trying even when it was difficult. Carr explains that this Learning Story will provide a focus for a discussion between Annette and Sean and, together with other Learning Stories, help both adult and child to see how well he is progressing in persisting with difficulty (15).

Other research studies have also played an important role in assessment. The Effective Early Learning (EEL), Accounting for Life-Long Learning (AcE) and the

Baby Effective Early Learning (BEEL) programmes are projects from the Centre for Research in Early Childhood in Birmingham. The projects are immensely valuable because they help early years practitioners to look closely at children and become aware of aspects of their behaviour. The EEL project introduced practitioners to a valuable observation instrument for identifying and measuring children's involvement. The Child Involvement Scale is based on the work of Ferre Laevers who studied how a child might be involved in deep learning as opposed to just being occupied and busy. Laevers defines the concept of Involvement as: 'a quality of human activity, characterised by concentration and persistence, a high level of motivation, intense perceptions and experiencing of meaning, a strong flow of energy – a high degree of satisfaction, and based on the exploratory drive and basic development of schemes' (16).

Laevers suggests that when children are involved in this way they show certain characteristics or signals, which can be graded to show the level at which they are working. These signals include:

- concentration
- energy
- creativity
- facial expression and posture
- persistence
- precision
- reaction time
- language
- satisfaction.

The EEL Project has very usefully adopted Laevers' work. The Child Involvement Scale enables practitioners in different settings to look closely at children and assess their level of involvement in activities through the absence or presence of the above signals (17).

The Involvement Scale which features in the EEL Project has helped practitioners to measure how well children are involved in learning – it concentrates on the process. The ongoing AcE Project is concerned with the outcomes or results of effective early learning. The project recognises children's dispositions to learn as one of four important indicators of effective learning. Part of the project is to help early years practitioners to identify and nurture the characteristics which appear to be linked with dispositions to learn (18). The BEEL project highlights the behaviour of children less than three years linked to three concepts – how infants demonstrate:

- social and emotional 'connectedness'
- exploration
- meaning making.

Practitioners are encouraged to discuss how their own approaches and provision help these behaviours (19). The projects have helped to make learning dispositions more visible and indicated ways of observing and assessing them.

DISPOSITIONS ARE CAUGHT RATHER THAN TAUGHT

Katz makes it clear that while skills can be taught directly, dispositions are learned in a more subtle way. Any visitor to a nursery setting will immediately be aware how readily most young children are inclined to learn and how engrossed they can be. Indeed, for the lay person it can appear deceptively simple; young children can be seen naturally to co-operate, persevere, think carefully and be well organised in what they do. However, practitioners know only too well that these positive dispositions do not just occur; the seeds are sown at home, while in the nursery setting and early school days positive learning traits are developed through interesting experiences and the interest and involvement of practitioners.

Real learning is not something that other people can do for us. However well constructed a curriculum programme may be, it cannot ensure that young children learn. It may, of course, result in children performing. Children can be taught the alphabet song, recite rhymes and numbers. This in itself is not necessarily bad – a measure of rote learning (which is what this is) will aid working memory (see Chapter 4). The dangerous thing is that a demonstration of rote learning can seduce lay people into believing that a great deal more has been achieved than is actually the case. In a hierarchy, rote learning is lower order learning. Higher order learning requires children to have the inner drive to learn for themselves. It is more than just tacking new learning onto what we already know. In order for children to make true progress in learning they need to make sense of new information by using what they know already and modifying, updating and rethinking their ideas in the light of new knowledge. This learning is creative, active and personal. It is also very hard work. Young children must feel that it is worthwhile investing their considerable energies. Practitioners know that they cannot coerce young children to learn actively; instead they try to understand how each unique child's natural inclination to enquire unfolds and provide scope for this to grow.

The High Scope method of working is well known for emphasising an active approach to learning. The High Scope study tracked children from the age of five to adulthood. It found that those children who had experienced an early education from five to seven years that encouraged a mastery orientation (see Chapter 1), choice and independence, became significantly more effective learners in the long term. The study concluded that helping children to develop a sense of 'personal control' is a key factor in enabling their progress in learning and subsequent success (20).

Any programme which supports children's inclinations to learn will do so by having regard to their interests. This means being aware of their schemes of thought (see Chapters 1 and 4). If schemas are recognised and supported they help young children to make links in their learning and so provide for continuity. Craig at 12 months repeatedly spilt his food on to the tray of his feeding chair and traced up-and-down lines in the liquid. When he started at toddler group he drew mainly vertical lines when finger painting. Later at a pre-school Craig constantly referred to the tall trees surrounding the building. His mum had discussed this with him and had taken a photograph of Craig standing by the side of one of the trees. Craig observed that, in the photograph, 'here is my head but you can't see the head of the tree'. Craig enjoyed drawing – mainly a series of vertical lines to represent the trees. In the reception class Craig practised his own writing which was largely composed of vertical marks of a broadly standard size. In physical play and in conversation he showed a good understanding of positional language, particularly 'up and down' and 'taller and shorter'. This small boy was also interested in other aspects of life, but here we see how an early pattern of behaviour persisted and was strengthened to support further learning.

As we have seen, sustained imaginative play is a sure way of building on children's interests and giving scope for young children to demonstrate their imaginative and creative powers should pervade the curriculum. The 5X5X5 arts-based action research project, which started in 2000, collects information on and gives support to developing children's creative capacities. This wonderful project is founded on recognising children as creative meaning makers, and practitioners and artists as enablers of their explorations, and was inspired initially by approaches in Reggio Emilia (see Chapter 2). The project works with children, educational settings and artists and consistently observes and documents the dispositions and behaviours demonstrated by young children when they are participating in creative experiences. For example, the practitioner at Longvernal Nursery reported 'concentration developed in all children and was particularly noticeable in children who had shorter concentration spans. In addition, children's independence has grown with children selecting and using resources more without adult direction. Their imaginative play developed at a deeper level due to space and freedom ... mixing resources ... concentration ... independence in relation to using materials/resources ... extended language and partnership with peers' (21).

Well-planned adult stimulus which follows children's interests will encourage them to dig deep into experiences and strengthen their interests. At Longvernal Nursery, observing that children (2–5 years) became interested in pirates, the artist introduced them to treasure maps. The adults then stood back and noticed how the children explored and used the materials and resources to communicate their ideas. The group made a map together and then the children worked on scorched materials to create their own maps. 'The results were unique, creative and purely magical! Treasure ... treasure!' (22).

The enterprises in the 5X5X5 project involve time for children to explore their ideas. In his thought-provoking book, *Hare Brain, Tortoise Mind* (23), Guy Claxton suggests that there is a very important place for allowing thoughts to incubate (see Chapter 7). In work with young children, we so often emphasise the need for rapid answers, for working at a brisk pace, for keeping busy. There is undoubtedly a place for encouraging young children to keep mentally alert. However, there is also a different and more creative way of thinking which is only achieved through consideration and mulling things over. Claxton acknowledges the importance of the fast and focused thinking of the hare brain in certain circumstances; he is, though, more interested in the slower processes of the mind where reflection is central. He suggests that play is significant for the tortoise mind in that it involves 'messing about' and figuring things out. This book makes a strong case for time for day-dreaming, for toying with thoughts, for sleeping on a problem and returning to it. In Reggio Emilia and in the many good quality settings in this country, practitioners believe that young children should have opportunities to allow ideas to arise slowly and naturally and they make provision for it.

Thus the type of curriculum programme offered will considerably influence children's inclinations to learn. In addition, the practitioner plays a powerful role. Over the years we have experienced doubts about where the practitioner featured in nursery settings. The understandable fear of not following the hard line of prescriptive teaching has led some settings to the mistaken assumption that warm relationships are an end in themselves – that the adult's main role is to be friendly, positive and loving. Clearly, warm and positive relationships have to be the foundation for any effective work with young children, but it is now realised to be not enough. If young children are praised frequently and indiscriminately, if everything they do is always regarded as intrinsically clever, then how are they going to learn? Our young children deserve more than this benign environment because it does nothing to challenge their intellectual development. The best work by practitioners, epitomised by the approach in Reggio Emilia, is three-pronged, based on relationships, observations and support (see Chapter 2).

The EEL Project provides an additional and similar emphasis on the role of the adult. The project includes an instrument for assessing how well practitioners nurture learning, namely the Adult Engagement Scale (24). This refers to three core elements:

- *Sensitivity*: how well the adult is 'tuned in' and the degree of response to the feelings and well-being of the child
- *Stimulation*: how effective the adult is when taking part in the child's learning
- *Autonomy*: the degree of freedom which the adult provides to allow the child to experiment, make judgments, choose activities and express ideas. It also includes the boundaries established to deal with conflict and behaviour.

This useful set of descriptors is further endorsed in the National Commission on Education (25) in the introduction to *Excellence and Enjoyment* (26) and in the EPPE project (27). The united and powerful message which emerges is that practitioners should and do impact on the way in which children approach learning. Early years staff understand that, by taking their cues from babies and children, they are more likely to be going with the tide of their motivation – going against it is hard and often unproductive, when children show signs of withdrawing their goodwill.

During the early steps in their life journey, young children will have experiences that begin to form their own rich mental environment. James Flynn, writing in the *Journal* for the Royal Society of Arts, suggests that this unique inner treasure can be 'caught':

> the things parents do at present for their children are all worth doing; reading stories, good diet and exercise, good schooling. But somewhere along the line children must fall in love with ideas ... so they will ... seek out friends who are alert, earn their living doing something cognitively complex, develop leisure interests that are challenging. And the best way to get them to fall in love with ideas is to fall in love with ideas yourselves. (28)

Lillian Katz echoes this:

> If teachers want their young pupils to have robust dispositions to investigate, hypothesise, experiment, conjecture and so forth, they might consider making their own such intellectual dispositions more visible to the children (29).

Practical suggestions

Observe
- Notice items that interest babies when they are lying on their backs or tummies – ensure that these items are part of continuous provision and where possible are accessible to touch.
- Note how far a mobile baby is prepared to move to reach an object; over time move the object to encourage and challenge further mobility.

Help children to concentrate and persevere
- Where possible, provide a quiet area where children can work without distraction. Provide notices for them to use, such as 'Please do not disturb'.
- Encourage older children to make stand-up signs, such as 'Please leave', which they can place on an unfinished piece of work to which they wish to return.
- Note when a child's perseverance is flagging. Offer practical help yourself or encourage another child to support the completion of an activity.
- Make clearing up tasks manageable by asking children to choose a specific area of responsibility to keep tidy. Encourage children to congratulate each other when they have completed their task.
- Introduce a vacant post in a reception class for an 'inspector to check clearing up' – a new appointee can be selected on a weekly basis.

Develop memory skills
- *Kim's Game*: place four objects on a tray; remove one object in turn and invite children to identify what is missing. Gradually increase the number of objects over a period of time.

Continued

Continued
- *Pelmanism*: make a giant game with matching pictures which link to the characters and objects in a favourite storybook, e.g. 'The Three Bears'. These are placed face down on a table; children in turn select a card and aim to collect a matching pair. Introduce the game with four matching pairs of pictures; increase this number over time.
- Regularly change an item of display in your room. Encourage children to spot the change. Give individual children responsibility for changing the display.

Encourage enquiry and help children to learn through their senses
- Take children on a sensory walk (wear old clothes!). Visit a quiet location; ask children to: crawl on the ground and describe what they can see; close their eyes and describe what they can feel; close their eyes and open their ears and describe what they can hear; close their eyes and open their noses and sniff and describe what they can smell (see Chapter 8).
- Provide a 'feely' bag with objects of different shapes and textiles which are changed each week. Play a guessing game when children in turn close their eyes and try to describe and identify the object.
- Play a listening game: children form a circle and a child is chosen/volunteers to be 'Peter'. 'Peter' goes into the centre of the circle and closes his eyes; the children pass a bell around and chant 'Peter, Peter, listen well. Peter, Peter who rings the bell?' When the chanting stops a child rings the bell. 'Peter' must point to the direction of the ringing.

Encourage organised approaches to learning
- Provide boundaries for using equipment/apparatus. Use circles and squares of material (small rugs can be used for larger construction) which can be laid out on a surface to provide the area on which to work.
- Help children to think sequentially when they set up, work at or clear away an activity. Ask them, what will you do first, what next?

Encourage reflection
Young children need lots of opportunities to be spontaneous and to share thoughts and experiences immediately. While adults should be available to allow this immediacy, it is also useful to help children to mull things over and to take time to think.
- Provide a thinking area in a quiet corner of the room; provide a couple of comfy chairs, interesting pictures/photographs, strange shaped stones/pieces of driftwood. Make it clear that this place is available for quietly growing thoughts; establish a culture which encourages children to share their thoughts regularly and informally.
- Help children to learn to visualise, e.g. when reading a story, stop from time to time and ask children to close their eyes and 'see the picture in their mind'.

Professional practice questions

1. How far does our sensory room (area) nurture or bombard a baby's sensory explorations?
2. How effectively do I act as a co-player to encourage babies' and children's interests?
3. What areas of learning do I most enjoy and what do I enjoy least? How does this affect the children's dispositions to learn?
4. How well do I show my key children that I am 'in love' with ideas?
5. What scope is there for children to persevere and follow through their ideas and discoveries?
6. How does our daily timetable help children to concentrate and persist?
7. How does the layout of my environment encourage children to reflect?

The following references in the *Early Years Foundation Stage* link to this chapter:
Statutory Framework and Guidance: pp. 12, 37
Practice Guidance: Appendix 2, Areas of Learning and Development
Dispositions and Attitudes (pp. 24–6)
Principles into Practice Cards: 1.1 *Child Development*, 2.3 *Supporting Learning*, 2.4 *Key Person*, 3.1 *Observation, Planning and Assessment*, 4.1 *Play and Exploration*, 4.2 *Active Learning*
The CD-ROM *in depth* offers further guidance on the above principles and commitments.

The following Early Years Professional Standards link to this chapter:
1, 2, 3, 7, 8, 9, 10, 12, 13, 14, 15, 16, 21, 22, 26, 27, 28, 29, 39.

REFERENCES

1. Katz, L. (1995) *Talks with Teachers of Young Children*. Norwood, NJ: Ablex.
2. Gopnik, A., Melzoff, A. and Kuhl, P. (1999) *How Babies Think: The Science of Childhood*. London: Weidenfeld & Nicholson.
3. Department for Education and Skills (DfES) (2007) *The Early Years Foundation Stage: Principles into Practice Cards 4.4 Learning and Development, Personal, Social and Emotional Development*. London: DfES Publications.
4. Carr, M. (2001) *Assessment in Early Childhood Settings: Learning Stories*. London: Paul Chapman, p. 23.
5. Fisher, J. (2007) *Starting from the Child*. Third edition. Buckingham: Open University Press, p. 10.
6. Bruce, T. and Spratt, J. (2008) *The Essentials of Literacy from 0–7*. London: Sage, pp. 14–18.
7. Katz, L. (1995) op. cit. (note 1).

8. Barrett, G. (1989) Introduction, in G. Barrett (ed.) *Disaffection from School? The Early Years.* Lewes: Falmer.
9. Katz, L. (1995) op. cit. (note 1), pp. 47–56.
10. Department for Education and Skills (DfES) (2007) *The Early Years Foundation Stage: Principles into Practice Cards* 4.1, 4.2. London: DfES Publications.
11. Bunting, J. (2004) *Learning through Sustained Imaginative Play at Tachbrook Nursery School,* Floor 13, Westminster City Hall, London SW1E 6QP.
12. Department for Education and Skills (DfES) (2007) *The Early Years Foundation Stage: Principles into Practice Cards* 4.1. London: DfES Publications.
13. Qualifications and Curriculum Authority (QCA) (2008*) The Early Years Foundation Stage Profile Handbook,* p. 9. www.naa.org.uk.
14. Carr, M. (2001) op. cit. (note 4) p. 21.
15. Carr, M. (2001) op. cit. (note 4) p. 96.
16. Laevers, F. (1994) *The Leuven Involvement Scale for Young Children* (video and manual). Experiential Education Series No. 1. Leuven, Belgium: Centre for Experiential Education.
17. Pascal, C. and Bertram, T. (1997) *Effective Early Learning: Case Studies in Improvement.* London: Hodder & Stoughton, p. 12.
18. Pascal, C. and Bertram, T. (2008) *Accounting Early for Life Long learning (AcE) Programme Pilot,* Amber Publications and Training. www.amber publications.org.uk.
19. Pascal, C. and Bertram, T. (2007) Quality and the under 3s: introducing the Baby Effective Early Learning (BEEL) programme, *Early Education,* No. 52, Summer, pp. 12–14.
20. Schweinhart, L.J. and Weikhart, D. (1993) *A Summary of Significant Benefit: The High Scope Perry Pre-school Study through Age 27.* Ypsilanti, MI: High Scope UK.
21. Bancroft, S., Fawcett, H. and Hay. M.P. (2007) *5X5X5 Researching Children Researching the World.* 5X55X5 = creativity, PO Box 3236, Chippenham SN15 9DE, Bath Spa University/Arts Council England, p. 20.
22. 5X5X5 (2007) *100 Words.* 5X55X5 = creativity, PO Box 3236, Chippenham SN15 9DE.
23. Claxton, G. (1997) *Hare Brain, Tortoise Mind.* London: Fourth Estate.
24. Pascal, C. and Bertram, T. (1997) *Effective Early Learning.* London: Hodder & Stoughton, p. 13.
25. Ball, C. (1994) *Start Right: The Importance of Early Learning.* London: Royal Society for the Encouragement of Arts, Manufactures and Commerce (RSA).
26. Department for Education and Skills (DfES) (2003) *Excellence and Enjoyment: A Strategy for Primary Schools.* London: DfES, p. 9, para 3.1.
27. Sylva, K., Melhuish, M., Sammons, P., Siraj-Blatchford, I., Taggart, B. and Elliot, K. (2003) *The Effective Provision of Pre-school Education (EPPE) Project: Summary of Findings.* Institute of Education, University of London.
28. Flynn, J. (2008) How to enhance your intelligence, *RSA eJournal,* April, p. 3, www.thersa.org.uk/journal.
29. Katz, L.G. (1995) op. cit. (note 1), p. 65.

Young Children's Behaviour

Summary of contents

- Young children should be helped to understand about right and wrong and to eventually develop their own moral code rather than simply be encouraged to comply with adult requirements to behave properly.
- Babies and toddlers become aware of behaviour in the home and they start to tune in to the feelings of others.
- Parents and practitioners set boundaries in line with their own beliefs about how far children should learn to develop a conscience for themselves and how far they should be directed to behave.
- In order for children to develop their own code of behaviour they must learn about cause and effect and motives for actions and develop empathy.
- Practitioners should be aware of factors which shape children's behaviour and always offer a positive example.

PAST AND CURRENT VIEWS ABOUT CHILDREN'S BEHAVIOUR

All parents and practitioners recognise that in the process of growing up children adopt different ways of behaving. However, views about what constitutes acceptable behaviour and how it is acquired have evolved as a result of increased knowledge and understanding about child development. Educational thinkers have held widely differing views about young children's moral development. In the fourth and fifth centuries, philosophers and theologians such as St Augustine supported the view of the child as a creature of original sin – small children were regarded as innately wicked and in need of careful moulding to lure them away from the devil. The most obvious way of suppressing the inborn tendency to sin appeared to be the use of corporal punishment. Portraits of medieval and Elizabethan school-

121

masters usually show them with the birch, described as 'God's instrument to cure the evils of their condition' (1). This doctrine of original sin was widely subscribed to until the eighteenth century, when Rousseau took an entirely opposite point of view. He portrayed young children as innocents – children were seen to be naturally good and in need of rescue from the bad world. He believed that children would be disciplined through natural circumstances. In some cases his suggestions are rather extreme. For example, in his most famous work, *Émile* (1762), Rousseau suggests that if Émile broke his bedroom window, he would have to sleep in a draughty room and the cold which followed would alert him to his wrong action. This suggestion ignores the fact that the consequence might also be that Émile catches his death of cold (2)! However, Rousseau's denial of original sin and his statement that all is good as it comes from nature, although extreme, did have the effect of bringing about a kinder and more sympathetic way of dealing with children's misbehaviour. Modern thinking has moved forward to recognise small children as powerful learners who are beginning to make sense of situations from babyhood and to develop their own moral stances from an early age. By the end of the Early Years Foundation Stage, children are expected to recognise the difference between right and wrong and understand the consequences of their actions and words for themselves and others (3).

FACTORS WHICH AFFECT YOUNG CHILDREN'S BEHAVIOUR

Newborn babies are not disposed to behave in a particular way but once exposed to the world they learn rapidly. Jenny Lindon gives a comprehensive outline of the major influences on early behaviour (4). Drawing on this work, four of these influences are examined below: family experiences, individual temperament, the way in which a child thinks and her emotional needs.

Family experiences

The first steps in learning about behaviour, are in the home. The young baby's main concern is for survival and his behaviour is heavily geared towards ensuring that he isn't abandoned (5). During his first year, he forms close attachments and learns to trust a few special people and needs their comfort and support. He also starts to manage his own feelings, for example, he manages to soothe himself and get himself to sleep. In the family very young children begin to see how the people whom they love behave and they try to copy aspects of this behaviour. Judy Dunn's early work (see also Chapter 4) shows how aware a baby and young child are about how family members act. In this way, through what she terms 'affective tuning', a one-year-old baby begins to learn about other people's feelings. A two-year-old child has a good idea of what annoys, distresses or pleases others who are close to them – this is apparent when they use this knowledge as a source of power in challenging and teasing behaviour during the 'terrible two' phase. However, although a young child will learn a lot through simply observing family conduct, she will learn a great deal more if she is helped to understand it. Dunn's studies suggest that in families where arguments are followed by talk about what went wrong and resolutions, this helps a young child to grasp moral issues (6). Where young children have family members who demonstrate consistent and reasonable expectations about how to behave, it is easier for a child to respond.

As well as watching and learning from the behaviour of others, young children start to find out what they are allowed to do – what is acceptable behaviour and what is not. In infancy children are dependent on older family members, and later, practitioners, to provide this information. Towards the end of the first year a baby looks to his mum or key person to see how he should respond – this is called social referencing. The information he receives is a crucial part of bringing up children in the home and setting, and it includes establishing boundaries for behaviour. Boundaries should be few, explicit and always in the child's interest. A one-year-old starts to understand what 'no' means. Around 18 months temper tantrums emerge as the child tests ground rules and wants to assert his independence. Frustrations emerge when the child is unable to complete something that he has chosen to do, commonly trying to dress himself, or where he does not yet have the language to express his needs or is over restricted. The way in which boundaries are set will determine how children learn about rules and, eventually, how they are able to regulate their own behaviour. For example, if a child is encouraged to understand the reason for a rule there is more chance of her respecting it. Moreover, given that she has a secure and strong relationship with an adult she will be willing to please. Isabel's mum had an easy relationship with her small daughter; she responded to Isabel's questions carefully and tended to share some of her views and thinking with Isabel. At two-and-a-half, although Isabel had no real grasp of cause and effect, she trusted her mother's rule about always wearing a seatbelt in the car. The different beliefs that parents and practitioners have about how to raise children will include what they expect of their behaviour and how they intend to help their children achieve it.

Adults' views of what constitutes acceptable behaviour from young children will be influenced according to their own religious, cultural and social and moral beliefs. For some parents, the main goal is for their children to follow religious precepts such as a Christian or Muslim code of conduct. Others may want their child to work out her own way of behaving based on care and respect for others. Yet other families' beliefs might cause them to want their children to become aggressive and defend themselves, to develop prejudices and to acquire dishonest traits as a way of coping with the world.

Parents may have given a great deal of thought to the approach they will take to bringing up their children. In practice, however, emotions such as fatigue, anger and love sometimes hijack the best thought-out strategies. Parents' approaches are also often influenced by memories of how they were brought up. Young mothers may admit to hearing themselves repeat what their mothers said when responding to their own children. Although the management of behaviour takes many forms, it is likely to reflect three different approaches which can be crudely categorised as the permissive, the negotiated and the directed.

Following Rousseau's philosophy, some parents and practitioners believe firmly that children should be allowed to be 'free spirits'. They feel strongly that the best way for children to achieve this 'freedom' is for them to be unfettered by adult requirements. Adults who follow this approach are fearful of crushing a child's spirit; they hold the view that it may be unnecessarily repressive to require good behaviour. Children raised in such an environment may be encouraged from a very young age to make their own decisions about matters of daily life such as what to eat and when to go to bed. Even antisocial actions may go unreprimanded as adults believe that a policy of laissez-faire will allow children to eventually come to sort out right from wrong actions for themselves.

Other families and settings may adopt negotiated approaches to managing behaviour in the belief that young children need authoritative guidance with this aspect of learning as with any other. Adults explain the reasons for rules and offer loving support to help children to achieve them. This helps the 'right' behaviour to stem from a basis of understanding. Moreover, in an easy and loving relationship, young children want to behave in a way which pleases the adults who care for them. As they practise this behaviour they grow to internalise it and, as they grow older, the behaviour stems from self-discipline.

Adults who direct young children's behaviour share the beliefs of the early thinkers who viewed children as being in need of strong moral exhortation. Strict external rules are imposed and threats of punishment used as a way of influencing how children behave. The need to control and require obedience stems from an authoritarian rather than authoritative approach. Adults may also adopt more subtle ways of directing behaviour through using emotional blackmail. In these cases young children are compelled to behave well because they are afraid of being punished or losing affection. Adults may also direct or control behaviour through heavy use of rewards. While young children need praise and encouragement to support good behaviour, too many tangible inducements will dampen children's own motivation to behave well.

Children who enter an early years setting may have experienced any one of these approaches to managing their behaviour or, more commonly, a combination of all three. It is useful for staff to gain insights into parents' views and approaches as well as making clear the approach that is adopted in the setting. Even where parents have different views about handling behaviour, they may respect a clearly argued counter-view from practitioners, which is based on the child's interests.

Temperament

We may understand a child's temperament as her nature or personality. Lindon suggests that temperament influences the way in which a child reacts to her early experiences. She gives the following examples of different types of temperament and how these can impact on behaviour (7):

- *Active-passive*: some children will take initiatives for themselves, will search for new stimulus and be physically robust; others wait for things to happen to them.
- *Sociable-withdrawn*: some children are very gregarious and need other children around them; others may be more self-contained, less outgoing, or may find it difficult to make friends (see Chapter 2).
- *Wary-impetus*: children vary in how they deal with new situations; some may be cautious and circumspect; others unheeding.
- *Negative-positive attitude*: while all children have to deal with irritations and upsets at some time, their capacity to cope and handle feelings differs; some children have a low threshold of tolerance.
- *Disinterested-involved*: some children appear to have a very brief attention span and are very easily distracted while others, given interesting activities, are able to focus and become involved.

Case study

On admission to the nursery it was immediately obvious that Gemma (four years) was fastidious about her clothes. She always arrived dressed in pristine outfits. Gemma refused to play with any messy materials and even after handling books she would wash her hands. On one occasion in the cloakroom, a faulty tap resulted in water being sprayed onto Gemma's dress. The little girl was inconsolable. She said that only naughty children dirtied their clothes and that the naughty children were not allowed to come to the nursery. The nursery superviser related this incident to Gemma's mum and suggested that they might work together to help Gemma to have a more relaxed attitude towards keeping clean. Gemma arrived at nursery the next day, smiling and enveloped in a pretty protective smock.

Comment

Gemma had taken very seriously her mother's strong cautions to keep her clothes clean at nursery. She clearly linked notions of right and wrong with cleanliness. Provision of a smock allowed Gemma to relax and gave her the confidence to take part in painting and water play (where she was very careful to wear additional protective clothing). However, early home influences remained. Gemma continued to disapprove of mess and was often in tears when sand or water was spilt. After two terms at the nursery, staff still needed to reassure Gemma that a mark on her clothes was acceptable and did not constitute naughty behaviour.

Thinking

Building on the social intelligence that they have gained from observing and experiencing the outcomes of family behaviour, on entry to a setting young children watch, listen and think. They note not only what adults say, but also what they do. They very quickly pick up on the expectations of adults and

Case study 🗁

Four-year-old Marcus had twin baby brothers and one older sister, Rose. Rose was very caring to her young brothers; she helped to dress and feed the twins and read them all stories when she returned home from school. Her mum had told Rose on a number of occasions that she was a good older sister. When Marcus started school he insisted that he share this caring role. He carefully put on the twins' socks and shoes and cleared up their toys. Sometimes, however, Marcus found this role difficult. On these occasions he wanted sole attention from Rose and his mum. On one of these days when his mum rebuked Marcus about his demanding behaviour, Marcus said that he only wanted a sister, he did not want brothers.

Comment

Marcus had learned a great deal from Rose about caring behaviour. However, understandably because of his own need for love and attention, he sometimes found it difficult to put others first.

the overall atmosphere in a setting. Children listen not only to words, but to the way in which a request is phrased or a tone of voice; they observe what happens if a request is not responded to – for example, what the adult does if the children do respond to a request to tidy up. Generally young children are very keen to please and a warm, consistent and harmonious ethos supports adults and children to behave well towards each other. However they are very sensitive to underlying currents, for example of friction between adults or a lack of interest in the children. Thankfully these are rare occurrences, but where they exist children can feel adrift and become anxious and demanding.

Emotional and physical needs

All of us are affected by the way we feel and this is shown in our behaviour for good or ill. Many young children are emotionally robust and show the effects of positive feelings in their joyous and vigorous approach to all that they do. Others are more needy and, even given the support of a loving family, they may still show helpless and dependent behaviour. We also recognise that children's feelings will change and this is reflected in behaviour. Often the reason for the change is obvious and it is a temporary episode. For example, we expect a child to show mixed behaviour when faced with the excitement, but also the threat, of a new baby in the family. Moving to a new house, having an illness or bereavement in the family or, perhaps even worse for a child, parents separating, pose huge disruptions and may cause a child to regress and adopt babyish behaviour until she has adjusted to the change. Once the cause of the new behaviour is recognised, often, a watchful eye, patience, understanding and additional attention from the practitioner are sufficient to 'tide the child over' during this difficult and turbulent period.

Physical factors also impact on behavior. Deprivation of opportunities for frequent and regular exercise will show in all aspects of children's well-being and learning (see Chapter 9). Lack of proper sleep can lead children to misbehave, underachieve, become restless and overactive (see section below). A newborn baby sleeps for around 16 hrs every 24 hours; this reduces over time so that a child of 3–6 years requires on average between 11–13 hours sleep every night. Dr Kati Hajibagheri from Imperial College London produced a review of research into sleep and concluded that 'if children are sleep deprived on a regular basis, it interferes with the processing of knowledge acquired during the day. And that has an impact on development and learning' (8). The type and amount of food given can also influence behaviour. Research studies continue to confirm that certain artificial colourings cause an increased level of hyper-active behaviour, particularly in three-year-olds (9). Moreover there is plenty of anecdotal evidence to show that hungry children can become restless and irritable.

COMMON TYPES OF BEHAVIOUR

Most young children are not fluent in spoken language and so the way they behave is their means of giving us messages. In a high-quality early years setting, children's joy and zest for life, their interest and involvement displayed in activities, are evidence of them feeling in harmony with their surroundings. Equally, if things go wrong for them or they feel badly within themselves, this will be reflected through their actions. We accept that most young children are still at an early stage of learning social behaviour – support for them to achieve positive social behaviour is a standard part of early years practice. It is also important to recognise when a child's behaviour may be difficult to cope with but is entirely appropriate for his age. Temper tantrums are a good example. They may emerge around 18 months and be violent and explosive. The cause may simply be frustration; the young child feels restricted and unable to achieve what he wants to do. Alternatively he may be tired or over-stimulated. Temper tantrums should be seen as reassuringly 'normal' around this age. Nevertheless certain worrying behaviours are increasingly evident in settings and require more understanding and attention. Emotional and behavioural difficulties is one of the four broad areas of special educational needs outlined in the 2002 SEN Code of Practice and may include some of the following behaviours (10):

1. *Distressed behaviour*: Some children appear to be overwhelmed by emotional distress and so unable to control the way in which they behave. In extreme cases this may show itself in screaming and crying or aggressive behaviour towards other children or adults. Some very young babies struggle to adjust and regulate their reactions, they may cry persistently, resist being fed and going to sleep and be unable to soothe themselves (11). One possible cause may be that the child has 'missed out' on having continuous care and love from birth and so has no strong attachment – this is most commonly seen

in children who have had different placements in care or where there are turbulent family relationships (12).

2. *Attention-seeking behaviour*: Some children constantly seek attention by behaviour which is difficult to ignore. Attention-seeking behaviour has negative connotations when it is probably more accurate to describe it as 'attention-needing'. For some young children (and older ones for that matter) any attention is better than no attention. And by four years a child may have learned that the one sure way of gaining attention is through negative behaviour. Demanding attention in this way may not be a conscious decision for the child, but it is what she has learned.

3. *Attention-deficit behaviours and sleeplessness*: Young children are exuberant and active; this is a normal aspect of their development. However, we hear increasingly of those who are extremely fidgety, unable to concentrate and who do not sleep well. We should be aware of changes in children's lifestyles and their responses that cause this to be highlighted. In the child's world today there is much more going on to assault the senses and so practitioners have a more difficult task to hold their attention. Moreover, there have always been those young children who have found it difficult to listen; the difference was that, in former days, these children were compliant but quietly switched off – now signs of lack of concentration are much more overt and noticeable. Whatever the reason, the effects of continual distractible behaviour and inability to sleep can be hard to deal with at home, and in a setting. Worryingly though, there seems to be a need to label this troublesome behaviour, as a first step to control it. Hence the increasing use of the terms 'Attention Deficit Disorder' (ADD), and 'Attention Deficit with Hyperactivity Disorder' (ADHD). It is important to understand the different behaviours of children with ADD and ADHD. The former disorder may cause children to be inattentive and 'flit' from one activity to another but they may be relatively unobtrusive doing this. Those children with ADHD are much more noticeable; they are often demanding and disruptive to others. Rather than look at the underlying reasons for the problem, too often the response has been through over-ready prescription of medication, notably Ritalin, to control the symptoms. Although these drugs can help to calm behaviour, they can also produce negative side effects such as mentioned below.

4. *Depressed behaviour*. Chapter 4 drew attention to increased signs of young children showing constant anxiety, depression and withdrawal. They may persistently fret about things or appear to find life a burden – this behaviour is particularly sad when shown at such an early stage in life. It is also easy to overlook in a busy early years setting but a key person should be aware of any body language and expressions which indicate 'sadness'. One apparent signal may be when a child regresses and returns to the comforts of being a baby. Children who are prescribed drugs to control hyperactivity may have a negative 'spin off' and become lethargic and depressed – it can be a matter of exchanging one disorder for another. In extreme cases young depressed children can appear to withdraw from the world and be unable to make contact with others.

The above behaviours signal that all is not well in the child's life and this is being communicated. We have outlined some of the contributory factors but we should not dismiss the impact of the effects of a child's experiences in an early years setting. For example, it may simply be that behaviour problems are compounded by a lack of physical activity in the programme. The most highly developed level of movement for young children is to stay still; prolonged sitting can cause undeveloped muscles to become cramped and painful; they need to use their bodies in order to focus and think (13). The lack of a strong play-based curriculum, is still too evident, despite current actions from the government. In her insightful study entitled *Listening to Four-Year-Olds*, Jacqui Cousins found that children talked of being 'too hurried to play'. When play is permitted, reception teachers admit to adopting a more controlling role. 'We cut it short ... stop them ... interrupt ... it must be irritating for the children ... ' One little girl's comments from the study poignantly sum up children's confusion about the pressure: 'Hurry up! Hurry up! It time! What it time for?' (14). Ten years since this study was completed, government directives for curriculum coverage and achievement targets (see Chapter 4) mean that teachers still struggle to adopt a relaxed pace with plenty of time available for children's own initiatives.

HOW CHILDREN START TO ACHIEVE INNER AND OUTER DIRECTED BEHAVIOUR

Although, as the early thinkers showed, it is possible to coerce children into 'good' behaviour, this has little to do with sound moral development. The ultimate aim must be to enable a child to understand about right and wrong and so to behave morally from her own motives. If we want children eventually to develop a strong moral code for themselves, then we must be concerned with more than them doing as they are told and parroting good manners. Their behaviour must come from the pull of their own conscience rather than from simply complying with instruction. Mia Kelmer-Pringle (15) describes this by referring to behaviour being inner or outer directed. Of course, inner-directed behaviour is a tall order for a three- or four-year-old, but it is then that the seeds are sown which are reflected in beliefs and behaviour in later life.

Most children under three are not yet able to appreciate another perspective. Sally Thomas suggests that a useful way of assessing this is to play 'hide and seek' or 'hunt the thimble'. If the child hides himself or the thimble in the same place that you selected this indicates that he can't yet understand that he can think differently from the adult (16). However, the three-year-old is beginning to recognise that other people or animals can be hurt or harmed; these empathetic understandings will grow when for example adults read and discuss situation stories with children. Before children start to regulate their behaviour they must begin to learn about cause and effect and intentions. The latter is a very difficult concept at such a young age and will only emerge over a period of time. A child starts to learn about cause and effect quite early on when she is able to project. 'If I throw that cup it will smash.' 'If I hit Carl it will hurt him.' Gradually she starts to understand about the consequences of her actions. Over time, she will come to recognise intention. Sometimes we intend to act wrongly and what we do is deliberate. At other times we do not mean to do anything wrong although the result is not good. We may not intend to drop a beautiful vase – it was an accident. Piaget's work showed that only children over eight years understood about intention (17). However, as Tina Bruce points out, more recent work with children, particularly by Margaret Donaldson, shows that these understandings can develop earlier when children are helped to learn in familiar circumstances (18).

As part of understanding another perspective, young children need to be able to empathise – to understand how others feel, and put themselves in their shoes. As we saw earlier, Judy Dunn shows that feelings of empathy develop very early in close family contexts. Here, babies and toddlers have had opportunities to be in close communication with people who care for them and have been with adults who share, explain and discuss feelings with them. Through growing to understand about the feelings of the people they love, children can later extend these understandings to empathise with others with whom they are less familiar.

Case study

Ibu, three years old, loved bathtime at home. He often came home from the nursery with specks of paint or clay on him and liked to wash them off in the bath. On getting out of the bath, Ibu would look at himself approvingly and say, 'all clean'. Ibu made friends with a new Traveller boy who had arrived at the nursery. Walter settled quickly into nursery life, but often when the two boys played, Walter would appear uncomfortable and complain of feeling itchy. On one occasion, Ibu looked at his friend and lovingly suggested 'Walt needs bath to feel nice'.

Comment

From his limited experience of being dirty, Ibu understood the reason for Walter's discomfort. He was already placing himself in Walter's position and wanted his friend to experience the same pleasures of washing that he did.

However, before children can have regard towards others they have to feel secure and loved themselves. Laevers' emphasis on the importance of personal well-being (19) is echoed by a group of primary teachers; in the context of their daily work, they recognised that the children who have positive self-esteem and a feeling of well-being will naturally recognise the work of others and praise them for it (20). This applies equally to adults. People are not likely to show this generous and caring behaviour when they lack the certainty of their own worth and so are hungry for recognition for themselves.

Case study 📁

Three-year-old Toby was collected from playgroup by his mum who picked him up and gave him a hug. Toby looked over to where Sean was still waiting for his mum who was late arriving. 'Hug Sean as well', Toby asked his mum.

Comment

Toby knew how much he was loved by his mum. He showed immense sensitivity in noting Sean's 'aloneness' and could afford to be generous in offering to share his mum's affection with the other little boy.

MAKING IT POSSIBLE FOR CHILDREN TO BEHAVE WELL

Having realistic expectations

Young children will only be able to behave in a way which is appropriate for their stage of development. As we have seen, if a two- or three-year-old has a temper tantrum, this is perfectly acceptable; at this age, emotions are powerful and difficult to control. Again, children under five find it difficult to mask feelings of frustration and boredom. Expectations both at home and in the nursery can be unrealistic. Adults may become upset or frustrated because three- and four-year-olds find it difficult to be quiet when adults converse, or to sit and listen to instructions or a story in large groups. It is important to recognise that children's social skills and powers of concentration will grow as they mature. At five and six years they may manage these things, but fidgety behaviour and interruptions before then are not necessarily signs of poor behaviour. Although a four-year-old can be encouraged to recognise that at times other people do need to talk without her, occasionally her own need for attention will be stronger.

Being consistent

One of the most confusing things for a young child must be to have contact with a number of adults who expect different things, or who require one thing of her on one occasion and something different on another. The former can happen when home and setting have markedly different expectations, or when adults at home or in the setting are not of one mind. The latter is most likely to arise when adults act pragmatically rather than considering what sense the child will make of their requirement. It is all too easy, when harassed under the pressure of time, to give in to a child's insistent demand for sweets or to overlook one child hitting another; in less stressful circumstances an adult might be more able to consider the consequences of her response for the child's future behaviour.

Early years practitioners should be alert to children's understandings of how they should behave. For example, where they have been used to directive language, 'do this', 'stop that', they may find it difficult to cope with indirect requests, 'would you mind clearing up please?'

In cases where there is no single clear message about what is acceptable behaviour, children may eventually develop double standards as they learn to use the different behaviours approved in each situation. This, however, provides no basis for a child to start to internalise a moral code for himself. This internalisation is more likely to develop if a young child can learn to predict that there is one constant expectation of how she should behave.

Encouraging conflict resolution

Until children learn to see another's perspective and to use language to express their feelings and needs they will use physical action to protect their rights. McTavish points out that 'Fighting and arguing help children to practise dealing with conflict and power and to develop social skills. This may also be the only way they know how to deal with anger' (21). Sometimes violent exchanges can lead children to resolve issues themselves and we should be careful not to intervene too quickly and so deprive children of how to deal with these situations themselves. However at times most children will benefit from learning ways of dealing with conflicts which include the adult:

- asking each child to describe or show what happened and to listen carefully to the other's point of view
- recognising and reflecting back what has caused the anger to erupt for each child, for example 'You are cross, Alma because Ana pushed you and took the red bike you were waiting for'. 'You are angry, Ana because you had been waiting a long time for the bike and Alma wouldn't let you ride it'
- encouraging the children to suggest what they could do now to make things better
- discussing the options with them in order to decide on the best suggestion.

Requiring children to say sorry is not helpful; the sentiment is often meaningless to a young child and McTavish suggests that it can detract from the source of the conflict (22).

Providing positive role models

Behaviour and the development of moral values, like dispositions, are heavily influenced by what children observe from adults who are close to them. Small children learn a great deal through imitation. If they love their parents and key persons they will want to be like them. This, of course, places a heavy responsibility on all of us who live and work with children. As Kelmer-Pringle pointed out, it is what we really are and how we behave which matters, not what we say or believe we say (23).

Case study 📁

Carl found that the cake in his lunchbox had disappeared. He discovered that James had taken it; James was hungry because his au pair had forgotten to pack his lunchbox properly. The teacher took both upset children aside. She gently asked James to think if there might have been any other solution to the problem. Together they agreed that a better line of action would have been for James to have told an adult that he was hungry. James himself suggested that in recompense he would bring Carl a cake from home tomorrow. At the end of the day (with the permission of James and Carl) the teacher shared this episode with the other children. Everyone agreed that taking things without permission was not good and should not happen in the nursery.

Comment

Later, when sharing this episode on a training course, Jane, the teacher, admitted that, although she was very aware that different standards were often accepted at home, she considered that her first task was to establish a clear moral code of conduct in the nursery. At the same time she worked with parents, using examples of children's behaviour such as this one to emphasise the need for the setting's code to be reinforced at home. In order for young children to strengthen their understandings about the behaviour of other people, they need to practise roles for themselves. This is possible in play where children can explore being a powerful adult and try out different relationships in total safety. Role play can help moral development in three ways:

- it can enable children to sort out their own feelings.
- it can help them to stand in other people's shoes (to decentre) and explore how they might feel.
- it places them in practical situations where they need to negotiate ways of behaving and treating other children.

Providing a programme which gives insights into behaviour

In a setting which has developed a positive ethos or climate for children's moral development, the adults will have considered carefully the types of experiences that will both introduce and help to reinforce notions of right and wrong. Although first-hand experience of behaviour is the most powerful way of influencing young children's actions, stories are also very helpful in introducing moral dilemmas and giving moral messages.

We know now that children learn all sorts of things better in situations that they can understand. It follows then that any nursery programme should make the most of those situations that occur in daily activities and routines. It is through helping to comfort a child who has fallen and grazed her knee, or being generous to a younger child who has interrupted an activity, that moral behaviour is practised. Discussion also plays an important role. Insightful practitioners will skilfully turn a minor catastrophe into a moral lesson.

Case study 🗁

Patri (three-and-a-half years) had few toys at home and the nursery staff were aware that he regularly hid small items and took them home. His key worker had discussed this issue generally in her small group. She explained that although everyone was tempted, it was not right for individuals to take things for themselves as this would mean that there were not enough things to play with in the nursery. She also suggested that anyone, including herself, could store things in their pockets and forget them; it was a good idea to check each day to see if this had happened. Patri did not respond to these messages and continued to take equipment home. Soon after the discussion, however, Patri was observed stuffing items under a teddy bear's blanket and whispering to teddy to hide them. Another discussion followed along the same lines. Approximately a week after this, Patri was observed again with the teddy. Using a similar tone and manner to that adopted by his key worker, Patri counselled the teddy to 'be a good boy and put things (again hidden under the blanket) back for the children to play with'. During the next month Patri was less and less inclined to take things home. He was keen to 'find' items in his pocket and share these with the staff, and was always warmly praised for his discovery.

Comment

Patri used role play with the teddy bear to work through his behaviour. Over a period of time he was able to overcome his temptation to take things without loss of face.

DEALING WITH CRITICAL BEHAVIOUR

In 2007 there were more than 4,000 suspensions of children aged five and under in England. Of the 400 suspensions of children aged two and three from nurseries, 310 involved accusations of physical assault or threatening behaviour against another child or an adult (24). It is surely an indictment on society that this should occur and there is a critical need to support settings against taking such drastic action. Gender can be a significant influence in identifying and labeling children's behaviour. The Ofsted report, *Managing Challenging Behaviour* (2005) praised early years settings for their sensitive support but found that in some settings up to 40 per cent of children had challenging behaviour. It noted that:

> Boys are more likely than girls to be defiant and both physically and verbally abusive ... Loud raucous behaviour by boys is often the focus of teacher attention, while inappropriate behaviour by girls is sometimes unnoticed or ignored ... A significant proportion of children with challenging behaviour have poor language and social skills and limited concentration spans. This association is evident in all the early years settings and in three-quarters of the primary schools (25).

In these circumstances, practitioners will find it helpful to:

- consider and deal with the reasons for some children showing low-level disruptive behaviour
- be aware that even though some boys' antisocial behaviour may be particularly noticeable, this should not lead to gender stereotyping.

It is imperative that all practitioners should have the skills to deal with more severe behaviour in order to prevent a young child having this experience of failure.

The Camden Early Years Intervention Team is experienced in taking positive action in this regard. They offer training to practitioners on strategies to lessen the likelihood of a child's behaviour becoming a crisis. The team points out that very challenging behaviour is complex and it is only too easy and not helpful to attribute blame to the child, parents or early years staff; this can be exacerbated when other parents complain about the behaviour. In fact there are always a number of factors which influence behaviour; it is both necessary to identify the underlying reasons for the child's actions and at the same time use skilled management to reduce the incidents. Basic rules require all the adults to keep calm and to reassure parents that the behaviour is being managed. Recorded observations will show the pattern and frequency of the incidents of the behaviour. It may be necessary to carry out a nursery risk assessment and, if the child is aggressive, for staff to position themselves between the child and other children. Sometimes a child will use her own methods of coping, for example the Camden team refer to a little girl who, in the build-up to a tantrum, would withdraw to sit on the floor in a toilet cubicle in order to calm down (26).

Supporting positive behaviour, loving the child

Learning to behave well can sometimes be quite an effort for adults and is a huge challenge for some young children. They do need guidance in the form of a few clear boundaries, which should help them to understand about what behaviour is wanted; despite this they will sometimes fail to meet expectations. If these expectations have been clear and constant, and communicated in a loving way, a child usually knows when she has transgressed and this is accompanied by a feeling of disappointment and letdown. Rather than simply rebuke the misbehaviour, it is important to help the child recover to a point when she can try again. Clearly, deliberate and persistent misbehaviour should be reprimanded but it should be the act that is disapproved of rather than the child. The child must be secure in the knowledge that she is loved, despite her wrong actions.

Practical suggestions

Listen and observe
- Be alert to signs of depression and anxiety in babies and young children, e.g. listlessness, withdrawal.
- Note the children who find it difficult to concentrate and consider the reasons why, e.g. over long periods sitting, lack of opportunity to play outside, story not pitched to their level of understanding.
- Observe children in role play in order to gain insights into their positive behaviour with others, e.g. able to share, include and praise others, give way – consider how these children influence others.

Be a step ahead
- Help children to think about their behaviour before the event; give a gentle reminder, call the child's name and make eye contact.
- Provide a special signal for a child who finds it particularly difficult to maintain social behaviour, e.g. 'Joe, your teddy wants you to do this really well', or 'Here is the flag, Joe'.

Reinforcing rules
- Introduce the children to a puppet who has recently joined the group; explain to the children that the puppet does not know how to behave and will need to be told about the agreed rules in the nursery.
- Use puppets to play out scenarios involving different aspects of behaviour, e.g. arguments about whose turn it is to have a toy/ride a tricycle. Ask children to offer the puppets possible solutions.
- Discuss how we need to behave in the nursery. Agree two or three key rules and display them pictorially in the nursery.

Provide a supportive environment
- Avoid temper tantrums, e.g. provide time and encouragement for a toddler to dress and feed himself.
- Create a programme which makes it practically possible for children to share and take turns, e.g. ensure that there is sufficient apparatus for all members of a group to have regular access; provide a 'pit-stop' and a means for children to 'sign up' (make their mark) to have a turn on a wheeled toy outside.
- Provide a substitute for very young children to release their aggression, e.g. suggest that, whenever they are angry, they pummel a cushion or some dough rather than a child.
- Help older children in the Foundation Stage to express their needs in words rather than physically. For example, Janine wants a turn on the rocking horse and is likely to push off Emma who is having a very long ride. Suggest that instead she goes to Emma and politely says that it is her turn now. Support Janine's request in order to reinforce that she has acted properly.

Continued

Continued

- Help children to settle conflicts: listen carefully to both parties and show interest and concern in what the children say and do.
- Provide children with many tangible examples of moral behaviour, e.g. discuss kind behaviour and encourage children to report their own and examples of others' kind actions.
- Start the day with a period of vigorous outside play which helps children to use up surplus energy and be more ready to focus on quieter activities.

Professional practice questions

1. What aspects of my behaviour offer a positive model for young children?
2. How much do we as a staff encourage and celebrate compliant behaviour rather than questioning and assertiveness ?
3. How many boundaries in the setting are totally in the interests of children's well-being?
4. How many boundaries are for the convenience of adults?
5. Which children find it difficult to behave socially and how do we help them ?
6. How far do we as a staff show common and consistent expectations of children's behaviour?
7. How well do we use our observations to: gain an accurate and balanced picture of young children's antisocial behaviour; plan effective action?

The following references in the *Early Years Foundation Stage* link to this chapter:

Statutory Framework and Guidance: pp. 22, 28, 37
Practice Guidance: Appendix 2, Areas of Learning and Development, pp. 33–4
Principles into Practice Cards: 1.1 *Child Development*, 1.3 *Keeping Safe*, 1.4 *Health and Well-Being*, 2.4 *Key Person*, 3.3 *The Learning Environment*, 3.4 *The Wider Context*
The EYFS CD-ROM *in depth* offers further guidance on the principles and commitments above.

The Following Early Years Professional Standards link to this chapter:
1, 2, 6, 8, 9, 10, 15, 18, 19, 25, 26, 27, 28, 29, 30, 33.

REFERENCES 📖

1. Curtis, S.J. and Boultwood, M.E. (1961) *A Short History of Educational Ideas.* London: University Tutorial Press, p. 278.
2. Ibid.
3. Department for Education and Skills (DfES) (2007) *The Early Years Foundation Stage: Practice Guidance* Appendix 2: London: DfES, p. 34.
4. Lindon, J. (2003) *Childcare and Early Education.* London: Thompson.
5. Thomas, S. (2007) *Nurturing Babies and Children Under Four.* London: Heinemann, p. 15.
6. Dunn, J. (1988) *The Beginnings of Social Understanding.* Oxford: Blackwell.
7. Lindon, J. (2003) op. cit. (note 4) p. 200.
8. Hajibagheri, K. (2008) quoted in 'Why we must wake up to sleepy pupils', *The Times Educational Supplement,* Research, 25 April, p. 38.
9. Committee on Toxicity of Chemicals in Food, Consumer Products and the Environment (COT) (2007) *Investigation of the Effect of Mixtures of Certain Food Colours and Preservatives on Behaviour in Children,* www.cot.food.gov.uk
10. Department for Education and Skills (DfES) (2002) *Promoting Children's Mental Health within Early Years and School Settings.* London: Stationery Office.
11. Barton, M.L. and Robins, D. (2000) Regulatory disorders, in C. Zeenah (ed.) *Handbook of Infant Mental Health.* Second edition. New York: Guilford Press, pp. 311–25.
12. Pryor, V. and Glaser, D. (2006) *Understanding Attachment and Attachment Disorders.* London: Jessica Kingley Publishers.
13. Goddard Blythe, S. (2000) Mind and body, *Nursery World,* 15 June.
14. Cousins, J. (1999) *Listening to Four-Year-Olds.* London: National Early Years Network/National Children's Bureau.
15. Kelmer-Pringle, M. (1974) *The Needs of Children.* London: Hutchinson.
16. Thomas, S. (2007) op. cit. (note 5) p. 114.
17. Piaget, J. (1932) *The Moral Judgement of the Child.* Harmondsworth: Penguin.
18. Bruce, T. (2005) *Early Childhood Education.* Third edition. London: Hodder & Stoughton.
19. Laevers, F. (ed.) (1996) *An Exploration of the Concept of Involvement as an Indicator of Quality in Early Childhood Education.* Dundee: Scottish Consultative Council on the Curriculum.
20. Fountain, S. (1990) *Learning Together.* Global Education 407. Cheltenham: Stanley Thornes.
21. McTavish, A. (2007) *Feelings and Behaviour: A Creative Approach.* The British Association for Early Childhood Education. Early Education, www.early-education.org.uk, p. 9.
22. McTavish, A. (2007) op. cit. (note 21).
23. Kelmer-Pringle, M. (1974) op. cit. (note 15).
24. *The Times* (2008) Nursery schools struggle with troubled and violent children, *The Times,* 7 November, p. 5.
25. Ofsted (2005) *Managing Challenging Behaviour.* London: Ofsted, pp. 8–9.
26. Camden Early Years Intervention Team (2004) Warning signs, *Nursery World,* 22 July, p. 13.

7

Young Children's Spirituality

Summary of contents

- Aspects of today's society severely constrain children's spiritual growth. Mass consumerism, the pressures on young children to achieve early in schools and the premature rush into adult life all contribute to a disenchantment with the wonder of childhood.
- And yet children have great potential to develop spiritually when they are young because of being open to new thoughts and ideas.
- If young children are encouraged to talk about their early beliefs, this will in time help them to learn about others' viewpoints.
- Although many children are bombarded by sophisticated experiences, most are very impressionable to everyday events.
- Young children will grow in spirit if they are supported by warmth, order and consistency, guided to appreciate the non-materialistic aspects of life and encouraged to develop their original ideas.

At a time when many churches are facing diminished congregations, interest in a spiritual dimension to life has strengthened in recent years. As the moral doctrines set down by organised religion appear to have less impact on people, many are struggling to find new meanings and guidance to ways in which they should conduct their lives. Despite this, there have been very few studies of young children's spiritual development, few insights as to what it comprises and little guidance on how it should be fostered. Although there is a reference to spiritual development in the section on health and well-being in the Early Years Foundation Stage there is no guidance about how to promote it. The 2008 Ofsted Common Inspection Framework for early years requires inspectors to make a judgement on children's spirituality as part of their Personal Development and Well-being but again there is scant help in regard to what constitutes evidence.

Nevertheless, Wales has made a brave attempt. The new Welsh Framework for the Foundation Stage has a section on spiritual and moral development. This includes requirements for children to have opportunities to reflect and experience quiet and creative times (1). Reflection and quietness do not come naturally to young children; they are such physical beings and so full of life and vitality that the term 'spiritual' does not appear to fit. Spiritual development can seem remote from the tenets of early education, which stress the importance of activity and 'being'. And yet during the early years of life children are not naturally weighed down by materialism (although some are in danger of being so, as described below) and are very receptive to thoughts and ideas. Clearly this is a good basis for beginning to recognise the things of quality and significance in life.

There is also a tendency to confuse the spiritual with the religious, although all religions share a sense of the sacred which is surely something worthwhile and precious to pass on to young children. In this chapter it is proposed that spiritual values can stand by themselves. There are different definitions about spirituality. Generic guidance from the Office for Standards in Education (Ofsted) suggests that

> spiritual development is the development of the non-material element of a human being which animates and sustains us and depending on our point of view, either declines or continues in some form when we die. It is about the development of a sense of identity, self-worth, meaning and purpose. It is about the development of a pupil's 'spirit'. Some people may call it the development of a pupil's 'soul', others as the development of 'personality' or 'character' (2).

Elaine McCreery offers a more straightforward definition of spirituality as awareness that there is something 'Other, something greater than the course of everyday events' (3).

The Ofsted definition includes some of the topics already covered in this book. Trying to narrow the meaning down I suggest that, for the purposes of this chapter, spirituality is about appreciating the journey through life in the deepest sense, particularly special moments, and recognising our own inner resources to help us cope with the journey. This is probably the most challenging aspect of development to promote when working with young children, but one of the most important, given that they are growing up in an increasingly soulless society. This is illustrated by three trends.

The first important example is the huge emphasis on consumerism which can massively distract children from recognising and enjoying the less tangible aspects of life. Mother Teresa, when visiting North America, observed that the whole society seemed to have an abundance of possessions (4) and Joanne Christolph Arnold, a passionate advocate for children, argues that our rich, Western society has enslaved children to consumerism.

> As advertisers tap the bottomless pockets of adults whose money is fueling the most prosperous economy in the history of the world, they are discovering the most lucrative market of all: their little (and not so little) boys and girls. At once the easiest targets and the most persuasive wheedlers, today's

children and teens have been successfully harnessed to pull their parents back to the mall week after week, month after month and year after year (5).

The Archbishop of Canterbury, Rowan Williams, continues to back up this view. In his powerful book *Lost Icons* Williams attacks the Disney empire which, he claims is turning children into consumers by its marketing strategies (6). Despite some notable exceptions of poverty in every country, there is no doubt that most young children in Western Europe and the USA have far more things than they need. Parents seem to work longer and harder to provide children with more and more luxuries. This reaches a peak at birthday and Christmas celebrations. Amanda Craig, a journalist and parent, describes vividly the orgy of pre-Christmas spending:

> Going into any high street now is like walking into Toy Story: shiny boxes piled high with Barbies in fluffy tinsel-pink or Smash and Crush Hulks in flak-jacket khaki. There are multi-coloured buttons, buzzers, clashing lights and remote-controlled flights; there are bells, yells, singing fish and howling owls. Crazed by greed and ignorance, children race about in a frenzy of indiscriminate desperation or log onto web-sites such as iwantoneofthose.com. The whole enterprise is a vision of hell (7).

But as we know too well, material wealth does not necessarily feed the spirit. Having witnessed affluent lifestyles in North America, Mother Teresa offered a stark message. She commented that she also had never seen 'such a poverty of the spirit, of loneliness and of being unwanted, that is the worst disease in the world today, not tuberculosis or leprosy. It is a poverty born of a lack of love' (8). As for young children, by giving them so much and making it so easy to replace and replenish things, we are denying them the need to really cherish and value what they have.

The second trend is linked to education. Williams also points the finger at the priorities of our early educational system. He suggests that current ideas about the purpose of childhood education is to give children the skills they will need to survive and succeed in a competitive and even dangerously cut-throat world (9). By implication, the Archbishop suggests that this means an emphasis on a relentless programme designed to improve children rather than one which understands and gently steers and strengthens their natural development. Although the Early Years Foundation Stage is supporting a relaxed, play-based curriculum, many practitioners feel under pressure to provide children with a heavy diet of literacy and numeracy too soon and some parents become too easily caught up with the need for their children to achieve as much as possible as early as possible.

This emphasis for children to acquire formal skills early is a small part of the third trend which is the move to rush them prematurely into the adult world. We hear a great deal nowadays about the 'loss of childhood' and this reflects a view that inevitably children are 'growing up' too quickly and become too knowing about the ways of the world at an early age. The media are quick to exploit this, particularly for small girls, and make-up, jewellery and sexually provocative clothes are heavily marketed. This perception of children as miniature adults becomes a vicious circle as it can affect the ways in which they are treated by parents and carers. The move has been slow and insidious. Twenty-five years ago Marie Winn identified this in her valuable book *Children without Childhoods*:

> as today's children impress adults with their sophisticated ways, adults begin to change their ideas about children and their needs; that is they form new ideas about childhood as adults act less protectively and as they expose children to the underside of their lives adult sexuality, suffering, fear of death, these former innocents grow tougher perforce, less playful and trusting, more skeptical, in short more like adults (10).

The above trends paint a grim picture also highlighted in The Good Childhood Enquiry which added that a culture of individualism is causing a range of problems for children. The report suggests that the over-riding belief that you need to take care of yourself is flawed, as evidence shows that unselfish people are happier. There is also a clear message for parents in the report who are urged to help their children to develop spiritual qualities (11). These messages indicate some important factors that we should face and try to combat if we are to protect and strengthen children's inner lives. I draw on two sources:

- a discussion paper published by the National Curriculum Council in 1993 (12). This attempts to highlight key aspects of spiritual development but in a way more applicable for older children.
- some headings in David Hay's thoughtful book *The Spirit of the Child* (13).

Some of the aspects considered such as relationships and feelings and emotions have already been dealt with in other chapters. The headings below have been interpreted in a way relevant for young children's spiritual growth.

AWARENESS

Although young babies rapidly recognise their mother's milk, her voice and smell, for the most part they live in the moment, having no sense of past or future. Margaret Donaldson suggests that this 'living in the moment' which she calls 'the point mode' is also apparent in older children (14). Hay describes a vivid, immediate experience in his family:

> One morning when he was very young our son Simon called excitedly for me to run to the window. When I hurried over he pointed triumphantly out of the window and ecstatically cried out, 'Grass!' One only has to think of how frequently small children are transfixed by the moment in this way to realize how natural and universal the point mode is to childhood (15).

Young children use their bodies and sensory experiences in order to focus on and sense situations. They find it difficult to describe what they experience but their awareness springs from listening to messages that spring from within them. Truly absorbed awareness is described by the social psychologist Mihaly Cskszentmhalyi as 'flow'. He suggests that this occurs when you are totally immersed in something that interests you and experience a liberating feeling of mastery (16). Young children's lives are filled with new challenges to conquer, most of which require their undivided attention: some joyous experiences of achievement may be linked to spirituality.

BELIEFS

As we have seen, children will already have some firm beliefs by the time they enter the reception class. These may include religious beliefs, including some hazy notions of deity; they will almost certainly include some values, for example, about how to treat people. Rebecca Nye's fascinating interviews with children about their spirituality included responses from 6-year-old Freddie as he discussed the importance of friendships and his difficulties in maintaining friends. His comment about God reflects core values. 'God's the kindest person I know, I think ... because he never shouts or tells you off, because he never even speaks to you apart from perhaps when you're dead' (17). It is important that we listen to children talking about their beliefs and values; in so doing they will start to recognise that not everyone thinks alike or attaches the same importance to particular issues. Informal conversations with individuals or in small groups are most appropriate where a good and trusting relationship has been established between the practitioner and children.

Children know when their thoughts and beliefs are acknowledged and respected. This can sometimes be difficult when the beliefs do not accord with those of the practitioner. However, insisting that 'you don't really mean that do you?' can easily undermine the child and will not necessarily change her way of thinking. The child should at least feel that she has been given a voice and that voice is respected. As Kahil Gibran says when talking of children, 'You may house their bodies but not their souls, for their souls dwell in the house of tomorrow, which you cannot visit, not even in your dreams' (18).

A SENSE OF AWE, WONDER AND MYSTERY

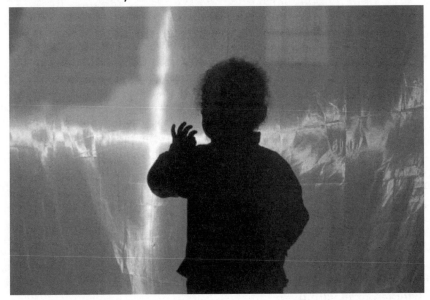

Figure 7.1 Emily full of awe and wonder

The roots of spirituality are founded in early experiences of awe, wonder and mystery. This is certainly the easiest aspect of spiritual development to foster, as young children are so very impressionable. They have lived for a very short time and to them most of life is still a mystery. Young children wonder at the mundane and constantly remind us more jaundiced adults of the joy of being alive. And yet the very process of growing up and experiencing more formal education can stifle the curiosity that leads to wonder and the exploration of the world. Wordsworth describes this beautifully:

> Heaven lies about us in our infancy!
> Shades of the prison-house begin to close
> Upon the growing boy (19).

The most successful examples of encouraging awe and wonder at all ages are when the adults themselves are open to the miracles and mysteries of life.

Case study 🗂

Alice, a pre-school worker, had planned to encourage children to observe and share thoughts about growing things. She also wanted to impress the group with the power and beauty of nature. Alice passed around some sunflower seeds for each child to look at closely through a magnifying glass. They talked about the shape and feel of the seeds and what might be inside the hard shell. Alice then asked the children to close their eyes and think hard about the little seed growing. When they opened their eyes, in front of the children were two huge sunflower plants growing in pots. Jamie gazed in amazement and whispered, 'It's grown into the sun!'

EXPERIENCING FEELINGS OF TRANSCENDENCE

The word 'transcendence' derives from the Latin word *transcendere* which means 'to climb over'. Young children do 'climb over' and reach out to the limits of their world as part of growing up. A child experiences her inner strengths when she summons up courage to venture into the playground alone for the first time. When Ahmed lay on the carpet, closed his eyes and listened to a brief extract of Beethoven, he said softly afterwards, 'the music burst out of me'. Children also go beyond everyday events in their imaginative play where they explore possibilities.

In our materialistic part of the world, children are bombarded with stimuli and invitations to expand their lives. They have sophisticated experiences at a very early age and this can lead them to look always for answers outside of themselves. We offer young children something of infinite value if we help them to look for resources within.

Although most young children are naturally noisy and exuberant, like all of us they can also thrive on peace and tranquillity. However, even if they need peace, not all find it easy to quieten themselves; some will find silence threatening and not all will be as prepared as Ahmed was to close their eyes in a group. Practitioners can help children to learn ways to relax, contemplate and concentrate but these habits will only be acquired over a period of time and in an atmosphere of trust. Many settings and schools now recognise the benefits of encouraging children to lie still and listen to music when they come into class following a noisy lunch break. Other settings teach simple yoga techniques to help relaxation. Observing these sessions it is striking to see how well young children respond, as if they crave these moments of calm. Joanna Haynes, who writes about children as philosophers, uses stilling techniques to help children focus. Describing how she uses the phrase 'make your bodies still and ready to listen' as a settling phrase, she says that one child commented that in order to really listen you have to be still both inside your body as well as outside. Haynes goes on to say that this led to children discussing what this comment might mean and a decision to alter the original phrase to 'make yourselves still, outside and inside' (20).

Helping children to meditate takes them a step forward to transcendence. At the Maharishi school in Lancashire, children at four are introduced to meditation and breathing exercises. Five-year-old children learn their Word of Wisdom and repeat this word as they walk to school or play with construction. At this age they do it for five minutes twice a day and after that they add one minute for every year in school (21). Caroline Sherwood in her book on meditation aptly describes it as 'making friends with ourselves' (22).

SEARCHING FOR MEANING AND PURPOSE

Bruno Bettelheim writes: 'Today, as in times past, the most important and also the most difficult task in raising a child is helping him to find meaning in life. Many growth experiences are needed to achieve this' (23).

And yet young children constantly search for meaning through their questions, many of which confront the big issues in life. Some of these may be related to the child's personal circumstances. 'Why doesn't my mummy live with us any more?' Others may be of a more philosophical nature – 'Why does the moon look at me?' Yet others may deal with more imponderable issues. 'Where do you go when you die?' or 'Who is God?' These last questions are the most difficult to deal with and there are no set answers. However, some basic principles are helpful. The first is to keep responses simple and honest. 'God is very special to a lot of people who believe that God made the world and all the things living in it.' That should be quite sufficient to satisfy an initial question and the child will probably move on to the next burning issue such as a request to play outside. The second is to admit when you do not have an answer but that you are really thinking about it. A child will be satisfied if you show that it is a very important question and that you are interested in discussing possibilities and finding out what he or she thinks.

Those who work with young children are frequently pained by the traumas faced by so many during their early years of life. It is amazing how some children do appear to withstand huge disruptions, as well as selfish and sometimes cruel behaviour shown towards them. Other children are, sadly, noticeably damaged and life is a confusion to them. Sometimes early years staff can help children deal with, and even come to terms with, aspects of suffering; a friend who is hurt or upset can be comforted and reassured; a pet dies and can be buried with suitable rituals. However, at times staff feel inadequate to deal with some hardships that children face outside the nursery. On these occasions, all that is possible is to draw on trusting relationships, to encourage children to talk, and try to point out any good and positive aspects that arise from pain. On all occasions it is helpful for children to recognise and share good memories and see them as one of life's gifts.

CREATIVITY

Bernadette Duffy reminds us of the universal human desire to be creative throughout history. She refers to how creation myths from religious and cultural groups express the profound need, satisfaction and pleasure in generating something new (24). Conversations with young children and observations of their models, drawings and paintings are a testimony to their original thinking and creativity. All but the most damaged children enter the nursery with creative talents, but it is during the early years that these talents blossom or wither. Practitioners know that, like any learning, growth in creativity does not just happen, but is crucially dependent on key factors which include the curriculum and the role of the adult.

Children under five are now entitled to creative development as one of the six areas of learning. However, in the government document *All Our Futures* the breadth of creative thinking is recognised. 'Creativity is not unique to the arts' (25). The Early Years Foundation stage makes clear the potential of creativity to make links across all areas. Good nursery settings and schools have always provided this, recognising that young children need a multiplicity of ways to represent their understandings. This is expressed beautifully in the title *The Hundred Languages of Children*, which describes the work of the pre-primary schools in Reggio Emilia (26). These Italian schools emphasise the ways in which young children use what the schools term 'graphic languages' to record their observations, ideas, memories and feelings. This type of curriculum is inclusive. It is worth remembering that a programme which only offers children narrow opportunities to record, perhaps simply to write or crayon is necessarily reducing opportunities for those who may need to show their learning in different ways.

Being creative involves emotions. The 5X5X5 Project (see Chapter 5), which encompasses many elements of spirituality, built much of its creative work with children on Ferre Laevers' research which highlights the need for a learning environment to focus on children's well-being. This includes offering children the chance to feel easy, spontaneous, safe, competent and satisfied. They should experience tenderness and warmth, social recognition, meaning in life and moral value (27). Young children can release powerful feelings and extend their emotional repertoire in dancing, stamping, twisting, in role play and mark-making (see Chapter 4). Sternberg also suggests that negative feelings, such as anxiety, can inhibit imaginative and creative thoughts and actions (28).

Creativity cannot be forced. Lesley Webb, a wise and informed educator of young children, once described the process of compost-making in the mind. Good compost, like ideas, needs time to ripen and mature. Guy Claxton echoes this when he argues that creativity is helped when people slow down and reflect; he suggests that deep and creative thinking is enhanced by serendipity (29). Probably all of us would relate to this, recognising, for example, the regenerative effect of a relaxing holiday in the midst of a busy life. The notion is particularly applicable to young children. During the early years when so much learning takes place children need to have plenty of opportunities to use and apply new ideas. In this way they become secure and confident with new information. In our current culture of targets and achievements, we are in danger of promoting a 'hurry along' curriculum. The result of this can be that children hang on by their fingertips to new knowledge without a chance to use what they know.

Given a broad and rich curriculum, the right emotional climate and time, children can become totally absorbed in creative activity. Csikszentmihalyi and colleagues observed artists, athletes, musicians and others who showed intense involvement in what they were doing. There appeared to be no extrinsic reasons for their involvement but the 'flow' of their energy or motivation. Whenever we are fully functioning, involved in challenging activity that requires all our skills and more, we feel a great sense of exhilaration. Because of this we want to repeat the experience. But to feel the same exhilaration again it is necessary to take on a slightly greater challenge and to develop slightly greater skills (30). When young children experience this flow they are tapping into their inner resources.

Once again, the adult is the most precious resource; she has a direct role in helping children to be creative and the role can best be described by using Bruner's term 'scaffolding'. The term implies support without constriction. Successful scaffolding requires the adult to make a sound judgement of what the child knows now, an accurate diagnosis of the next step in learning and provision of suitable support to help the child achieve it. The support could include:

• offering appropriate stimulus; this may be through provision of sensory experiences, through aiding memory skills, fostering imagination or by the provision of materials

- teaching the subskills of handling tools, mixing and managing materials
- listening, questioning and commenting, encouraging the child to bounce ideas or talk through her activity
- encouraging the child to combine materials and link different ways of representing experiences (31).

As with all talents, some children will prove to be more creative than others. Nevertheless, all have potential. Given the time and resources, access to informed adults and some good quality stimulus, this will free young children's creative abilities in, to use Robin Tanner's words, 'making the ordinary and trivial arresting, moving and memorable' (32).

THE CONTRIBUTION OF STEINER SCHOOLS

Although many early years settings both plan and seize opportunities which support children's spirituality, some provisions make this a keystone for their work. Telling examples are seen in the Rudolph Steiner schools. Around 800 Steiner schools exist around the world. They are very child-centred and the aim is for the spirit of the school to be created by the mutual co-operation of everyone. There is a heavy accent on the use of natural materials and learning about natural crafts. Imaginative play has a high profile (typically children use very simple props, such as drapes and blocks). The sense of community is tangible, through the ritual gathering around a lighted candle at the start and end of the day. Other rituals recognise and celebrate the natural cycle of life; children regularly bake their own bread and work in the garden and observe living things. The practitioner is not there to explicitly teach, but to demonstrate or model certain behaviours. According to Freya Jaffke, a renowned Steiner kindergarten teacher, these behaviours include a sense of order and rhythm, good habits and loving consistency. Jaffke suggests that when the adult exemplifies these behaviours she creates a 'mantle of warmth' which protects the child from the outside world and strengthens the child's inner resources (33).

Caroline Von Heydebrand was a distinguished teacher trainer and supporter of the Steiner philosophy in the early part of the twentieth century. Her words capture overwhelming reverence and respect for the child and the need to trust in the power of the spirit.

> Compulsion in the life of the spirit is unendurable. If the child is given the nourishment proper to him, one which does not constrain but nurtures, then in later life, his soul will have power to investigate and discern and come to find the spiritual foundations of the world through his own reasoning and insight – the means suited to his nature and stage of development (34).

This belief remains fundamental to Steiner practice. It also has relevance for all practitioners today who are trying to balance the dictates of planning and adult-directed activities with providing space for the child.

Practical suggestions

Observe and respond
- Be alert to times when very young children delight in the moment.

Nurture children's inner resources
- Help young children to appreciate stillness. Establish a few moments daily when children close their eyes and are totally quiet. Help them to recognise silence as a gift of life. Encourage them to relax: lie on the floor and breathe deeply; make their bodies like flippy, floppy scarecrows; suggest that they think of beautiful things which they might share afterwards (it is always important to respect all responses, even non-contingent ones!).

Provide places for quiet reflection
- Make spaces available inside and outside for children to withdraw from activity and be alone. It can be a tent or curtained-off area indoors or simply a bench near some flowering shrubs or underneath a tree. It needs few resources – some comfy cushions as a minimum – but can be enhanced by a vase of flowers, scented herbs, soft lighting and music, all of which provide a calming atmosphere. The purpose of this space needs to be made clear to children – it is there for each one of them if they want to think or just to be quiet by themselves.

Share precious memories
- The adult shows a small group of children her memory box. She pulls out one or two items: a photo of a dog she had when she was a little girl or a fir cone that her own child had given her some years ago as a gift. The adult talks about why these things are valuable for her although they do not cost much or any money. She introduces a memory box for the nursery. Children are invited to bring in some item that reminds them of a special time. The items are placed in the memory box and shared at a certain time each week. A sense of occasion can help to set the tone for the gathering, e.g. quiet music, lighting a candle, the box placed on a piece of carpet, the child sharing the memory sits on a particular cushion. If the item is passed around it should be handled with respect and care. It is important that each presents her 'memory' as she wishes. The adult may also continue to share her memory items with the group and share presentations with those less confident individuals.

Encourage a sense of values
- Encourage older children to talk about what are the most important things in life. Start a story about a girl/boy who was able to wish for the three most precious things to have forever in her/his life. S/he could choose from (provide a tray with a selection of the following, either portrayed in photographs or the real objects): a large bar of chocolate, a bike, a loving mum/dad/carer, a popular toy, a large ice-cream, good friends, a cat. Ask the children in turn to make their choices and so open discussion about what sorts of things are important and why. This will also give the adult useful insights into the children's developing values. *Continued*

Continued

Follow the child
- Listen carefully to children's thoughts and views; affirm them when they struggle with ideas and give them time to respond to stories and daily situations which have some links to spirituality.

Professional practice questions

1. What do I do to take care of my own spiritual life?
2. Am I sufficiently aware of the contexts which encourage babies and young children to feel calm and peaceful?
3. How do we best provide for children to reflect?
4. How strongly do beautiful things (music, art, aspects of nature) feature in our setting?
5. How do our environments and interactions with children inspire them to be creative?
6. How well do we encourage children to value the real treasures in life – love, laughter, friendship, giving?

The following references in the *Early Years Foundation Stage* link to this chapter:

Statutory Framework and Guidance: p. 37
Practice Guidance: Appendix 2 Areas of Learning and Development, p. 23,
Sense of Community, pp. 37–8, *Language for Thinking,* pp. 48–9, *Communities,* pp. 87–9
Principles into Practice Cards: 1.4 *Health and Well-being,* 2.4 *Key Person,* 4.1 *Play and Exploration,* 4.3 *Creativity and Critical Thinking*
The EYFS CD-ROM *in-depth* offers further guidance on the principles and commitments above.

The following Early Years Professional Standards link to this chapter:
2, 3, 8, 11, 15, 17, 22, 26, 27, 28, 29.

REFERENCES

1. Department for Education, Lifelong Learning and Skills (2007) *Foundation Phase: Framework for Children's Learning for 3–7 year olds in Wales,* Welsh Assembly Government.
2. Ofsted (2001) *Inspecting Pupils' Spiritual, Moral, Social and Cultural Development: Guidance for Inspectors.* London: Ofsted.
3. McCreery, E. (2006) quoted in D. Hay and R. Nye, *The Spirit of the Child.* London: Jessica Kingley, p. 60.

4. deBertodano, T. (1993) (ed.) *Daily Readings with Mother Teresa*. London: HarperCollins, pp. 62–3.

5. Arnold, J.C. (2000) *Endangered*. Robertsbridge, E. Sussex: Plough Publishing House, p. 16.

6. Williams, R. (2000) *Lost Icons*. London: Continuum International Publishing Group.

7. Craig, A. (2003) What children really need, *Sunday Times, News Review*, 30 November, p. 5.

8. de Bertodano, T. (1993) op. cit. (note 4), pp. 62–3.

9. Williams, R. (2000) op. cit. (note 6).

10. Winn, M. (1984) *Children without Childhoods*. New York: Penguin, p. 6.

11. Layard, R. and Dunn, J. (2009) *A Good Childhood: Searching for Values in a Competitive Age*. London: The Children's Society.

12. National Curriculum Council (NCC) (1993) *Spiritual and Moral Development: A Discussion Paper*. London: NCC.

13. Hay, D. and Nye, R. (2006) *The Spirit of the Child*. London: Jessica Kingsley.

14. Donaldson, M. (1992) *Human Minds*. London: Allen Lane/Penguin Press.

15. Hay, D. and Nye, R. (2006) op. cit. (note 13), p. 66.

16. Hay, D. and Nye, R. (2006) op. cit. (note 13), p. 68.

17. Hay. D. and Nye, R. (2006) op. cit. (note 13), p. 105.

18. Gibran, K. (1927) *The Prophet*. London: Heinemann, p. 20.

19. J.O. Hayden (ed.) (1990) Intimations of Immortality from Recollections of Early Childhood in *William Wordworth: The Poems*. London: Penguin Books.

20. Haynes, J. (2002) *Children as Philosophers*. London: RoutledgeFalmer, p. 69.

21. Selby, A. (1998) The little school of calm, *The Times Magazine*, 5 September, pp. 78–80.

22. Sherwood, C. (1997) *Making Friends with Ourselves: Introducing Children to Meditation*. Kidsmed, 10 Edward Street, Bath BA2 4DU.

23. Bettelheim, B. (1975) *The Uses of Enchantment*. New York, NY: Random House, p. 3.

24. Duffy, B. (1998) *Supporting Creativity and the Imagination in the Early Years*. Buckingham: Open University Press, p. 4.

25. National Advisory Committee on Creativity and Cultural Education (1999) *All Our Futures*. London: Department for Education and Employment and Department for Culture, Media and Sport, p. 27.

26. Edwards, C., Gandini, L. and Forman, G. (1993) *The Hundred Languages of Children*. Norwood, NJ: Ablex.

27. Bancroft, S., Fawcett, M. and Hay, P. (2007) *5X5X5 Researching Children Researching the World*. 5X5X5 = creativity, PO Box 3236 Chippenham SN15 9DE.

28. Goldberg, K. (2003) Are we all potential Einsteins? *TES Primary Campaign*, 2 May, p. 24.

29. Claxton, G. (1998) *Hare Brain, Tortoise Mind*. London: Fourth Estate, p. 52.

30. Csikszentmihalyi, M. (1988) *Optimal Experience: Psychological Studies of Flow in Consciousness*. Cambridge: Cambridge University Press, p. 367.

31. Dowling, M. (1995) *Starting School at Four: A Joint Endeavour*. London: Paul Chapman.

32. Tanner, R. (1985) *The way we have come*. From a talk at the opening of the Arts Centre at Bishop Grosseteste College, Lincoln.

33. Jaffke, F. (1996) *Work and Play in Early Childhood*. London: Floris Books.

34. Von Heydebrand, C. (1942) *Childhood: A Study of the Growing Soul*. London: Anthroposophical Publishing Company, p. 181.

8

Living in the Wider World

Summary of contents

- The early years setting can help young children to become aware of the world beyond their immediate environment; to learn about others from a basis of tolerance, respect and open-mindedness.
- In order to learn to respect others, children must see this demonstrated positively by adults and must also respect themselves.
- Staff expectations have a powerful effect on what children feel they are capable of, and this in turn influences their feelings of self-worth.
- Staff should plan for children to have access to many different experiences; they should also follow individual children's interests, provide them with ways of learning which suit them and establish the foundations for them to become young global citizens.

Babies and toddlers thrive in the love and security of their homes. The earliest environment is intimate and constant. The three- and four-year-old continues to need that secure environment, but she is very mindful of and curious about the world around her. She becomes aware of this wider world through what she hears and observes within the family, through books, the media and perhaps being taken on outings to different places; when she joins an early years setting she meets other adults and children. All these experiences contribute to the child's growing understanding about herself in relation to a wider context. This chapter deals with how settings can encourage young children to think and start to understand about aspects of the wider world. This includes understanding about different ways of living and matters of equality.

LEARNING ABOUT THE WORLD OUTSIDE

Early on young children recognise that there are other families apart from their own; through travel they begin to understand that people live in different places – nearby and sometimes far away. Through visits to family and friends they see at first hand people living in different ways and they learn more about this through books, stories and television. The Early Learning Goals expect that, by the end of the Early Years Foundation Stage, children 'understand that people have different needs, views, cultures and beliefs that need to be treated with respect'. Also that children 'Understand that they can expect others to treat their needs, views, cultures and beliefs with respect' (1). Some children will learn these lessons easily and naturally; others, dependent on their early lifestyles, may need a lot more support. Children will have very different personal experiences of diversity; by the time they start at nursery some will have witnessed a rich cosmopolitan range of lifestyles; others may have only encountered the cultural traditions in their own community. Nevertheless, all children who will be living in the world tomorrow need to develop an understanding of how other people live. It is during the early years when children are naturally curious and receptive to new ideas that these understandings should take root. Some early years settings have a wide cultural mix of children or a deliberate policy to include children with special educational or physical needs. In these groups the issues of difference are ready to be grasped. Practitioners have a greater challenge in finding ways to raise children's awareness of diversity in settings with a more homogeneous intake, with families from only one culture or from a narrowly defined social class. However, even in these contexts children can be helped to see how others vary from them as well as what they have in common.

BEING OPEN-MINDED

Everyone builds up a set of beliefs about others. These beliefs are influenced by personal experiences but also by fear of strange or different characteristics. Beliefs may also arise from developing fixed views about others and labelling or stereotyping them.

People often fear the unknown and prejudice can flourish in a climate of ignorance. There are tales of 'closed' societies where 'outsiders' are discouraged. I encountered this in an outlying village in East Anglia in the 1960s; the staff in the school were hostile to any new families being admitted other than the locals and termed them 'foreigners'. The basis for this belief was the result of one family who had moved into the village and whose child had some difficulty in making the transition from a large town school. As a result of this experience the teachers had generalised an expectation of all new families. They were genuinely worried that standards of discipline in the school would suffer if 'foreign' children with different ways were allowed to contaminate the others. Their intolerance included a fear of dealing with strange parents and children, who they believed would have different values and lifestyles from the families they knew intimately in the village. They failed to recognise that families with young children are likely to share many things in common no matter where they come from. They also considered the idea of difference in a very negative sense in that it could only disrupt the status quo rather than add to it.

In this instance the staff had built up negative assumptions of others simply based on where they came from. Fears and suspicions also arise when people look and act differently. This may be because of the colour of their skin, a disability or their behaviour which is linked to a cultural identity.

The teachers in the village school had also developed a fixed or stereotyped view of 'outsiders'. Jenny Lindon points out some important characteristics of stereotyping, which are summarised below:

• they are usually unfavourable
• even positive stereotyping restricts, e.g. 'black boys are natural athletes'
• stereotyping depends on a belief that other groups are less varied than one's own, e.g. people are more likely to say of another social or ethnic group 'she's a typical ... ' but they will say of their own group 'it all depends'
• experience of individuals who do not fit a stereotype are not thought to give any reason to adjust a view, e.g. 'you're my friend, I don't count you' (2).

The extent to which young children will learn to stereotype others and regard them with fear and suspicion depends on their own experiences and how they see people they know behaving. Children who mix with a wide variety of people from different cultures and who have encountered disability from a young age are more likely to be open-minded about differences. However, this will only happen if they see open-mindedness demonstrated by the adults they know and love. If homes do not offer this model then it is all the more important that the early years setting provides it.

EARLY INFLUENCES WHICH AFFECT UNDERSTANDING ABOUT BEING EQUAL

We saw in Chapter 1 how young children start to develop a picture of themselves very early through their relationships within the family. This building up of a self-image continues when a child joins a group setting; she sees then how she is regarded by a wider group of children and adults.

Young children's early life chances are deeply dependent on adults' views and behaviour towards them. This can affect all aspects of their development.

Children who are clear about who they are and are at ease with this identity will feel comfortable and positive about themselves. This is likely when children have been encouraged from the start to feel proud of themselves, their backgrounds and their early achievements. However, some children come to develop their self-esteem at the expense of others. Some families may have encouraged their children to feel naturally superior to others who are not from their social or cultural background. Other children may come from families who themselves suffer from a poor self-image. This may be for reasons of unemployment or lack of social standing. Children from these backgrounds may have been taught to boost their own position by rejecting others deemed less fortunate than themselves. They may have learned particularly to disparage other children who look different or act differently. If practitioners detect any of these signs in young children, they have a responsibility to demonstrate each child's worth and to counterbalance any feelings of superiority.

Case study

Ben, a toddler, was regarded as fragile and was physically over-protected by anxious parents. He had fewer opportunities to develop balancing and climbing skills than other children in the neighbourhood who were encouraged to play actively and take physical risks from babyhood. He also grew to be fearful of hurting himself. By the time he started at a nursery, Ben already regarded physical activity as something to avoid; when he saw other children, confident and assured in using their bodies, Ben strengthened his view of himself as physically incompetent.

After falling from a low rung of a climbing frame, for one term Ben flatly refused to use any apparatus or to use the outside play area in the nursery. By the age of four years Ben had developed a clear picture of his physical limitations which had sprung from his parents' behaviour towards him. His lack of confidence in his body led him to develop a very cautious disposition. Other children initially avoided including him in any boisterous play and then Ben started to exclude himself from any other activities apart from 'safe' pencil and paper work. Ben became increasingly isolated. He showed no interest in other children and told his mother that 'the nursery was full of nasty people who tried to make him do things'.

Comment

Three- and four-year-olds are very concerned with finding out who they are and what they can do. They need to feel that they matter. Ben's self-esteem was diminished initially by being over-protected and not being encouraged to build up his physical confidence. This led him to withdraw into himself and become negative about others.

Despite heightened awareness on the part of many people, prejudice and discrimination are still deep-rooted in British society. The grounds are widespread. They include what sex, race or ethnic group you are, your religion, age, ability/disability, social class, how you speak, what you wear and the work that you do. Some of these grounds are covered by law; all contribute to people being regarded and treated in different ways. We are concerned here with equality issues that affect young children. It is not a matter of treating children the same, but rather ensuring that, whatever their inheritance, all children have a similar entitlement in life. It is in the preschool years that children first receive messages about how they are valued and give these messages to others. Some children are particularly vulnerable. Those children who are in a minority in a group will find it difficult if they are labelled or stereotyped by others.

It is a mistake to think that young children are immune from prejudice. Jane Lane points out that 'Just because we hope children will not learn to be racially prejudiced we must not delude ourselves into believing such hopes will be fulfilled and that therefore we need to do nothing about it. Every racist attacker was once a child'. Lane quotes a case study of a three-year-old boy who was physically and verbally abusive to a black woman on a bus and whose mother refused to intervene. When this was pointed out to the mother she accused the black woman of 'having a chip on her shoulder' (3). The Macpherson Report on the Stephen Lawrence murder noted that inquiry members had heard 'about the racist attitudes of very young children' during the public hearings (4). These findings are immensely disturbing and practitioners need to be vigilant to all aspects of children's behaviour that indicate prejudice. Initially, however, children may be simply interested in difference. Three-year-olds may comment openly that 'that man has a black face'. Four-year-olds will be socially more aware and whisper this comment to the adult they are with. In both cases this is simply an interested observation and not a value judgement or indeed the start of racist attitude. As we support young children in sharing their observations in other situations we should not encourage them to turn a blind eye to physical differences. When carefully handled, these observations can become expressions of worth. Children will learn easily about bigotry and prejudice if it is modelled for them. Parents can provide a powerful role model for children. It is only natural that they should take their values on all sorts of issues from what they observe from people who are close to them.

Case study 🗁

In conversation with Hugo, aged four years, he told me earnestly that he knew that he must never ever get into a car with a stranger. 'Except', he said, 'if the person was driving a Volvo or Mercedes car because only rich and good people drive those cars'.

Comment

Hugo loved and admired his father very much; his one ambition was to become like his father who was a wealthy and successful businessman. I did not know the make of car that Hugo's dad drove but I could guess.

As a consequence of what very young children observe and hear and assimilate within the family setting, they will arrive at a nursery with their individual package of beliefs which influence how they view themselves and their attitudes towards others. This includes the way in which children view children with physical disabilities.

Case study 📁

I was sharing with four-year-old Rosie a book about a small boy who was restricted to a wheelchair. Rosie pointed out that this was like Dom, a boy in her class. 'I know that he can't walk', she said, 'but instead of good legs he is very good at painting. I told him that'. The previous month, Andrew, a new boy to the reception class, had refused point-blank to sit next to Dom at circle time. When pressed, he protested that he was not going to sit next to someone with poorly legs – 'it's not nice'. As Andrew became used to life in the nursery, he observed Dom's good relationships with the other children. He also watched Dom painting with confidence and skill. A few weeks into the term Andrew stood painting next to Dom. He looked at Dom's work and leaning over said, 'You've drawed a good man, Dom – do you like my picture?'

Comment

On her first visit to the nursery Rosie had noticed Dom. She had talked about his 'bad legs' with her mum who had explained that some people have bits of their bodies that do not work very well. Rosie's rapid and genuine recognition of Dom's difficulties and talents helped Dom to see himself as a full member of the nursery group. Andrew's fear of physical disability had an equally powerful effect. Initially Dom responded to Andrew's negative comments about poorly legs by refusing to remain in the circle; he repeatedly asked to be wheeled into the book area where he sat silently watching the group. Staff rapidly realised the reason for Dom's action; Andrew's attitude had made him for the first time in the nursery feel different and deficient. As Andrew became more familiar with Dom he began to realise and admire his social skills and talents in painting. The wheelchair became irrelevant; Andrew wanted Dom for a friend.

ADULT EXPECTATIONS

The staff in an early years setting need to find out about children's beliefs about themselves and others. They will also work to strengthen each child's self-image, particularly those who may be vulnerable to bias and prejudice. One of the most effective ways of doing this is through staff demonstrating their high expectations of all children. Practitioners are invariably skilled in this aspect of work. However, occasionally where a young child is led to believe that the adult has only a low opinion of what he can do, like Ben who truly came to believe himself to be physically incompetent, the child's confidence drops and he only achieves what is expected of him. This then becomes a self-fulfilling prophecy.

Cooper distinguishes between self-fulfilling prophecies and sustaining expectations. He suggests that the self-fulfilling prophecy occurs when an inaccurate expectation of a child influences the behaviour of that child so as to make the expectation accurate. A sustaining expectation follows an initially accurate judgement, which is maintained despite other influences (5). The concern is that a self-fulfilling prophecy can lead to an expectation of a child which is sustained in later years.

Most nursery settings make shrewd and accurate judgements about their children based on skilled observations and sound information about what the child knows and understands already. However this process takes time. Staff in reception classes know that they must determine each child's starting point for learning in order to pitch experiences appropriately and provide suitable and sensitive support. Nevertheless, hasty assessments made too early often mean that judgements are being made and recorded before the child has made a sound transition to school. The consequence of this is that those children are not yet sufficiently confident and settled to demonstrate their skills and competencies. This is compounded where a practitioner has received insufficient information about a child's previous experiences and is unable to spend much time with individual children because of a large class size. In these situations practitioners themselves know that there is a danger of making an inaccurate judgement about a child's abilities and potential for learning.

These circumstances can, of course, occur in any setting. Furthermore, without any other information, the adult's judgement may be unduly influenced by the child's social competencies rather than what he or she can do. A resulting halo effect can operate and cause over-optimistic views. For example, one Scottish study of multicultural nursery schools suggests that, in the absence of detailed observations of individual children, teachers made assessments of them based on their ethnic group membership. Thus a quiet, hardworking and well-behaved Asian child was regarded as competent and her difficulties with language were overlooked (6). The converse can also apply. A child who is awkward with people, who finds conversation difficult or who speaks colloquially, may, in the absence of other evidence, be judged to be of limited ability. Expectations are also influenced by what people find familiar and identifiable. Practitioners may spot ability in middle-class children more easily than they do in children from less advantaged backgrounds, simply because they are more attuned to the former. On the other hand, children who have English as an additional language may have their behaviour misinterpreted or their abilities underestimated because of their struggle with a new language. Reflection and puzzlement may be interpreted to be sulky and uncommunicative behaviour. Children's difficulties with expressive language may lead adults to be unaware of the extent of their understanding of spoken language. Those children who are not only new to a school or nursery, but also face a new culture and have communication difficulties, need to be observed particularly carefully and given the necessary time to adapt. The importance of home language is wholeheartedly recognised in government guidance for early years practitioners. 'Bilingualism is an asset, and the first language has a continuing and significant role in identity, learning and the acquisition of additional languages' (7).

Practitioners have a very real responsibility to make sensitive, informed and accurate judgements about children. They also need to make sure that they are knowledgeable about different cultural groups and consider their attitudes to people who are different to themselves (8). Without this, some children at least will have too much or too little expected of them.

EQUALITY BETWEEN BOYS AND GIRLS

Any setting concerned about equality should be aware of how they make it possible for boys and girls to have a similar entitlement and learn to adopt positive attitudes towards each other. Young children's awareness of their gender develops over time. Three-year-olds are usually able to recognise and label themselves as boys or girls but it can take another couple of years before they begin to understand that their gender is stable, e.g. I am a boy and boys don't grow up to be a mummy.

Children may also learn in the home how to behave differently as boys and girls and will take this behaviour into the setting. As Siraj-Blatchford wisely comments, many parents and staff conclude from children's behaviour that they are naturally different, without considering their own contribution to the children's socialisation or considering the impact of role-modelling (9). The ways in which parents dress children, talk with them, decorate their rooms and the toys they buy them will give messages about their sex identity. Some parents can have strong views about children having what they consider to be unsuitable responses for their sex, for example they can subject their child to public ridicule. Banjeree suggests that this type of reaction can be a strong inducement for the child to behave in a gender stereotypical manner (10).

In these instances it is difficult for parents to accept that there is a very different approach in the setting, based on the belief that children should be encouraged to develop all aspects of their personality. Margy Whalley, head of the Pen Green Centre, recounts an episode one Christmas when the mother of a four-year-old child was angry and distressed as a consequence of Father Christmas presenting her son with a picnic set which was what he wanted. Whalley concludes that it is necessary to move slowly when attempting to influence parents. Young children will only become confused if values at home and nursery are in direct opposition (11).

Case study 📁

Andrea was sitting, sorting out cutlery in the kitchen area of a well-resourced role-play area. Aaron entered and settled himself in an armchair to 'read' the newspaper. He went through all the motions of a reader; turning the pages and appearing to scan the print. Glancing up from the paper he saw Andrea. 'Get off your bum and make me a cup of tea', he ordered. Andrea promptly picked up the kettle and looked for the teapot. On observing this Ann the teaching assistant asked Andrea if she could come in to join them for a cup of tea. 'Perhaps we could ask Aaron to wash up afterwards?' she suggested. Frowning slightly, Aaron agreed.

Comment

Aaron's behaviour reflected what he had observed at home. (When the episode was recounted to his mum she wryly admitted that Aaron would have heard similar comments directed to her from his three much older brothers.) Clearly it was not consistent with the equal opportunities ethos that the nursery was trying to develop. Ann promptly invited herself into the area in order to steer the play towards giving Aaron a more equal role. Ann also hoped that she was offering a role model to encourage Andrea to be more assertive in future situations.

EQUALITY TO IMPROVE EDUCATIONAL ACHIEVEMENT

A starting point towards greater equality is to ensure that all children have access to similar provision. However, it is important to recognise that the provision is optional and parents' wishes should be respected. A number of children with English as an additional language achieve low scores at the end of the reception year; commonly, these children for various reasons will have remained at home and not taken up the offer of free nursery provision. In the interests of equality, Local Authorities are required to ensure that no child is excluded from provision because of difficulties in accessing a nursery place (12).

Gypsy/Roma and traveller children are among the most disadvantaged groups in our society. These groups are most at risk of failing in our education system largely due to their mobile way of life and a continuing lack of understanding of Gypsy/Roma and Traveller lifestyles. Research has found that the best way of combating this low achievement is for children to participate in early years settings; despite this there is a low take-up of early years services among these communities. In both of these groups, parents may not recognise the benefits of early years provision or may feel that their cultures are not understood or respected. An audit carried out in 2003 by Save the Children emphasised the need for practitioners to have opportunities to share experiences and information and so come to recognise good practice with Gypsy/Roma and traveller families. This resulted in a government-funded project being set up in 2004 to promote inclusion of these communities in early years settings and the publication of a practical guidance booklet (13).

National data from the Early Years Foundation Stage Profile suggests that boys continue to achieve less well than girls across all areas of learning and that more girls are working well within the early learning goals than boys (14). Government guidance for practitioners points out that boys are not less capable than girls and suggests that the quality of relationships and the attitudes that practitioners have towards young boys may contribute to this unequal achievement (15). This is supported in an Ofsted survey of 144 Foundation Stage settings published in March 2007, which recommends that practitioners could take more responsibility for creating the conditions which engage boys to learn (16). The current priority on early achievement in reading and writing is not helpful to boys who develop these skills later than girls. Maria Robinson draws attention to some significant differences between boys and girls in their early learning and development. Quoting different studies she highlights the diverse areas of maturation, for example a two-year-old boy is three times more likely to be able to build a bridge out of blocks than a girl of the same age, while girls at around three-and-a-half can read facial expressions often better than five-year-old boys. She refers to findings which indicate that boys prefer colder temperatures, louder voices and opportunities for movement than girls (17).

In regard to boys' lack of achievement there is a case to be argued for some early and sensitive intervention. It may be that if children in the setting are simply allowed freely to choose their activities, this in itself can set the scene for differences in later achievement. One study pointed up that it is the choices that boys and girls make from early years onwards rather than their innate ability that influences what they do later. In playgroup, given free choice, children observed selected stereotypical activities; for example, boys racing around the garden and showing an interest only in books about tractors and dumper trucks; girls engaged in role-play, and quietly drawing. On arrival in reception some boys were reluctant to draw and write, having had little experience with pencils. They were also more interested in information books rather than fiction; as a result the study suggests that boys may find reading schemes which involve stories more difficult to follow. In reception classes where reading and writing are regarded highly, boys who have had little relevant experience are immediately vulnerable. As children move through school the stage is set for them to develop different styles of writing based on the books that they read (18). Increasingly in early years efforts are made to encourage boys to mark make, drawing on their interests, particularly super-hero play.

While it is important that children are encouraged to succeed in all aspects of learning, practitioners also know that if children are able to learn in ways which suit them, they will want to learn more. Research by the Campaign for Learning on different learning styles found that small boys initially respond more to kinaesthetic or active learning (19). Adults living and working with young boys are very aware of their energy and exuberance; a sedentary curriculum programme is not conducive to most young children but small boys can find it particularly trying. This is exemplified by comments from two boys being interviewed on their transition from the Foundation Stage to Year 1:

> Researcher: 'Is there anything you don't like about being in Year 1?'
> First boy: 'Being on the carpet for a long time.'
> Second boy: 'Neither do I because it's very boring.'
> First boy: 'And it wastes our time playing.'
> Second boy: 'It wastes your life' (20).

Annabel Dixon, an exceptionally sensitive teacher and author, would have understood these comments. Dixon stressed the importance of using what we know about children to nurture positive attitudes from the time that they start their nursery and school careers. 'If boys gain a positive attitude to learning, in my experience they will take on a wider range of interests as they get older. So, if we are focused on difference earlier, there might be less division between boys and girls later on' (21).

These findings emphasise the need to tune in carefully and build on children's early preoccupations or schemes of thought. They also concur with guidance in the Early Years Foundation Stage:

> While there are patterns of development and learning that most children follow, the pace and character of children's learning can differ from one child to another as children have different interests, skills and knowledge that they have built up from their experience. This means that children can learn the same thing in different ways or learn the same thing in different times in their development (22).

It can be too simple of course to look at this issue only in terms of gender. Some boys achieve well in school and still some girls do not thrive. Research by Keele University for Ealing Council shows the influence of social class. Looking at the home life of 5,000 children from the age of four years, the study found that both girls and boys from working-class backgrounds were less likely to achieve as well as those from middle-class backgrounds. Other studies of both working-class and young black students found that the boys rejected school authority and invited confrontation although for reasons to do with class and race rather than gender. Interestingly, although black girls distanced themselves from the school system, they were careful not to jeopardise their education (23).

All aspects of equality in early years and later are concerned with making sure that children are enabled to do their best. This involves much more than providing the same activities for all. Any reasons for a child's lack of interest or achievement must be teased out and the experiences on offer and teaching styles suitably adapted.

Early years staff offer new experiences and learning in a range of forms. By using a wide repertoire of teaching styles this should ensure that every child is given the means by which they can understand best. As we know, young children learn initially through their senses and then affirm and deepen their learning as they start to use symbolic representation. Ideally, learning approaches should be matched to the needs of individual children. However, use of a broad range of methods will help to cover a range of needs and importantly also introduce children into new ways of learning.

PROMOTING A GLOBAL DIMENSION

Practitioners have a huge responsibility in shaping the ideas and attitudes of our youngest children at a time when much of the world is in turmoil and peace is threatened. The future is in the hands of these children and we must prepare them in the best way to be global citizens.

Responding to encounters with violence

Disasters and acts of terrorism are now replayed again and again through the media and viewed by children on a daily basis. We know that children play out what they experience in an attempt to make sense of it; frequently play, particularly that of boys, includes elements of aggression. This rough and tumble play has always been the case and boys blend their understandings of reality with flights of imagination as they vigorously replay their versions of superheroes and goodies and baddies, much of which they have experienced in stories, television, film and through commercial games (see Chapter 11). Smith's study suggested that this kind of play contrasts with girls' play preferences which are based more on domestic themes (24).

Accepting that forceful and energetic play is always a challenge to manage, Adams and Moyles usefully debate the impact on children's play of increased incidences of violence which have occurred since the attack on the World Trade Centre in 2001. The escalation of conflict, bombings and intransigent killings are now horrendously witnessed as part of daily life in the world. Adams and Moyles lay out some helpful focus points which help practitioners to explore how young children respond to and represent global violence and what action they might take. Points include recognising children's entitlement to expressing their feelings about what they experience, and practitioners being responsible for protecting all children in their setting and for actively handling issues of conflict (25).

SUPPORTING INCLUSION

Resources

We know that the young brain is extremely receptive to all the experiences that are on offer. This highlights the fact that all adults do, say and provide can make a difference to children's attitudes about others. For example, children will respond to a setting's environment. If the environment conveys values and principles, what messages do settings offer young children and their families about different cultures and backgrounds? While young children are still struggling with written language the impact of images is strong and they will encounter many negative media images – listless, unhappy, tired and hungry families. These should be counterbalanced by affirmative posters and paintings of people from different races and cultures involved in everyday events – shopping, cooking, eating and going to work.

Resources for play are important, but a word of caution about dressing-up clothes. These need to reflect clothes worn for everyday life in different cultures rather than 'national costume'. As Iram Siraj Blatchford wryly observes, we might be fairly surprised if we went to an Indian nursery to find that the only English dressing-up clothes were those of Morris dancers (26). Children will play what they know. Different cooking utensils and household items need to be introduced – even better if there are children or parents who can show others how they are used in their homes.

Language

Language powerfully influences how we think and feel about ourselves. Young children should be able to see and hear various languages and alternative scripts. Children find it easy to learn sign language and enjoy using it to respond in small groups. As they get older, they love to learn to count a few numbers, sing a song, reply to the register or greet their friend using different languages and identify symbols in Braille. Over time, and naturally, they come to realise that these different sounds and signs are equally useful ways of communicating.

Other people

We know only too well now that young children will learn so much by themselves but sometimes they need informed adults to bring them to the next steps in understanding (see Chapter 2). Informative displays and good resources will only have good impact if they are brought to children's attention, if practitioners encourage children to explore them and to make connections between what they see and hear with their own experiences. 'Oh, my daddy digs the garden like that man in Africa but he grows flowers.' It is only when children make these sorts of comments that we can see that they are beginning to recognise both similarities and differences in peoples' lifestyles.

However hard practitioners work they cannot afford to do it in isolation. Working with families is explored in Chapter 10. It is touched on here in the knowledge that some families may hold strong and fixed views on global education for their children. To quote one father, 'I want to protect my little girl from all that muck in the world – her eyes will be opened soon enough'. And yet, we cannot really succeed in influencing children's attitudes, helping them to have a positive view of the unfamiliar, unless we work in tandem with parents and carers.

Working in mono-cultural areas

The danger of living in a closed or insular group has already been discussed. As Elinor Lynch points out, our culture is like a second skin; most of the time we are not aware of it but it becomes visible when we encounter one that is different (27). Where children only mix with others who come from similar backgrounds their first meeting with a person who looks different or behaves differently can be a momentous experience.

In a mono-cultural setting there can be a view that it is not necessary to look outside and that 'global education is not relevant for us'. But this attitude neglects to understand that our world has shrunk: people travel easily for work and leisure across continents. Although some of our young children may not leave their locality during their lives, many more at some time in their lives will be thrown into contact with people from different walks of life. All of our children will be affected by world events and their lives will be richer as a result of thinking about the world rather than only about their own little environment.

The reality is that where a setting is unable to offer children the first-hand experience of living and learning within a mixed community, staff have to devise scenarios in order to raise awareness and encourage children to share their views. The obvious routes to this work are to purchase resources and focus on different celebrations. However, these approaches alone are not going to achieve real understandings. Development of global education is a process and as such it should infiltrate into all aspects of work. It can be woven into register taking, through music, songs, and stories and in cooking. Different experiences of travel can be shared. A global approach in the Early Years Foundation Stage is not a bolt-on, but more another way of looking.

Balancing choice for children with adult guidance

A setting which aims to help children accept and care for others must develop a climate in which everyone feels welcome and included. This is reasonably easy to achieve when the adult oversees activities and routines. In most circumstances young children respond naturally to plenty of warm encouragement for them to be generous and open to others. However, in a democratic nursery, understandably children will also choose for themselves who they play with and this may occasionally lead to exclusion. Although some children in a nursery will opt to play with others of either sex, by three and four years of age they will increasingly play in single-sex groups. Some children also have particular difficulties in joining groups because they are perceived as being different. Alice was very overweight and sometimes clumsy; Jaru had a cast in his eye and often disconcerted children by talking to them while appearing to look in another direction. Both of these children experienced being on the perimeter of the setting's activities and had at times been hurt by comments from other children.

Interestingly, a study of early years settings in six European countries showed that very few adults had received training to support children to play and work collaboratively. Practitioners were worried about children who were in danger of being bullied and excluded but they felt that this problem related to the individual rather than the whole group. Overall, with the exception of Sweden, children in other countries received very little help to engage with others (28).

This finding is of concern and practitioners do have a responsibility at times to be proactive. Any hurtful or insulting remarks require sensitive but firm intervention. They should be dealt with promptly with the children concerned when the adult can make her views clear. 'I don't think that Jaru should be called "funny-eyes". It's really interesting that his eyes look different, and we have all got different coloured eyes.' Although children should be allowed to exercise their choice about who they will play with, it is a different matter if the decision stems from discrimination. It is also necessary to help those children who are vulnerable to being excluded; for example, to learn the skills of friendship and ways of entering a group (see Chapter 2).

Nevertheless, although the aim for any setting should be for all children to be fully included in activities, when children make decisions in play they may offer only minor roles to certain individuals. Thus some children will play a full part and others may be only partially included. Typical examples in role play are when children are regularly given token parts such as the baby or the dog. Although it seems to the outsider that these children are being marginalised, it may satisfy the children themselves. One researcher, when studying social inclusion, made the important point that inclusion is a two-way process (29). Both the person wanting to be included and the person who is the includer must agree to a situation comfortable to both parties. Even if it appears unfair that a child is always given something unimportant to do, the significant fact is that it is acceptable to the child. These issues concerning the wider world may appear remote, but young children experience many of them at a personal level. Children are regularly involved in issues of fairness and discrimination – the use and discussion of these experiences will sow seeds of understanding and codes of behaviour which can be explored in more depth at a later stage. It is unrealistic to expect early education and care to address all of society's problems. Nevertheless the foundations of equity and tolerance can be laid. Vivien Paley, working with her kindergarten children in the USA, suggests that 'maybe our classrooms can be nicer than the outside world' (30).

Practical suggestions

Listen and observe what children think
- Observe how babies respond to meeting different people and to different experiences.
- Listen to children as they play with each other and share books; what do they notice and what observations do they make? Note any derogatory names that children use towards each other if they are angry or upset.
- Use these comments to develop teaching points, e.g. a comment overheard 'Lisa's fat' might lead to the adult bringing in posters of children and well-known media figures of different sizes in order to talk about the range of physical shapes and relative importance of body shape and size against what a person is really like.

Respect every child
- Ensure that you use children's correct names which are pronounced properly.
- Take care to record full names when a child enters the nursery. Ask parents how they and their children would like to be addressed and listen carefully to how the name is pronounced. For the benefit of other staff, a child's personal name should be underlined on the record and if necessary spelt out phonetically.
- Show a genuine interest in children's backgrounds. Ask them to bring in something that is special for them from their home. Share these precious things informally during circle times (most effectively organised for older children in small groups of six to eight where all children are encouraged to join in and ask questions).

Help children to see themselves in relation to others
- Create a personal book for each baby which has photographs of them with other close family members – talk to them about each photograph and the loving relationships that are depicted. Add more photographs as they bond to new adults and children.
- Use images (photographs/pictures/postcards) which show children in their own homes, other children and their families in the local environment and from other parts of the world. Use these images to interest children in other people and places and to develop balanced views.
- Display and discuss examples of similarities in the stages of growing up, in the daily aspects of life (washing, dressing, eating, celebrating) and common emotions we experience; common problems experienced in all countries (people who are homeless and poor); differences in homes, physical appearances and dress and different customs.
- Use routines to help children identify how they are alike and how they are different, e.g. when grouping children or dismissing them from a group use physical characteristics as well as items of clothing – 'all those with red socks, black, curly hair, two thumbs'. *Continued*

Continued

Provide role play settings to reflect different lifestyles
- Provide materials which encourage children to construct different types of homes (tent, caravan). Help children to appreciate the special circumstances of living in these homes (cooking, washing, collecting water) in order for them to use their play to develop understandings.
- Provide examples of men and women doing different jobs. Invite adults into the nursery whose roles help to counter stereotypes, e.g. a father with a baby, a woman bus driver, a man who assists with a cookery activity.
- Use stories, jigsaw puzzles and photographic displays to show adults in different roles.

Confront exclusion
- Using photographs of the adults and children in the nursery, make stick puppets. Introduce these to the children; ask each child to select his own stick puppet and then choose other puppets whom he wants to play with that morning. This activity may identify the children who are excluded – discuss what it feels like to be left out; make brief but clear reference to any issues which involve ethnicity or disability.
- Leave the puppets in the book area for children to play with; observe any activity with the puppets or change in the children's play partners. Repeat the activity after two weeks.

Develop a global perspective
- Help children to empathise with those who arrive new to a setting from another country – e.g. how would they feel if they didn't know anyone, they didn't understand what people were saying and they had to leave their grandma behind when they moved?
- Pick up cues and comments from parents about their views of inclusion in order to be aware of where they stand on this issue.
- Be clear and honest about the stance that you take in your setting and justify this in the children's interests. Make your views explicit through displayed images and statements.
- Use workshops, discussions and video to raise parents' interest/awareness of the need to introduce global education at a young age – at least some parents will become interested and are then likely to support work.
- Help families to recognise how young children are influenced by the portrayal of images of violence through the media.
- Find out what parents/family members could offer to give children insights into different ways of living such as dress, cooking, singing, stories. Value all contributions, e.g. through thank-you cards, a thank-you picture from the children, a simple thank-you party.

Professional practice questions

1. How far do we as a staff understand the issues behind promoting equality of opportunity for all children?
2. How far do we as a staff work in a similar way to achieve equality?
3. Does my response to children depend on whether they are boys or girls?
4. How visible are men in the nursery; how are they used?
5. How aware am I of my own culture and how does it influence my behaviour with children?
6. How much do I use my knowledge of each child's cultural background in my work with them?
7. What tangible things do we do in our setting/class to create a warm and welcoming climate to all new children and their families?

The following references in the *Early Years Foundation Stage* link to this chapter:

Statutory Framework and Guidance: pp. 12, 15, 37
Practice Guidance: Appendix 2, Areas of Learning and Development,
Sense of Community (pp. 37–8), *Communities* (pp. 87–8)
Principles into Practice Cards: 1.2 *Inclusive Practice*, 2.2 *Parents as Partners*, 2.3 *Supporting Learning*, 3.4 *The Wider Context*, 4.1 *Play and Exploration*
The CD-ROM *in-depth* offers further guidance on the above principles and commitments.

The following Early Years Professional Standards link to this chapter:
1, 2, 3, 4, 8, 10, 12, 15, 16, 27, 28, 29, 30, 35, 38.

REFERENCES

1. Department for Education and Skills (DfES) (2007) *The Early Years Foundation Stage Statutory Framework*. London: DfES Publications, p. 12.
2. Lindon, J. (1998) *Equal Opportunities in Practice*. London: Hodder & Stoughton, pp. 11–12.
3. Lane, J. (2008) *Young Children and Racial Justice*. National Children's Bureau, p. 85.
4. Macpherson, W. (1999) *Inquiry into the Matters Arising from the Death of Stephen Lawrence* (The Macpherson Report): http://news.bbc.co.uk/1/hi/_special report/1999/02/99/stephen_lawrence/279746.stm
5. Cooper, H. (1985) Models of teacher expectation communication, in J.B. Dusek (ed.), *Teacher Expectancies*. London: Lawrence Erlbaum Associates.
6. Ogilvy, G.M., Boath, E.H., Cheyne, W.M., Johoda, E. and Schaffer, H.R. (1990) Staff attitudes and perceptions in multicultural nursery schools, *Early Childhood Development and Care*, Vol. 64, pp. 1–13.
7. Department for Children, Schools and Families (DCSF) (2008) *Supporting Children Learning English as an Additional Language: Guidance for Practitioners in the Early Years*

Foundation Stage. London: DCSF, p. 4.

8. Department for Education and Skills (DfES) (2007) *The Early Years Foundation Stage: Principles into Practice* 1.2. London: DfES Publications.
9. Siraj-Blatchford, I. (2006) Diversity, inclusion and learning in the early years, in G. Pugh and B. Duffy (eds) *Contemporary Issues in the Early Years*. London: Sage, p. 111.
10. Banjeree, R. (2005) Gender identity and the development of gender roles, in S. Ding and K.S. Littleton (eds) *Children's Personal and Social Development*. Oxford: Blackwell.
11. Whalley, M. (1994) *Learning to be Strong*. London: Hodder & Stoughton, p. 53.
12. Department for Children, Schools and Families (DCSF) (2008) *Supporting Children Learning English as an Additional Language: Guidance for Practitioners in the Early Years Foundation Stage*. London: DCSF, p. 2.
13. Save the Children (2007) *Early Years Gypsy/Traveller and Roma Families Project*. Sure Start/Save the Children, www.savethechildren.org.uk
14. Department for Children, Schools and Families (DCFS) (2008) *Foundation Stage Profile Results in England 2007–8*, 20 September 2008, www.dcsf.gov.uk
15. Department for Children, Schools and Families (DCFS) (2007) *Confident, Capable and Creative: Supporting Boys' Achievements*. London: DCFS, p. 3.
16. Ofsted (2007) The Foundation Stage: A Survey of 144 Settings. www.ofsted.gov.uk.
17. Robinson, M. (2009) Why gender matters, *Nursery World*, 8 January, pp. 26/27.
18. Macleod, D. (1997) The gender divide, *Guardian*, 17 June, Schools Section, p. 3.
19. Rodd, G. (2001) Can young children learn to learn? *Early Years Educator*, Vol. 3, No. 6, pp. 16–18.
20. Department for Children, Schools and Families (DCFS) (2007) *Confident, Capable and Creative: Supporting Boys' Achievements*. London: DCFS, p. 3.
21. Dixon, A. (1998) quoted in *TES Update*, 13 November, p. 9.
22. Department for Education and Skills (DfES) (2007) *The Early Years Foundation Stage Statutory Framework*, CD Rom 4.2. in depth, p. 3. London: DfES Publications.
23. Hinds, D. (1998) Don't be trapped by gender stereotypes, *TES School Management UpDate*, 13 November, p. 9.
24. Smith, P.K. (2004a) Social and pretend play in children, in A. Pellegrini and P.K. Smith (eds) *Play in Humans and Apes*. Mahwah, NJ: Erlbaum.
25. Adams, S, and Moyles, J. (2005) *Images of Violence*. Husbands Bosworth: Featherstone Education Ltd.
26. Siraj-Blatchford, I. (1996) Why understanding cultural difference is not enough, in G. Pugh *Contemporary Issues in the Early Years*, Second edition. London: Paul Chapman.
27. Lynch, E.W. (1998) Developing cross-cultural competence, in E.W. Lynch and M.J. Hanson (eds) *Developing Cross-cultural Competence: A Guide for Working with Children and their Families*. Baltimore, MD: Paul H. Brookes, p. 24.
28. Kutnick, P. et al. (2007) The role and practice of interpersonal relationships in European early education settings: sites for enhancing social inclusion, personal growth and learning? *European Early Childhood Education Research Journal*, Vol. 15, No. 3, September, pp. 379–406.
29. Sherman, A. (1995) I hardly feel like I am playing: differing intentions with regards to social inclusion, *Early Years*, Vol. 16, No. 1, pp. 51–4.
30. Paley. V. (1992) *You Can't Say You Can't Play*. Cambridge, MA: Cambridge University Press, p. 22.

Outdoors – a Haven for Personal Growth

Summary of contents

- There are rich opportunities for children to grow and develop personally when playing outside but the realities of modern life mean that many have too little chance in their home lives to encounter and enjoy the outside environment.
- Early years practitioners have a responsibility to offer an outside curriculum to children in the knowledge that it is part of their entitlement. Each setting should make its outside accommodation and resources fully accessible to children.
- Where young children are involved in planning and developing their outside environment, they are likely to be more motivated to use it.
- As they become familiar with the natural world, young children can be encouraged to value and care for it.

When asked to recall their childhoods, many adults have only piecemeal memories but admit that some of their best and most vivid recollections are linked to being outside (1). They talk with pleasure about their fantasy play, making dens and using whatever was on hand as props. Messy play seemed to be understood and accepted by parents, and adults remember the joys of digging in the earth, making mud pies and, sometimes, wading in streams. Adults recall being given a lot of freedom from a young age although older children were responsible for ensuring that younger ones did not come to harm.

Dan, now 65 years, looks back on his childhood in a small Midlands town as a time almost exclusively spent outside.

> We played near to the railway bank and cheered the trains as they passed by. The big boys taught us games of tag and leapfrog. They laid down the rules but we knew that they would keep us safe. We all took some food, biscuits, sandwiches and a bottle of drink – you shared what you had if someone for-

got to bring their grub with them. Often I would return at the end of the day, whacked out with torn trousers and muddy shoes, but longing for tomorrow to come in order to do it all over again.

Adults such as Dan recognise only too well the value of these early experiences in helping them to enjoy a robust childhood and to grow up. In today's world it is a different story; there are many issues in young children's home lives that lead to a danger of them being deprived of the memories of outdoor play which their parents still enjoy. These issues, now well rehearsed, include:

1. *Over-protection.* In today's society, many parents are worried about the safety issues of being outside. Traffic has increased immensely in residential areas and, despite efforts to clamp down on speeding, many cars are driven too fast and pose a hazard to children playing in streets. Although there is no direct evidence that children today are in more jeopardy from encounters with strangers, the grim stories sensationalised in the media have certainly influenced parents to think that their children may be in danger, and they are understandably not prepared to allow them to play out of sight. As a consequence children are not able to enjoy 'risky freedom' – that heady feeling of tasting adventure which encourages personal growth (2). Western societies are also obsessed by hygiene and increasingly homes, settings and schools try to protect young children from dirt and germs. This can backfire in later years as Clare Warden describes, quoting a study from Norway:

   > Children in their teens are being exposed for the first time to germs and bugs that they should have encountered in childhood, where they have the increased ability to produce more antibodies. When a group of children were monitored by parents at the Norwegian Barharge, the incidence of cold and infections actually went down as the time they spent outside increased (3).

2. *Lack of experience of being outside.* The pressure of time and the convenience of cars mean that children walk very little on a daily basis; it is common for children to be taken by car to their nursery or school even if it is located within a few minutes' walking distance; walking as a weekend leisure activity for families is now rare, and particularly unusual in cold or wet weather; for those families without cars, daily journeys on foot to settings and shops can be a rushed experience in the attempt to fit in these outings with the many other demands of the day.

3. *Lack of hard physical exercise to develop young bodies.* While some families arrange physical activities for young children through attending leisure centres and clubs, many are prevented from so doing because of expense. In addition, most homes with gardens do not have facilities or space for children's energetic outside play; and not all families live near to or use the facilities of a park.

While we have to face the realities of modern life and parents' concern to protect their children, the outcome is that many children do not have the opportunities to exercise their bodies or to encounter the excitement and challenges of the outdoors. As a consequence an increasing number of children have weight problems. Current figures suggest that 22.9 per cent of four- and five-year-olds are either overweight or obese. The head of policy for the British Heart Foundation suggests that a generation of children is paying the price for society's inaction (4).

During the early years of life when a vast amount of physical development is taking place and when habits of life are being laid down it is critical that children are able to be active. Early years settings and schools have a fundamental role to play here. This was recognised by the Chelsea Open Air Nursery opened in 1929 in order to provide challenge for over-privileged children, whom the benefactor asserted were crippled by not being allowed to take risks outside. The introduction of the Early Years Foundation Stage has emphasised the value of outside play and learning. Although sadly there is no legal requirement to have an outside area, the statutory guidance does urge providers to have access to an outdoor play area (5). Most early years practitioners now recognise that experiences which stem from being outside are every young child's entitlement. Although it is perfectly possible for young children to make progress in all areas through learning outside, some of the main justifications for an outdoor curriculum relate to aspects of personal development.

CONFIDENCE

We know that, in the sequence of development, children first have to experience the world actively through their senses before they can think in the abstract and hold thoughts and memories of things in their heads. If we bring an interesting new object into the classroom children's responses make it clear how they need to learn about it. 'Let me touch it, let me feel, let me see, let me listen', they cry. Provision of sensory experiences is part and parcel of the early years curriculum. In a carefully planned inside environment, children are invited to receive information through tasting, smelling, touching and listening to sounds, and rich visual displays are evident in classrooms. The good practitioner will ensure that these experiences are provided inside. However, the outside area lends itself much more easily to sensory learning; such contrivance and planning is not so necessary as much of the provision is already to hand. Children can observe minibeasts in their natural environment, they can match leaves of different colours, feel their textures and listen to the sound of their feet crunching on dry leaves. They can experience the effects of different weather at first hand, smell flowers and, under supervision, they can grow and taste different herbs.

As with any other learning children need support to identify each sense and make full use of it. But the important point is that sensory learning is natural for young children; through smelling, touching, tasting, listening and looking children pick up information in a way that makes sense to them. This relevant and often intuitive learning helps them to grow in confidence and self-esteem.

Movement is initially the natural way of learning, for young children. They may be seen to be boisterous and noisy but this behaviour is entirely appropriate for their age. Maria Robinson suggests that adults should be careful not to try to make young children do specific things that they find physically uncomfortable at a time when their bodies are growing. These can include: expecting children to 'write' before their wrist bones are developed (usually around five years); insisting that they sit still (a very demanding level of movement); or have them adopt positions that they find awkward, such as kneeling or sitting cross-legged (6). It is not that they are unwilling to do so but simply that they do not find it easy to have this degree of control over their bodies.

Children urgently need to become adept at using their bodies and they want to do so. Their physical skills are closely linked to other aspects of development. Those children who are clumsy, now diagnosed as developmental co-ordination disorder (DCD), are found to do less well in school than their intellectual abilities would suggest. Conversely, children who have good control of their bodies tend to have high self-esteem. Movement involves much more than just physical development. Chapter 2 referred to children's schemes of thought or preoccupations which are linked to different movements. These early patterns of behaviour help children actively to experience the world. Children use their bodies in all areas of learning; they use and extend gross and fine motor skills when working practically and creatively. Over time their gross motor movements become refined and support mark making. From an early age they also learn to solve problems through practice, trial and error. All of these efforts result in children experiencing achievement and developing a positive view of themselves.

INDEPENDENCE

A well-planned outdoor area, like an indoor area, can offer tremendous scope for children to become self-reliant and make choices and decisions. The outside area can, however, offer the child more scope for challenge: opportunities to take risks in climbing and balancing, in having more spaces to hide, in experiencing the weather, in building and constructing on a larger scale than possible inside. Moreover, the nature of outside play means that children are more likely to instigate activities for themselves rather than being reliant on the adult. At a basic level, if outside play is available throughout the session children are able to select where they want to play. As they get used to setting their own challenges and making decisions when playing outside, children will strengthen their powers of independence and grow in responsibility.

Children can also play a part in developing their outdoor environment. A project in Kent supported 22 settings to develop the outdoors. The project involved the community and children's views were listened to carefully. Initially children described what they liked to do in their current space; they then contributed ideas for planning new outdoor spaces. The various design options were discussed with children who also took part in carrying out the agreed changes. Adults who managed the project found that by encouraging and responding to the children's views, new possibilities arose for the outside (7).

SOCIAL SKILLS

Although some younger children are not yet ready to play with others and some are naturally inclined to play alone, much outside play is social and co-operative. A guidance document from the National Strategies suggests that 'Settings that have prolonged periods of free access to a challenging outdoor environment report that generally children behave more cooperatively, particularly boys' (8). Large construction and resources for imaginative play including making dens in trees and in clumps of bushes all foster collaborative play. The most basic of outdoor areas can use the natural elements to encourage children to enjoy puddle jumping and sharing and comparing their shadows. Sarah Knight, who has had extensive experience of forest schools, stresses how the outdoor environment can improve behaviour and social skills (9). Waller looks at the particular benefits for social development when children aged 3–7 are given scope to play in natural and wild environments (10).

EMOTIONAL DEVELOPMENT

The indoor environment, particularly where there is a confined space, often means that there is concern to button up children's emotional expression in the interests of the rest of the group. Earlier studies show that when children work in overcrowded conditions they can become irritable and aggressive (11). Outdoor space is more accommodating and allows children to express their feelings more openly; they can squeal with pleasure and excitement or explode with a temper tantrum without undue disruption. Super-hero play is a con-tentious issue but one that needs to be faced. Practitioners, while sympathetic to the need for young boys in particular to take part in vigorous, super-hero play, admit to finding it difficult to cater for this in classrooms. Outside it is eas-ier, not only to allow this play but to enter into it – noise and vigorous activity are able to be accommodated. Outside play is also very inclusive. There are cer-tain groups of children who feel more at ease out of doors. Helen Bilton refers to traveller and refugee children: 'for them, they need to be outside as this is where they feel empowered' (12).

One of the most profound lessons that children can start to learn outside is about the pattern of life, of birth, death and renewal. It is important for them to understand that their environment is forever changing, even in the depths of winter. As they sweep away dead growth in the winter they start to find new shoots underneath. In one nursery children found a dead sparrow and planned its funeral in some detail. One child suggested that other birds were looking at the burial from the single tree in the garden and they felt sad.

MOTIVATION

Perhaps the greatest justification for outdoor learning is that children are strongly inclined to learn outside – studies show that it is a preferred activity and invites curiosity, investigation and the pleasure of growing things. Learning through Landscapes suggests that the freedom involved is a great incentive. 'Because of the freedom the outdoors offers to move on a large scale, to be active, noisy and messy and to use all their senses with their whole body, young children engage in the way they most need to explore, make sense of life and express their feelings and ideas' (13). One small-scale study provided young children with Polaroid cameras and asked them to record what they liked best about their nursery. The children voted firmly for being outside. 'One little boy took a picture of a crawl-through tunnel and another photographed a football. They really valued the open space, especially if there were things like climbing frames and bikes …' (14).

Case study 🗂

Two-and-a-half-year-old Noah was fascinated by snails that inhabited the dry stone wall in his childminder's garden. He lay on the ground watching them for ages and gently touching their shells. He discovered how they ate young plants and left shiny and slimy snail trails. Noah announced to his childminder Zoe, 'I make home for snaileys – lots', and without more ado he started to collect the snails in a large plastic bowl. Without prompting, Noah handled the snails carefully and placed each one deliberately in the bowl. He then set about collecting various leaves and twigs 'for dinner' and placed several stones in the bowl 'for bed'. Noah observed the snails crawling up the sides of the bowl and was clearly worried as two clambered over the rim and escaped. He readily agreed to Zoe's suggestion that they place a net cloth over the bowl to keep the snails safe. However, despite this, the next morning the bowl was empty – not a snail in sight! Noah was initially daunted and asked again and again 'Where they gone?' Noah then decided that the snails had 'gone play – I see them'. He patiently caught further specimens and this time gave them different food – grass, mud and some fir cones. Noah also decided that the snails 'need drink' and added a saucer of water to the bowl. This time Zoe found a piece of rigid plastic to place over the bowl.

For three days Noah was absorbed with his snail friends – he talked to them, brought them more food and was fascinated by the way they clambered up the sides of the bowl. He gave them names: daddy, mummy, big boy Toby, baby. He was initially not interested in using a magnifying lens provided by Zoe, but by day two he started to use it, intrigued by how it enabled him to change the size of his view of the creatures.

After three days Zoe suggested that the snails might like to be freed in order to find their friends. Noah reluctantly agreed. He placed each one on the stone wall and bid it goodbye. 'They happy go home', he announced.

Continued

Continued

Comment

Noah's absorption with the snails led him to learn a great deal about their movements and eating habits. Zoe was careful to allow him uninterrupted time to study the snails and develop his concentration. Noah showed care and concern for the snails in the way he handled them and made provision for their comfort. He persisted with his interest by collecting them again and this time made a personal link by giving each one a name. Although he needed some persuasion to release the snails, having done so he seemed to have sated his curiosity. However, his interest in minibeasts continued and within an hour Noah was searching a pile of damp logs for woodlice and beetles.

Given these undoubted benefits, settings have a very real responsibility to offer children experience of outside activity but, as with any provision, the quality of learning and development will be dependent on the amount of thought and preparation that is invested. Any planning for outdoor play will need to consider provision of a safe environment which is available to children. This should ensure many gains in personal development, one of the main ones being early experiences in caring for the world that they live in.

GETTING SAFETY IN PERSPECTIVE

It is reasonable to accept that, during the time they are in early years settings priority must go to keeping young children safe. The outside early years environment needs to be a particular focus for safety as children are likely to be more active. However, while this means protecting a child from obvious hazards there is also a dual and longer-term responsibility, which is to help children to learn about keeping safe and dealing with possible danger. As Jenny Lindon suggests, if we want to protect children in the longer term it is not sensible to keep them away from every risk. Children, from an early age, need to gently learn from trusted adults about some of the dangers in their environment and how to deal with them (15). Being *in loco parentis* means taking on the role of the sensible and responsible parent, but this does not mean wrapping children up in cotton wool. In one sense if we wrap children up in cotton wool we are not so much protecting them, as ourselves from taking the responsibility of helping them to understand what it means to grow up and to be safety conscious.

Even at a young age children can understand the need to be safe, to check for themselves if a structure is secure or a plank is properly balanced. Most will take this responsibility very seriously and grow in self-confidence as they make the decisions.

Not only is it undesirable, it is impossible to create an environment that is risk-free. However, staff have to be aware of liability and now it is standard and recognised practice to undertake a risk assessment. This should apply to the layout of the grounds, different surfaces and the type and positioning of equipment. A risk is usually assessed through careful observation and shared information about incidents or perceived potential to harm children. However assessment of risk does not mean imagining the worst possible scenario that could happen. While it is not acceptable to tolerate high risk, any environment that provides opportunities for challenge and excitement will, for some children, be slightly risky. A useful approach is to consider risk benefit assessment where providers consider carefully some of the advantages of the risk for children (16). By providing our youngest children with elements of freedom and challenge outside we encourage them to become resilient. Tim Gill, in vigorous defence of this type of provision, suggests that in our interactions with children we have lost the art of benign neglect (17).

MAKING THE MOST OF WHAT YOU HAVE GOT

There have always been lots of good reasons for not providing an early years curriculum outdoors. Some common ones are a lack of space, limited staffing and insufficient time. However, with increasing recognition of the value of the outdoor environment these limitations are being faced and dealt with.

Space

Outside spaces are rarely ideal but the important point is what children and adults make of it. Many settings have limited outdoor provision but with imagination they can provide for a range of experiences in a very small area. One benefit of a small outside area is that it is likely to be easier to supervise.

The aim should be as far as possible for the outside area to complement what is available for children inside in order to allow for the flow and elaboration of ideas and to make it as accessible as possible.

Increasingly children in reception classes have their own designated outside space which can be planned and resourced as an outside classroom; during the first few weeks in school this should be the child's protected play space at all times of the day. Staff will plan a gradual transition for children to mix with older peers in the main outdoor area and keep a watching eye for individuals who find this experience daunting.

Staffing

Staffing ratios can vary from 1:3 for children under two to 1:30 in a reception class (staffed by a qualified teacher) and this is clearly going to influence the amount of oversight and degree of involvement of adults with outside activities. Staff who restrict outside provision to set times in the day might be persuaded to allow more access if they recognise that:

- a well-planned outside environment should involve no higher risk and thus no greater level of care for children than if they work inside
- free access to outside will mean an end to the rush to go out en masse, which can create difficulties for children sharing provision and for adults in allocating their time fairly.

Children's personal development is heavily dependent on staff understanding the benefits of being outside where children can create noise and mess. Practitioners will also recognise the type of materials that offer the most scope for creativity, social play and adventure. Less experienced staff need to understand children's needs in order to value certain resources such as mud, water, ropes and boxes.

> The adult perception can be that materials designed by adults have a greater value. Adults who are knowledgeable about the way that young children learn can see beyond the plastic façade and see that beyond many of these resources lies limited exploration and learning (18).

Time

Practitioners never complain of excess of time – there is always a scarcity and often a feeling that we rush young children through activities each day. However, if we focus on what children are experiencing rather than what they are doing, this helps us to look at the programme in a holistic way, hopefully to plan a little less content but to concentrate on providing the most fruitful experiences that will help children to grow personally. As with indoor activities, children will be more inclined to concentrate and persevere if they have time to pursue interests. The brief playtime is not conducive to this and McAuley and Jackson suggest that interrupting 'children's absorbed activity' can subvert learning almost as much as allowing disruptive behaviour (19).

Time is a finite commodity. There is of course time for anything but not time for everything. If we recognise the rich benefits of outside experiences for children, this leads to the conclusion that we cannot afford to reduce time for this provision even if it means less time spent on other daily routines.

Case study

A nursery class in an inner city area had limited space inside and access to only a tiny yard outside, which until then had been used as a space for three-wheeled toys. The arrangement was not satisfactory as each child only had access to a vehicle twice a week and then could only ride it in a small circle round and round the yard, which caused both staff and children frustration. The nursery staff recognised the need for change. Having closely observed the children's play they decided that they had very little scope to play imaginatively in the classroom. The 'home corner' occupied a corner of the classroom, and the small space meant that it was very poorly resourced. When asked what they would like to do outside if they did not

Continued

Continued

ride the vehicles, some children said that they would love to make dens.

Staff started to share stories with children about dens, hidey-holes and caves. One of the favourites was *Can't You Sleep Little Bear?* by Martin Waddell. The children thought that the bear's cave looked very cosy. They were invited to draw pictures and plans for building a cave and to decide what they might need to have inside it. Together, staff and children made a 'cave' which took up the entire out-side space. They built a willow construction which they covered with waterproof cloth. Inside it was equipped with bedding, torches, cushions and a large stuffed bear sitting on a chair. Children had free access to the cave and the play that developed was complex and focused. The home corner inside was dismantled and this freed up some much needed inside space to be used for construction and small-scale play.

One child reflected the views of many others when he commented that 'our bear cave is the very best thing in school and it's our very own'.

Comment

The nursery staff had sensibly researched through observations and through dis-cussions with children what they needed outside. They also made the most of two small spaces by regarding them as a total environment. The children's close involvement in setting up the cave is reflected in their high-quality play and their expressed sense of personal satisfaction.

HELPING CHILDREN TO LOOK AFTER THE WORLD OUTSIDE

The need to respect and conserve our environment is now acute and is a recog-nised aspect of the National Curriculum. Most young children have a strong affinity with the natural world. A two-year-old will amble along a road and stop for a maddeningly long period to examine a weed growing out of a wall. The attractions of water, mud and minibeasts never fail. This early interest provides a very sound basis for extending their understanding and developing a respect for the environment in which they live. Even given a small patch of earth children can still learn how important it is to care for it, to keep it looking beautiful by being careful, tidy, gentle in handling things and leaving nature to grow.

However, some nurseries will be interested in catering in more depth for this aspect of personal development. Three successful approaches working with young children outside are described briefly below.

Earth education

The Institute for Earth Education was set up in America in the 1980s as a nonprofit volunteer organisation. It aims to provide programmes to help individuals 'live more harmoniously with the earth'. The basic programme is one of acclimatisation, which in summary is to feel at home with the natural world, to be aware of one's place in life's processes, and to become more aware and understand more of the natural world.

Although the programmes are designed for all age groups, many aspects are particularly suitable for young children, as there is a heavy focus on feelings and learning through the senses. Some of the main principles of an acclimatisation programme reflect the tenets of early childhood practice. These are that: people learn best when they feel what they are learning; the best learning starts where the learner is; the wide worlds of perception and emotion cannot be measured or described in words; in a good learning experience the medium should be the magic of discovery and wonder and joy (20). The programme of activities is designed to take place out-of-doors and to be organised for small groups. With under-fives, one adult for every four children is desirable. This enables easy conversation and for the adult to respond to each child's discoveries and observations. An essential requirement is that the adults themselves enjoy the wonders of the natural world. (See below for practical suggestions for an earthwalk.)

Forest Schools

In Denmark, Forest Schools have been an important aspect of early years education for the past 30 years. They were introduced initially for children of five and six years in Copenhagen to provide them with some nursery experience in the year before they attended school; a bus would collect children daily and take them into the local forests simply because there was no space to build conventional nursery units. The benefits of this type of provision were quickly recognised. The Forest School developed based on the belief that young children could be educated to appreciate the natural world and to begin to understand the need to care for nature. There is also a heavy emphasis on helping children to become autonomous – to become physically independent, explore for themselves and not be afraid of getting dirty.

In 1995 Bridgwater College Early Years Centre of Excellence followed the Danish model and started its own Forest School for three- and four-year-olds and the centre now leases a secure woodland site and a minibus. The children visit the forest for one day nearly every week they are in the nursery and in all sorts of weather. The aim is to encourage them to grow in confidence and independence, to learn to take risks and to gain skills in, and knowledge of aspects of, the outside environment. They develop observational skills, learn how to whittle sticks, light a fire and extinguish it safely. After one year of these experiences the children camp in the woodland, with some of the parents, staff and students. In recent years the project has expanded vastly and Forest School centres are established in many parts of the country (21).

Figure 9.1 Looking after our world

Figure 9.2 Young children develop skills in the Forest School

The Rising Sun Woodland Project

This project drew both on the philosophies of the Forest Schools and the Reggio Emilia pre-schools. With the aid of a grant, children from a nursery class in

Northern England were transported to a countryside park with a team of specialist workers (including artists, an environmental officer and early years staff). The richness of their experiences depicted in beautiful video materials shows opportunities for children to gather and collect natural objects, encounter water, ice, mud and fire, challenge their physical skills in climbing banks and trees, build dens and live with an imaginary dragon in the woodland. The project records the children's huge range of personal development. Caring attitudes were encouraged in protecting plants and trees. This ethos influenced children's attitudes to each other, for example when one child stung his arm on a nettle, his friend said 'Don't worry, I'll look after you, we'll find Mrs B or Mrs N' (22).

Practical suggestions

Listen and observe
- Note which outside areas babies and children prefer to use.
- Observe what experiences they choose outside, e.g. what surfaces babies like to touch and crawl on.
- Listen to how children engage others in their large-scale outside play.

Start from the child's perspective
- List the things that you enjoyed doing outside as a child – climbing, jumping, digging, make-believe, making dens, hiding, collecting.
- Discuss with your children what they would like to include in an outdoor play area; ask them to tell you or draw a picture of this.
- Take a small group of children to visit a neighbouring early years setting which has a good outside area; walk around and discuss the different features; provide them with cameras and ask them to take a photograph of a favourite feature outside that they would like to include in their setting.
- Crawl around the setting and take photographs of different aspects of your outside environment to reveal the child's perspective.

Develop a quiet sanctuary
- Place a baby in a pram under the branches of a tree.
- Provide a sheltered/screened area for children to rest from activity and reflect; provide low seating/rugs and cushions; make sure that children recognise that the purpose of this place is to be able to withdraw from noise and activity to enjoy peace.

Provide transportable resources which encourage children to work together and give vent to their feelings
- Have a trolley on wheels with transparent or wire baskets; label and resource each basket with different equipment, e.g. for gardening – small forks, rakes, trowels, watering cans, gardening gloves, plastic kneelers; for windy days – streamers, windmills, bubble mixture and wands, paper for making paper planes, small kites; for imagining – small play scenarios and mats.
- Provide a wide range of found and natural materials for children to use to reflect and transform their ideas.

Continued

Continued

Plan outside play which is developmentally appropriate for babies and children
- Provide outdoor treasure baskets and bouts of heuristic play for babies which include natural materials.
- Extend this form of play for older children using large-scale materials, e.g. planks, pipes, boxes.

Plan your outside area to teach about environmental issues
- Even a very limited space can provide for a raised bed or tubs of plants and bird feeders or a bird table; trees and vegetation to attract butterflies and insects; rocks or logs as homes for minibeasts; an area sectioned off to contain cobbles and stones for children to arrange in different patterns; regular activities which include looking at shadows at different times of the day, noting the different position of the sun and clouds at different times of the day.
- Think carefully about what environmental experiences you want to provide for children, rather than simply what you want to grow.

Plan specific activities to nurture acclimatisation with the earth
- Prepare a series of simple activities to allow children to experience and enjoy the environment through their senses. The following three activities have been adapted from the Earth Education Acclimatization Institute. The walk should be for no longer than twenty-five minutes on the first occasion and ideally there should be one adult available for a group of three children. The venue would ideally be a patch of woodland but it is possible to use a 'wild' area in a local park. It does not have to be an extensive area; you do not have to walk very far but do ensure that the environment is suitable for the activities. You should aim to link the activities to provide the children with an enjoyable and unified experience of the natural world.

Explain to the children that you are going on a very special walk when they will be using their eyes, ears, fingers and noses to explore things.
Activity 1: Using your nose. Start the walk if possible near a fragrant spot (damp moss, bluebells, wild garlic). Explain to the children that some things are easy to smell but others have secret scents; show them how to scratch a root or patch of damp soil in order to allow it to share its perfume. Encourage them to share their favourite 'smells' with their helper and others in their small groups.
Activity 2: The little people's garden. Resources required: cardboard tubes which are cut down to provide a viewfinder for each child. Prepare for this activity in advance by identifying the little garden, a mossy and secluded patch with interesting features such as boulders, ferns, pieces of bark and fungus. Cover this with a black cloth. Tell the children a story about a group of little people who have a garden nearby and lead them towards the cloth. When you arrive explain to the children that in order to see the garden they must first collect a gift for the little people – it should be the smallest thing they can find nearby – a twig, leaf, tiny stone. When the children have gathered

Continued

Continued

their gifts they return to the cloth. Before you reveal the little people's garden you give a viewfinder to each child. Show them how they can have their own special view of the garden. Encourage each child to decide where to place their gift in the garden.

Activity 3: Wind dancers. Demonstrate to the children how a leaf twirls through the air. Talk about all the little things that dance in the wind. Suggest that children find their own. They have to look carefully for twigs, blades of grass, seedpods and feathers, and test them to see which are the best dancers. They return to the group and each child demonstrates his or her dancer.

Professional practice questions

1. How much do we know about our children's previous experiences of being outside?
2. What messages does our outside area give to children as users; how do you know?
3. How much do we know of parents' attitudes to their children being outside? How have we managed to reassure and convince more reluctant parents of the benefits of outside play?
4. How well does our outdoor area allow children to express and extend their thoughts and ideas?
5. How do we encourage toddlers and children who are more reluctant to use the outdoors?
6. How well does our outside area challenge our oldest and most experienced children?
7. How well do we as a staff demonstrate enthusiasm for being outside?

The following references in the *Early Years Foundation Stage* link to this chapter:

Statutory Framework and Guidance: pp. 33, 35, 37
Practice Guidance: p. 17 *Appendix 2; Physical Development*, pp. 90/91
Principles into Practice Cards: 3.3 *The Learning Environment (the Outdoor Environment)* 4.1 *Play and Exploration*, 4.2 *Active Learning*
The CD-Rom *in-depth* offers further guidance on the principles and commitments above.

The following Early Years Professional Standards link to this chapter:
1, 2, 3, 4, 5, 7, 8, 9, 10, 11, 12, 14, 16, 25, 26, 27, 31, 38, 39.

REFERENCES 📖

1. Edgington, M. (2002) *The Great Outdoors*. Early Education, 136 Cavell Street, London E1 2JA.
2. Ouvry, M. (2000) *Exercising Muscles and Minds*. National Early Years Network.
3. Warden, C. (2007) *Nurture through Nature*, p. 23. Mindstretchers, www.mind-stretchers.co.uk
4. *Nursery World* (2008) Government statistics on four- and five-year-olds, *Nursery World*, 28 February, p. 3.
5. Department for Education and Skills (DfES) (2007) *Statutory Framework for The Early Years Foundation Stage*, Section 3. London: DCSF , p. 35.
6. Robinson, M. (2008) *Development Birth to Eight – A Child's Journey Through the Early Years*. Buckingham: Open University Press.
7. Ryder-Richardson, G. (2006) *Creating Spaces to Grow: Developing your Outdoor Learning Environment*. London: David Fulton.
8. Department for Education and Skills (DfES) (2008) *The National Strategies Early Years. Social and Emotional Aspects of Development (SEAD): Guidance for Practitioners in the Early Years Foundation Stage*. London: DCSF. www.standards@dcsf.gov.uk
9. Knight, S. (2009) *Forest Schools and Outdoor Learning in the Early Years*. London: Sage.
10. Waller, T. (2007) The Trampoline Tree and the Swamp Monster with Eighteen Heads, *Education 3–13*, Vol. 35, Issue 4, November, pp. 393–497.
11. Bates, B. (1996) Like rats in a rage, *The Times Educational Supplement*, Vol. 2, 20 September, p. 11.
12. Bilton, H. (2004) *Playing Outside: Activities, Ideas and Inspiration for the Early Years*. London: David Fulton, p. 5.
13. Learning through Landscapes (2004) *Early Years Outdoors: Vision and Values for Outdoor Play*. Winchester: Learning through Landscapes.
14. Finch, S. (1999) quoted by J. Moorhead in Out of the mouths of babes, *Guardian*, 2 June, p. 9.
15. Lindon, J. (1999) *Too Safe for their Own Good*. London: National Early Years Network.
16. Gill, T. (2007) *No Fear: Growing up in a Risk Averse Society*. London: Clouste Gulbenkian Foundation.
17. Gill, T. (2008) in a keynote speech presented at Early Years 2008, Roehampton University, London, organised by EYE in association with Practical Pre-school and Child Care.
18. Warden, C. (2007) *Nurture through Nature*. Auchterarder: Mindstretchers, p. 18.
19. McAuley, H. and Jackson, P. (1992) *Educating Young Children: A Structural Approach*. London: David Fulton, pp. 46–7.
20. Van Matre, S. (1979) *Sunship Earth*. Earth Education Acclimatization Institute, PO Box 288, Warrenville, IL 60555, p. 11.
21. Bridgwater College Children's Centre brochure, Bath Road, Bridgwater, Somerset TA6 4PZ.
22. Rising Sun Woodland Preschool Project (2000) *Time Out in the Woodland*. Newcastle: Sightlines Initiatives, p. 24.

10

Working with Families to Support Young Children's Personal Growth

Summary of contents

- Whatever form a family takes, it is immensely important for each child.
- Parents will have their own views about bringing up their children and these may not always coincide with the aims of the nursery. If each party knows where the other stands, this is more likely to lead to shared tolerance and respect.
- If early years settings are to support parents, they need to value them and recognise the pressures of parenthood.
- Although recent government initiatives are providing an infrastructure and increased funding to help families, the successful nurturing of young children is dependent on practitioners and parents working closely together on a day-to-day basis.

The Early Years Foundation Stage reminds us that families are unique. 'Children may live with one or both parents, with other relatives or carers, with same sex parents, unmarried partners, divorced and married partners with families' (1). However, generally families are smaller and the role of the extended family in many cases has dwindled. For children their family consists of the people who are closest to them and who care for them on a daily basis. These may include neighbours, family friends and partners or birth parents, and in settings, the key person. Any one of these may be the 'significant' person for the child; these are the people that we as adults remember so vividly when recalling major influences in our childhood. Early years staff are also significant for young children but they can never take the place of the family. However, if families and staff work closely together the child will benefit.

This chapter explores the particular role of families in the young child's personal and social development. It also considers how early years staff can learn from families, support them and work closely with them.

FAMILIES MATTER

However it is made up and however imperfect, for a young child her family is critically important. The relationship between a young child and her immediate family is recognised by its very nature to be personal, intense and long lasting.

> Parenting has a strong influence on emotional and physical health and well-being in adult as well as child life. There is a growing body of evidence that the quality of care that babies and toddlers receive depends on the sensitivity, insight, attitudes and resilience of parents or carers (2).

Parents invest so much in their children because they matter to them. They are, and should be, biased in favour of their child. The Newsons, writing over 30 years ago, stressed how important this is.

> The best that community care can offer is impartiality – to be fair to every child in its care. But a developing personality needs more than that; it needs to know that to someone it matters more than other children; that someone will go to unreasonable lengths, not just reasonable ones, for its sake (3).

Throughout this book we see how adult models of behaviour impact on the way children think and behave. Long before a child starts at a nursery, her early personal experiences in her family will be a powerful influence on her attitudes to living and learning as one of a group.

Case study

Rick was used to making decisions about how to use his time in play and sharing with others while he stayed with a neighbour who was his childminder; his dad, a single parent, encouraged Rick to help with the daily chores of clearing up after meals and sorting clothes out for washing. Rick and his dad also talked about what they had done each day and sang songs and looked at books before bedtime. Dad took Rick and the neighbour's child swimming every Saturday morning. Rick was used to taking some responsibility and being treated with respect. At four, Rick was confident and secure within himself.

Jez was seemingly also confident but at four years of age he was learning different lessons. His older brother shoplifted regularly and he taught Jez how to easily transfer a bar of chocolate from the shop counter into his pocket. When these episodes were recounted at home Jez's dad was tolerant and amused, saying that he 'had done the same as a kid'. Jez initially settled into a nursery well but was confused and angry when he was gently taken to task for taking toys and sweets from other children's pockets and lunchboxes.

We can be sure that the family provides the young child with an influential example of what things are important and interesting in life, how to conduct oneself and how to live with others. Most significantly, the ways in which the family members regard and treat the child provide her with a view of herself.

The value of the home and family life in helping young children to develop emotional insights and to learn about right and wrong behaviour has already been discussed (see Chapters 4 and 6). In addition, studies have shown the significance of daily life at home where children listen, converse, interrupt, question and learn from members of their family (4, 5). The EPPE study has found that parents' interest and involvement in their child's early learning at home has a significant impact; the quality of the home environment was the key factor – in short, what parents do with their children is more important than who they are. For example, one of the numerous factors that seemed to lead to children developing higher intellectual, behaviour and social skills is the opportunity to have friends to play with at home (6). Moreover it seems that initial investment in the early years can have long-term benefits. The ongoing EPPE research has shown that parental involvement with their young children can have positive advantages which are still apparent for children at age seven and ten (7). Charles Desforges' study for the DfES suggests that parental engagement can account for up to 12 per cent difference between the outcomes for individual children (8). Increasingly, we recognise that fathers matter to young children and can have a profound impact on their children as they grow up. Studies show that where dads are involved early in their child's life:

> there is a positive relationship to later educational achievement
> there is an association with good parent-child relationship in adolescence
> children in separated families are more protected from mental health problems (9).

The research evidence for all ages of children in school is constant in showing that when schools, families and communities work together to support learning, children tend to do better, stay in school longer and enjoy school more (10).

In regard to young children the sheer amount of time they spend with their families is persuasive. Even though family members work, or are at school, in the long-term most of them have a lot of contact with their youngest children. Apart from those in full-time daycare, children spend the bulk of their time at home.

APPROACHES TO PARENTING

We have all had parents, and if and when we become parents, our experience of being 'parented' is probably the strongest influence on our attitudes and behaviour. This can work in two ways. Some people may, consciously or not, dismiss their parents' approach, believing that their own style of parenting is preferable to what they had. Others, deliberately or unconsciously, will base their style of child management on what they have known.

Although parents may have clear views about their preferred way of raising a child, there is a growing awareness that others may adopt a different approach. Jane Lane points out that this wasn't always the case. For example, in the past it was considered good parenting practice to establish a routine of a set early evening bedtime. Where this didn't happen parents, commonly from black or working-class families, were often regarded as irresponsible or inadequate. Now more relaxed attitudes are evident, the more important concern being that children have enough sleep and awake refreshed. Lane concludes that 'the idea that there is one best way … is rightly being questioned … So long as a child is content and thriving most parents accept that there is no definitive way to bring up a child and feel little pressure to conform to specific ways' (11). Parents may also have different views between them about how to raise their children. Blamires reminds us of this with particular reference to those parents who have children with special educational needs. She suggests that when parents are faced with highly emotional issues and significant issues regarding provision for their child who has difficulties, they may think and react very differently (12).

Whatever parents believe about and do with their children, it cannot be assumed that this will coincide with what happens in early years settings. Unless staff and parents are aware of each other's beliefs and practices, they could be working at cross-purposes. Early years staff do not have the right to tell families how to bring up their children or indeed to insist that the setting's way is the right way. However, both parties need to know about each other's views. Early years settings and schools take great pains to inform parents about their priorities and practices. It has been less common, though, for settings to find out about what families consider to be important for their children. The Early Years Foundation Stage now makes clear the need for a reciprocal dialogue. 'Successful relationships become partnerships when there is a two-way communication and parents and practitioners really listen to each other and value each other's views and support in achieving the best outcomes for each child' (13).

Case study 🗁

Four-year-old Wang-Hoi was waited on heavily by his three older sisters at home. They tidied away his toys and clothes and responded to all his needs. At the nursery Wang was required to learn to be self-sufficient; he found this very difficult and resisted all attempts to encourage him to fend for himself. When changing clothes to go outside, Wang would dangle his wellington boots in front of a member of staff; he became confused and cross when asked to tidy equipment away and started to hide at tidy-up time. It was not until his mother and teacher discussed Wang's behaviour that they became aware of each other's different expectations. After that they agreed that Wang should be helped to conform with nursery practices and his family would encourage him to 'do as his friends did'. However, his mother insisted that at home Wang would remain the 'little prince' and his sisters would continue to do things for him.

Comment

The nursery and the family respected each other's viewpoint, although initially Wang-Hoi found it difficult to adjust to these dual expectations. However, he carefully observed what other children did. Three weeks later, Wang joyfully pulled

Continued

Continued

at one of the helper's hands and showed her how he had stacked bricks away. After that, he appeared to have accepted the nursery routines and took great pleasure in learning how to cope for himself. Wang's mother laughed when she heard this development and reported that his dependent behaviour was unchanged at home.

PRESSURES ON YOUNG FAMILIES IN TODAY'S SOCIETY

Being a parent of a young child is an unmatched wonder; all parents experience the joy, excitement and fun of sharing life with a newly emerging personality. These are the precious rewards for the difficulties and challenges of parenting. It is tempting for professionals working for limited and planned periods of time with children who do not belong to them, to criticise what parents do and do not do. The reality is that bringing up children today is not easy even when one has the support of a loving partner or family, no financial worries and your children are loved and wanted. Being a parent can be a frightening, exhausting and lonely job if the parent concerned is young, inexperienced or alone. Most parents, whatever their circumstances, find the job a heady combination of delight, frustration and despair; some of the time it is simply tedious. Being a parent has always meant responsibilities; in a complex and fast-changing world the job has become even more demanding. Lillian Katz wrote:

> Many of the stresses of parenting stem from the wide range of choices, alternatives and options available to modern Americans in virtually every aspect of life. It is not difficult to imagine how many fewer arguments, heated discussions and reductions in demanding behaviour on the part of children would follow from having to live with minimal or even no choices in such things as food, television shows, toys, clothes, and so forth (14).

These stresses are evident in the UK and have certainly not lessened in the last 34 years (15, 16). A particular issue for parents is the way in which even very young children are seen as targets for television advertisements (17) (see also Chapter 7). Parents are also not helped by society where often we see dual standards. For example, there are pressures for all parents to contribute to the workforce, and yet the public finger is still pointed at parents who place their children in daycare in order to remain in employment. People like to see young children behaving properly in public; they complain that today's children are 'spoilt' by being given too much. And yet the media bombard children with messages about the latest toy that they should have; children are constantly beset by temptations in supermarkets where sweets and toys are set out on low-level shelves accessible to small hands. Busy parents, sometimes only too aware of the lack of time they can spend with their children, try to compensate by providing their children with material possessions, whether they be sweets or other goodies advertised by the media as essential to make every little boy or girl happy. Asha Phillips, an experienced child psychiatrist, while sympathising with the parents' need to indulge their children, suggests that this may actually deprive a child of learning the important lesson in life of doing without. 'Without this ability, he (the child) will always be at the mercy of wants that can never all be satisfied. Having and discarding possessions easily also robs him of the feeling that anything is special' (18).

Parents invariably want the best for their children but sometimes their own circumstances prevent them from acting in their child's interests. Financial burdens can take their toll on young families; unemployment and poor housing can lead to adults having low self-esteem and seeing little point in striving for improved conditions for them and their children. Often these families live in areas with weak community links and general acceptance of antisocial behaviour. Many women are now more assertive about achieving what they want in life while men are less certain of their role in the home, particularly where they are no longer the breadwinner. In turn these circumstances can cause stress and family rows which are so damaging emotionally for young children. Family members may also suffer from poor mental health shown in symptoms of anxiety, depression and erratic behaviour. Stephen Scott, Professor of Child Health and Behavior at King's College, London, shows in his studies how the behaviour of parents closely influences the life chances of their children. He suggests that lack of money is only one negative factor and suggests that 'it seems to be poverty of parent-child experience ... that leads to poor child outcomes rather than poverty of a material kind' (19). This book refers to plenty of evidence for very young children needing consistent love and care from close adults; those children coming from families who are beset with the problems described above often do not receive nurture from good enough parenting and this can penalise their futures.

There are then a minority of families who are most vulnerable. A wider group of parents cope with the turbulence and demands of separated partnerships, single parenthood and full-time jobs and careers. While none of these factors in themselves is necessarily harmful for children, they can mean that it becomes difficult at times for parents to provide their young child with the undivided attention and unqualified love that is needed. Constant disharmony between parents can be particularly disturbing. When parents stay together, but in an acrimonious relationship, children can be hurt emotionally. Goleman's work shows that the way a couple handle feelings between them will have a clear effect on their children, who from a young age are very sensitive to the feelings of people close to them (see Chapter 4). The alternative – parental separation – can also damage, particularly if children are faced with this as a fait accompli. If parents do decide to go their separate ways, even young children need to have matters explained to them and to feel involved in decisions if at all possible. This was proposed in a government paper on parental separation (20). The Good Childhood Enquiry Report goes to the heart of the matter when it recommends that, in order to reduce conflict in families, parents must give more priority to relationships (21).

The challenges of being a parent go across all sectors of society; with grossly unequal distribution of work, children may be living with parents who, as Charles Handy describes, may have plenty of resources and no time, or plenty of time and no resources (22). Young children need access to both.

In wanting the best, most parents are ambitious for their children to achieve well. Seaman et al. found that many parents saw doing well in education as a key measure for their children's success and wanted their children to do better than themselves (23). Liz Brooker's study of a group of 'hard up' Anglo and Bangladeshi families whose children were starting school showed that all recognised the importance of education for their child's future and believed that parental involvement in their child's learning had an influence on their academic success (24). These positive aspirations and support are surely helpful for children who are likely to be better motivated by the encouragement from parents. However, where this develops into a culture of competition, aspirations can cause stress. Contributing to evidence for the Cambridge University Primary Review, parents of young primary children described feeling under intense pressure to read to their children and help them with school work. They struggled to find the time but felt guilty if they did not do so (25). There has also been plenty of anecdotal evidence from parents and practitioners and from the results of national surveys to show that young children do feel pressurised by targets and having to undertake tests at as young as seven years (26). Some children are required to jump the first hurdle even earlier. Joan Clanchy, former head of North London Collegiate School, describes her observations of young parents in the park with their three-year-olds as they discuss selection procedure.

> They exchange data on the success rates of different primary schools and prepreps, on which teachers they have decided are 'simply hopeless', on where to send Little Treasure for beginners' French, tennis, ballet, swimming, violin and, often, speech therapy ... The time on the swing seems to be a rare moment of peace for some three-year-olds.

Clanchy's sympathy is for these parents who, she suggests, are driven by the message that early achievement is all that matters. However, she ends her article on a warning note: 'Most of the current small victims ... will brush it (the pressure) all off and cope. But some will long resent the hurdles that are constantly erected in front of them and the hurt will go deep. Teenagers can exact a terrible revenge' (27).

Penelope Leach shares the concern for those young children whose parents are only interested in their offspring achieving things. She paints a picture of the child who comes to recognise that she is only loved for what she does rather than for who she is. Leach suggests that this has extremely damaging consequences for any child's self-esteem (28).

OFFERING SUPPORT FOR FAMILIES

There is increasing acknowledgement that raising a child in today's world is not easy. Despite this it is only very recently that there has been anything done by the government to intervene in the family. Until 1997 there was very little support for childcare. Tricia David suggested that British family policy was dominated by the belief that 'an Englishman's home is his castle' and that any state intervention was thought to intrude on and erode family life (29). However, since 2005 the government has publicly recognised that parents play a critical role in their children's development and learning. This view was formally reiterated in 2007 in the publication *Every Parent Matters* and a partner publication designed for parents (30, 31). These documents explicitly faced up to some of the challenges of being a parent in today's society and described a range of initiatives which would guide and support parents. The Children's Plan followed, reinforcing these moves and clearly stating the respective roles of parents and government. The first principle of the Children's Plan is that 'government does not bring up children – parents do – so government needs to do more to back parents and families' (32).

SOME MAJOR DEVELOPMENTS

Reaching the most vulnerable families

The politically stated intention to support families heralded considerable moves particularly aimed at reaching families most at risk. The government has identified groups of families where children may be at risk of not achieving (among other things) good levels of well-being. These are teenage parents, lone parents, families living in poverty, unemployed households, those in temporary accommodation, parents with mental health, drug or alcohol problems, those with a parent in prison or engaged in criminal activity, minority ethnic families, asylum seekers, families with disabled children or disabled themselves (33). However there are dangers of making simplistic assumptions about families based on membership of groups; there is increasing recognition that where there are complex needs these must be carefully considered on an individual basis in order to offer effective and accessible services. Togther4Children, a national children's charity, published a useful toolkit aimed at local authorities and managers of children's centres which includes some helpful advice for making links with priority and excluded families (34).

The government recognises the potential of charities in family work. Findings from the Early Learning Parenting Project (ELPP) showed that voluntary bodies can play an important role in supporting parents to be involved with their children's learning, in this case with children under three years who were at risk of learning delay. However these initiatives were likely to be short-lived and the report had a strong message for local authorities to work more closely with voluntary agencies and mainstream the effective work being carried out (35).

A major policy report *Turning up the Volume on Child Poverty* published by Together4Children identified shared agreements on issues by the major political parties and suggested five important areas for action that should be taken to support the poorest families, halve child poverty by 2010 and end it by 2020. All of these are very relevant for families with young children and were listed under the following areas:

To increase tax credits and benefits

Politicians recognise that low incomes determine low living standards and that there are weaknesses in the current benefit systems. The current means testing arrangements are complex and confusing and some families are worried about dire consequences of unknowingly being over paid. At the time of the report £14 billion a year in tax credits and benefits was not being claimed by families who were entitled to them.

The actions suggested were for the government to immediately invest £3 billion more into tax credits and benefits; extend child benefit to favour second or third children or to be biased in favour of the youngest children; increase working weekly tax credits to £91.31 per couple and to keep child benefits and child tax credits in line with earnings and the cost of living.

Support parents into decent and sustainable jobs

All parties agreed on the importance of work not only in helping families escape from poverty but also to raise their self-esteem and confidence, which can have a positive impact on their children. It was also accepted that in order to maintain a quality of family life, parents needed the type of work that both recognised and made provision for them to carry out family commitments. The particular needs of lone parents were acknowledged, studies having shown that they were more likely than other parents to abandon their jobs because of family pressures. The actual move into a basic job proved a challenge for many parents when faced with the reality of a minimum wage of £5.52. This commonly means that a low paid job offers a family less money than the benefits they have been accustomed to.

The charity recommended that: parents should have more support not only in finding and getting a job but in continuing work; that benefits should continue on a phased basis during the early months of employment; and that as parents continued work they should receive advice on becoming more skilled and learning more to enable them to develop careers.

Offer an early years childcare guarantee

There was universal recognition that childcare is required not only to assist parents in work but to provide a quality provision for children during the early years of life. However, the complex system of allocating and funding childcare meant that the neediest families are often debarred from taking up the offer. Nearly 100 per cent of parents accessed childcare when the entitlement was free for two-, three- and four-year-olds.

Together4Children recommended simpler systems and means of payment that will mean that early years childcare is made more accessible to vulnerable parents.

Narrow the gap in achievement

Politicians agreed that the gap in achievement starts in children's earliest years and continues to widen. One study shows a comparison of two groups of two-year-olds – those who have poor cognitive scores from wealthy backgrounds and those who are bright from poor households. At ten years, the children with low cognitive scores from wealthy families achieve better than the bright children from poor homes (36).

The report recommended that schools should be helped to support and assess children's progress in order to reduce the gaps in achievement.

Build a system of support for parents and families

Throughout the report, there is acknowledgement of the corrosive effective that poverty has on families and their children, coupled with a recognition that this will not end without government assistance and intervention.

The charity suggests that government initiatives may range from general practical advice on managing budgets and raising children to intensive targeted support. Whatever is offered should build on families' own capacity for self-reliance – in other words, families should be respected and helped to help themselves (37).

This report and recommendations are particularly timely given the impending recession in the country and the fact that poor families are very fragile in times of financial crisis.

One stop centres for families with young children

Historically, social care, health, childcare and education have operated separately; too often parents have had to negotiate their way through different services, replicate information for different professionals, and often receive conflicting advice and support. The notion of bringing together agencies to support families in a unified way gained impetus in the late 1990s with the introduction of early excellence centres and Sure Start programmes. These paved the way for children's centres with their central agenda to put children and families first.

The Sure Start principles for Children's Centres are unquestionably well intentioned:

• working with children and their families
• providing services for everyone
• flexible at the point of delivery
• starting very early in a child's life

- operating respectful and transparent procedures
- community driven and professionally co-ordinated
- influenced by outcomes (38).

The most recent evaluation of the early Sure Start local initiatives found that their impact on young families has been unequivocally positive. The longitudinal study of 9,000 three-year-old children originally started when they were involved with Sure Start projects at nine months. When matched with children of the same age who had not been involved, the Sure Start children showed more positive gains in social development and independence. Families had also gained, being less negative towards their children, providing them with a better environment and using more services designed to support young families. Importantly, in contrast to an earlier study, there was no evidence that children from more disadvantaged backgrounds did less well – the benefits were generalised across all types of family groups. One possible reason suggested for this last finding was that the later family programmes were more carefully thought out and there had been more concerted effort to reach the most needy groups. The authors admit that gains were small but showed overall evidence that the impact of Sure Start services was improving (39).

However, as Sure Start programmes have been extended across the country and developed into Children's Centres, practice has varied particularly in regard to later phases of children's centres. The notion of integration, well established in the first phase of centres, is not so apparent as the programme has been rolled out. Children's Centres developed in phases two and three commonly have services which are co-located, making it more difficult to provide a cohesive provision for families. Moreover, increasingly there appears to be insufficient funding to provide for the original vision of centres. There are also continual problems of staff recruitment particularly of senior staff who are capable of managing a centre on a day-to-day basis and having and sharing a long-term view of development. Where centres are working with families who have complex problems (always seen as a key aspect), there are heavy demands on professional and administrative staff which are not always recognised by local authorities. Importantly there is insufficient time for staff to meet, to share and develop their practice. The former Early Excellence Centres often started from a low base and grew over four or five years to cultivate effective integrated provision for families. Children's Centres need time to evolve, to get everyone on board, build trust with families, try out initiatives and allow those that are successful to take root and act as a model for others.

The Statutory Framework for the Early Years Foundation Stage now requires practitioners in all settings to work closely with other agencies in the interests of young children and their families and this message is echoed in the developing frameworks in Northern Ireland, Scotland and Wales (40). Although this way of working is almost universally accepted as indicated it is not always easy to achieve. Pat Broadhead's findings from her research based in Sheffield (41) include the critical point that the most successful examples of partnership are based on all those involved sharing the same values and principles, for example, signing up to the principles and commitments of the Early Years Foundation Stage.

Improved options for parents during their children's start in life

Options for parents have increased steadily in recent years. In 2003, new legislation on maternity and paternity leave and flexible working made it more possible financially for parents to stay at home with their children from birth to two years. Alternatively, if parents do return to work early, rather than look to group childcare, some prefer to have their babies and toddlers cared for in their own homes or to be with a childminder. From April 2005 this was made easier when parents were able to claim tax credits for home-based childcare. As from 2009 expectant mothers can claim universal child benefit from the 29th week of pregnancy. Moreover the government intends to increase additional paternal leave and additional statutory paternity pay which can be taken in the second six months of the baby's life. The Working Families website is just one of a number which publishes a range of very useful fact sheets for young families although because these are online it should not be assumed that they are easily accessible to all (42).

Guidance for parents to support their children

At times, being a parent can be difficult, distressing and confusing, particularly for young and inexperienced adults. General and specialist help were set up in 2004 from various funded parent helplines. A recent service, *Parent Know How*, provides an ambitious range of ways for families to receive help – through a telephone helpline, using the web and social media, through print and online information (43). In addition, children's centres include a wide range of courses for parents to help them to understand and support their child's positive learning and behaviour. In centres where this type of support is well established, parents grow to lead discussion groups and meetings for themselves to share some of the problems and pleasures of bringing up young children. Government grants, coupled with the skills and dedication of skilled trainers, are having an impact on families. Evaluations of work with parents in early excellence centres had suggested that the lives of parents and children were genuinely transformed (44). Findings from the national evaluation of local Sure Start programmes (now children's centres) were more modest. 'Differences between the impact of various parenting programmes were small ... but where they were observable they were consistent with the belief that areas providing good parenting were achieving better parenting outcomes' (45).

In summary, some parents are already receiving considerable financial help for childcare, others are gaining from easier access to different services, some parents of very young children are beginning to have choice of home care and the task of parenting is now recognised as worthy of support.

PRACTITIONERS AND FAMILIES WORKING TOGETHER

Against this picture of government backing, the nursery and school have the responsibility and challenge of working with families practically on a daily basis. All parents should certainly benefit in some way from the scope of the government schemes, but it is the direct contact that they have with the practitioners that can influence the way in which parents feel supported to bring up their children. Similarly, the effect of the setting on what happens to children is largely dependent on what parents are prepared to condone or actively support.

Staff in nursery settings have traditionally understood the inextricable links that exist between the young child and her family. When Margaret McMillan opened her nursery school in Deptford in 1911, she was a firm believer that parents should take a strong role in all aspects of the work (46). Margaret McMillan was ahead of her time. Although over the years nursery settings have developed some exciting and innovative ways of working with families, it has taken almost a century to ensure that this work is beginning to become common practice. Even now, terms such as 'parental involvement', 'partnership' and 'open door policy' are used in a variety of contexts and to cover different purposes in discussing and documenting aspects of nursery life. Some nurseries and schools cautiously acknowledge that parents have a right of access but little more. Others are proud of the daily presence of a number of parents tackling different tasks with children during the nursery day. When one looks more closely, though, it is often difficult to see any planning or purpose to this involvement, other than the view that 'an extra pair of hands is always useful'. Yet other nurseries may have a detailed written policy for parents – a stack of paperwork may be produced to keep parents informed but this does little to generate the spirit of working together.

Work with parents can take many forms and will be undertaken for different and legitimate reasons. These can include meeting the requirements of government in order to be eligible to receive nursery grants, or capitalising on parents' fundraising initiatives. However, if staff really wish to work closely with parents and share in the upbringing of their child during the critical early years, this requires an approach with three important ingredients:

- exchanging information with families
- tuning in together to understand children's personal and social development
- respecting and supporting families.

Exchanging information with families

All settings and schools are required by law to provide information for parents. The Early Years Foundation Stage Statutory Framework requires this as part of close partnership working. The framework stresses that when children attend more than one setting information sharing between providers and with parents is important in the interests of ensuring that the child receives a continuous and coherent experience. Exchange of information is also important in order to identify children's learning needs (47). However, no legislation is likely to meet the real concerns any new parent will have when their baby or child moves from home for the first time. Any parent of a young baby will be anxious that the key person has understood the baby's non-verbal signals. Those with older children may worry about how their child will adapt to a new regime and environment; what will be expected of the child; how he or she will get on with other children and adults; how much the child will miss the familiarity of home life.

When parents hand over their child they are demonstrating a great act of faith in the people who will be acting *in loco parentis*; in turn, they should be informed about what they regard as important. It is not surprising that their child's welfare, personal development and behaviour feature highly. Essentially, although parents need to be given information about policies and daily procedures, what they want is reassurance about the staff who will be working with their child. When settings asked parents what they need from practitioners their responses included: someone who really likes my child and knows them well, gives me time to talk, has a sense of humour and keeps me informed (48).

It seems, then, that in order to respond to parents' real questions and concerns, the nursery must try to communicate the ways in which staff bond with the children, get to know them, support their behaviour and help them to develop good relationships. The key person should be available to talk informally; in this way parents will get to know the qualities of the key person, observe how she relates both to their child and to others and see how their child might make an attachment.

In some family circumstances, for example where parents have separated, it can be difficult to keep both partners informed. It is worthwhile for a setting to try to maintain contact with both parents and, so long as there are no access issues to the child, to encourage involvement from both.

Case study

Three-year-old Jake's parents had terminated an acrimonious relationship and his dad, Gus, moved 70 miles away to start a new job; this severely restricted his access to Jake. The boy clearly missed his dad and on several occasions said sadly that he had dreamt about his daddy.

The children's centre were holding a 'dads and kids' day as part of their programme to encourage fathers to take a key role with their children. Following several discussions with Jake's mum they found out Gus's address. With her agreement they wrote a personalised invitation for Gus to attend the day and in consultation with Jake, attached a recent photo of him to the invitation. Gus managed to take a day off work and travelled to spend the entire day with Jake at the

Continued

Continued

centre. The little boy was delighted to see his dad and wanted to show him everything. By the end of the day Gus had chatted at length with Jake's key person and arranged to attend future dads' days which were held monthly. The key person also promised to send Gus regular updates of Jake's well-being and progress.

Comment

All parties gained from the arrangement which continued for nearly two years when Jake moved into the reception class. A few months after Gus's initial visit to the centre, Jake's mum in discussion with Jake's key person admitted that Jake had really benefitted from seeing his dad more often: 'he tells me that he shows his dad his pictures and gives daddy a big kiss when he sees him'. Gus was delighted to feel that he was 'playing his part as a proper dad and seeing my son grow up'. The centre's initiative had enabled partners in a fractured relationship to maintain an aspect of their role as parents.

Settings are also aware that the exchange of information is two way. Staff need to tap into the fund of knowledge that families have about their children; for example, how children have spent their time during the earliest years of life. Have they been used to being parted from parents – perhaps staying at granny's for occasional nights, spending weekdays with a childminder, or staying with a whole range of neighbours or friends on account of parents' busy social or work lives? The establishment of children's hotels means that some young children will have had the experience of being 'boarded out' while their parents are away. Contrast this with children who have never been separated from their parents until they join a nursery.

Parents potentially play the ace card when it comes to having information about their children's personal development. Because of the close relationship that they have, they know about their child as a person in a way that no outsider could. Parents and other close family members are aware when children feel pleased with themselves, when they are confident or fearful and when they are truly interested. Unless parents are estranged from their children they know how they tick and can predict how they might feel and act. They may not be aware of how their child is prepared for early literacy and numeracy but they have invaluable and intuitive knowledge about their child's personal attributes. It is unlikely that an adult working with children in a group setting will easily have access to such intimate information. Early years staff sorely need this information from parents in order to help them to form a rapid and meaningful bond with each child. The information can highlight children's behaviour in different situations and throw light on a completely different world of learning at home. It can complement the information that staff glean in the nursery or school and can contribute towards a three-dimensional view of each individual. Staff and parents need time together in order to encourage parents to respond to the request, 'Tell me about your child'. Parents will respond if they are convinced that their knowledge is not only valuable for staff, but important to help their child to settle happily, to feel that she is known, and to make progress. 'The key ingredient to a successful meeting will be the teacher's evident and genuine interest in getting to know their child' (49).

Tuning in together to young children's personal and social development

Although parents and carers are likely to have unparalleled information about their children, there are times when they find it difficult to interpret why they behave as they do. As children struggle to find out and understand their world they become absorbed in certain activities and ask what appear to be bizarre questions. Parents love their children; they find many of their responses endearing and amusing as they repeat them to friends. However, they do not always recognise the significance or the underlying messages behind what they are describing. Early years staff who have been trained in child development may understand better the reasons for a child's actions; nevertheless, they only see a very limited slice of behaviour while the child is in the nursery. If staff and parents share their observations of children in the nursery and at home they will be in a stronger position to understand what is happening.

Chris Athey's classic work with parents in 1990 introduced them to their children's schemes of thought. The study aimed at gaining further information about how young children developed their understandings at home and in the nursery. Information was shared freely with parents, who were asked to attend discussions and outings with their children. Parents were also asked to note what their children did and said at home. Chris Athey admits that initially parents treated the professionals as the experts. However, as they became better informed and gained confidence, parents were able to take an equal part with staff in tracing their children's patterns of understanding. Although parents' levels of understanding and participation in the project varied, Athey stresses that all became more and more interested in observing their child. 'Nothing gets under a parent's skin more quickly or permanently than the illumination of his or her own child's behaviour' (50).

Respecting and supporting families

The government has stated clearly that it recognises the challenges of parenthood. 'There is no doubt that children enrich our lives but raising them is hard work. The hours are lousy, there's no annual leave and crucially you don't get training' (51). Perhaps it was always naive to assume that the biological fact of producing a child made for good parenting. However, now parents are urged to consider their responsibilities and to capitalise on their child's responses from birth to such a degree that the joy and spontaneity of the role is in danger of disappearing. Some parents are confused as they become steeped in literature which may offer conflicting advice; others are isolated and in danger of feeling desperate and powerless as a small child appears to take over their lives. By sharing the child with parents the early years setting is in a key position to help.

Adults can indulge children as a consequence of their own guilt. They may naturally be worried about the effects on a young child of family break-up or the lack of time that they spend with their child as a result of their long working hours. As a result they may condone behaviour which they would normally regard as unacceptable. This can lead a child to feeling in an uncomfortable position of holding power. Parents sometimes need reassurance that a good way of showing their love for their children is to establish clear boundaries. This helps young children to feel secure and cared for, while a lack of guidance can lead a young child to a freedom which is heady but frightening. Lillian Katz reminds us that it is not so much the different family pattern that the child grows up with that will affect her psychological and social development, as the way in which she regards that arrangement (52).

Despite the unique role that they have, parents are at least very modest about their influence, and in some cases still remain unaware of how essential they are to their children's personal growth. Perhaps the one most important thing that staff, particularly key persons, can offer all parents is to help them recognise this.

Work with families is complex and sometimes frustrating. Being realistic, the single largest variable that affects children's lives is the one over which practitioners have the least control – the child's home circumstances. So there is a stark choice – to give up or to regard it as a fundamental challenge. Edwards points out that committed practitioners see this aspect of their work as a long-term investment (53). If parents are respected, supported and informed during the earliest years of their child's education, they are likely to be stronger parents as their child grows older, and their parenting skills will also be used with younger children in the family.

Practical suggestions

Listen and observe
Note how relaxed parents are when they enter the setting and how easy they are when approaching you. Occasionally a parent will need time to talk to you immediately and in private and staffing arrangements should allow for this.

Ensure that your environment is family friendly
- Have clear signposts to the office/reception area and to a parents' room.
- Design paths which are wide enough for double buggies, and a covered area for prams and pushchairs, provide photographs of all staff members with brief descriptions of their roles (including domestic and administrative staff).

Continued

Continued

- Have comfy chairs and a playpen with toys for parents who wait in the reception area.
- Display a prominent welcoming sign in different languages.
- Display information about meetings/courses for parents (in different languages) with photographs of any recent family events.
- Provide a library of books/booklets for families to borrow.

Share respective standpoints about young children's personal and social development

- Through informal chats/discussions/seminars (whatever term is likely to appeal to your family group), invite parents and carers to share their views about how they would like their children to develop, e.g. how important is it for their children to become self-confident, assertive, sensitive, competitive, obedient, self-critical?
- Ensure that families are clearly informed about the setting's aims for fostering personal and social development.
- You may never reach a full consensus but open discussion can help all parties to reflect on their views.

Help families to support their children in personal and social development
When you have established a trusting relationship with parents it may be helpful if you encourage them to consider some of the following questions (it is extremely important that these are offered in a spirit of mutual discussion and that any suggestion of 'testing' parents is avoided):

- *Helping confidence.* How carefully do you listen to what your child is telling you? How do you show that you respect (i) your child's views (ii) your child's drawings/paintings/models? How do you show your child that she is very special?
- *Supporting behaviour.* How consistent are you in how you expect your child to behave? When are you likely to be too hard on your child? When are you likely to be over-indulgent? What rules are non-negotiable? How often do you praise/give attention to your child when she is behaving well?
- *Aiding independence.* How well do you encourage your child to be personally independent, e.g. dressing/washing/going to the lavatory? How much choice does your child have in daily routines, e.g. choosing a cereal for breakfast, clothes to wear, which walk to take? What decisions does your child have in how she uses her time at home?
- *Developing social skills.* How many other adults and children does your child meet during the week? How often do you invite other children to play with your child at home? How often does your child visit other people's homes?
- *Encouraging tolerance and interest in others.* How well does your own social circle reflect a mix of people from different backgrounds and cultures? How do you help your child to learn about how other people are different and similar, e.g. from within your neighbourhood, through your family accommodating foreign students, from books, pictures and television?

Continued

Continued

- *Encouraging care for the environment.* How do you help your child care for growing things, e.g. through having her own patch of garden/window box, providing food for the birds, helping to care for a pet? How do you help them to become responsible for keeping the environment tidy, e.g. through picking up litter in the park, on camping holidays?
- *Priority.* How much of your time do you show that you really enjoy being with your child?

Set up communication links to suit parents
- Parents' very different circumstances will influence the way in which they will wish to exchange information about their child with the nursery. For example, some will prefer a daily and informal personal contact with their child's early years practitioner; others will relish completing a home diary or having a visit at home. It is helpful if the nursery makes clear that there are a number of options. The most effective link will have good regard to family preferences.

Professional practice questions

1. How much do you know about parents' aspirations for their children?
2. How much do you know about what young children enjoy and learn about at home?
3. How well do you convince all of your parents how important they are to their children?
4. What are the barriers to dads participating in their young children's lives in your setting?
5. How do you show families that you use the information they share with you about their children?
6. How do you know that parents are fully satisfied with what you provide for their babies and children?

The following references in the *Early Years Foundation Stage* link to this chapter.

Statutory Framework and Guidance: pp. 9, 23, 24, 25, 26, 27, 41
Practice Guidance: pp. 6, 9
Principles into Practice Cards: 2.1 *Respecting Each Other*, 2.2 *Parents as Partners*, 2.4 *Key Person*
The CD-ROM *in depth* offers further guidance on the principles and commitments above.

The following Early Years Professional Standards link to this chapter:
1, 2, 3, 5, 6, 24, 29, 30, 31,32, 38, 39.

REFERENCES 📖

1. Department for Education and Skills (DfES) (2007) *The Early Years Foundation Stage: Principles into Practice Cards*, 2.2. London: DfES Publications.
2. National Service Framework for Children, Young People and Maternity Services (NSFC) (2007) *Rationale for Standard 2*. London: Department of Health.
3. Newson, J. and Newson, E. (1976) *Seven Years Old in the Home Environment*. London: Allen and Unwin.
4. Tizard, B. and Hughes, M. (1984) *Young Children Learning*. London: Fontana.
5. Wells, G. (1984) *Language Development in the Pre-School Years*. Cambridge: Cambridge University Press.
6. Sylva, K., Melhuish, M., Sammons, P., Siraj-Blatchford, I., Taggart, B, and Elliot, K. (2003) *The Effective Provision of Pre-school Education (EPPE) Project: Summary of Findings*. Institute of Education, University of London.
7. Sammons, P., Sylva, K., Melhuish, E., Siraj-Blatchford, I., Taaggart, B., Grabbe, Y. and Barreau, S. (2007) *EPPE 3–11 Project. Influences on Children's Attainment and Progress in Key Stage 2: Cognitive Outcomes in Year 5*. DfES research brief RB828, February.
8. Desforges, C. and Abouchaar, A. (2003) *The Impact of Parental Involvement on Pupil Achievement*. DfES Report 433.
9. Department for Children, Schools and Families (DCSF) (2006) *Sure Start Children's Centres Practice Guide*. London: DCFS, p. 81.
10. Department for Children, Schools and Families (DCSF) (2007) Haris, A. and Goodall, J. *Engaging Parents in Raising Achievement. Do Parents know they Matter?* in DCSF research report RW0O4. London: DCSF.
11. Lane, J. (2008) *Young Children and Racial Justice*. National Children's Bureau, p. 132.
12. Blamires, M., Robertson, C. and Blamires, J. (1997) *Parent-Teacher Partnership: Practical Approaches to Meeting Special Educational Needs*. London: David Fulton.
13. Department for Education and Skills (DfES) (2007) *The Early Years Foundation Stage: Principles into Practice 2.2, CD ROM in depth*. London: DfES Publications.
14. Katz, L. (1995) *Talks with Teachers of Young Children*. Norwood, NJ: Ablex, p. 162.
15. Palmer, S. (2006) *Toxic Childhood*. London: Orion Books.
16. National Children's Society (2008) Good Childhood Inquiry reveals mounting concern over commercialisation of childhood in *Good Childhood Inquiry*, February, National Children's Society. www.childrenssociety.org.uk
17. Large, M. (2003) *Set Free Childhood: Parents' Survival Guide to Coping with Computers and TV*. Stroud: Hawthorne Press.
18. Phillips, A. (1999) How to raise a confident child, *The Times*, 18 February, p. 21.
19. Reeves, R. (2008) Society's challenge to build character, *The Sunday Times News Review*, 24 August, p. 7.
20. Department for Education and Skills (DfES) (2004) *Parental Separation: Children's Needs and Parents' Responsibilities*. www.dfes/gov.uk/childrensneeds.
21. Layard, R. and Dunn, J. (2009) *A Good Childhood: Searching for Values in a Competitive Society*. The Children's Society.
22. Handy, C. (1994) *The Empty Raincoat: Making Sense of the Future*. London: Hutchinson.
23. Seaman, P., Turner, K., Hill, M., Stafford, A. and Walker, M. (2005) *Parenting and Children's Resilience in Disadvantaged Communities*. York: Joseph Rowntree Foundation.
24. Brooker, L. (2002) *Starting School: Young Children Learning Cultures*. Buckingham: OUP.
25. Curtis, P. (2007) Hard pressed parents struggle to help with school work, *Guardian Unlimited*, 23 November. guardian.co.uk/primaryeducation/story.

26. Northern, S. (2003) Play, *Times Educational Supplement*, 2 April, p. 7.
27. Clanchy, I. (1998) I'm late! I'm late! I'm only three, but I must achieve, *Independent*, 8 October.
28. Leach, P. (1994) *Children First*. London: Michael Joseph.
29. David, T. (ed.) (1999) *Young Children Learning*. London: Paul Chapman, p. 209.
30. Department for Education and Skills (DfES) (2007) Every *Parent Matters*. London: DfES publications, ref: LKAW/2007.
31. Department for Education and Skills (DfES) (2007) *Every Parent Matters: Helping you to Help your Child*. London: DfES publications, ref: LKAW/2007.
32. Department for Education and Skills (DfES) (2007) The *Children's Plan: Building Better Futures*. London: DfES, p. 5.
33. Sure Start (2006) *Sure Start Children's Centres Practice Guidance*. London: DfES, DH and Sure Start.
34. Together4Children (2007) *Toolkit for Reaching Priority and Excluded Families*, version 4, August 2007, Together4Children, www.4children.org.uk
35. Evangelou, M., Sylva, K., Edwards, A. and Smith, T. (2008) *Supporting Parents in Promoting Early Learning: The Evaluation of the Early Learning Partnership Project*. London: DCSF, Research Brief ref: RB039.
36. Feinstein, L. et al. (2008) *Reducing Inequalities: Realising the Talents of All*. London: National Children's Bureau, ref: 28.
37. Together4Children/Financial Services Authority (2008) *Turning up the Volume on Child Poverty*. www.4Children.org.uk
38. Department for Children, Schools and Families (DCSF) (2008) *The Impact of Sure Start Local Programmes on Three year olds and their   Families*. National Sure Start Team, London: DCSF.
39. Anning, A. and Ball, M. (2008) *From Sure Start to Children's Centres: Improving Services for Young Children and their Families*. London: Sage.
40. Early Education (2008) *Planning for Quality in the Early Years*, Leaflet 5, Roles of adults, pp. 3–4. early-education.org.uk.
41. Broadhead, P., Meleady, C. and Delgardo, M.A. (2008) *Children, Families and Community: Creating and Sustaining Integrated Services*. Maidenhead: OUP.
42. Working Families Website, www.workfamilies.co.uk.
43. Department for Children, Schools and Families (DCSF) (2008) *Parent Know How: Working Together, Supporting Families*. London: DCSF.
44. Bertram, T. and Pascal, C. (1999) *Early Excellence Centres: First Findings*. London: DfEE.
45. Anning, A. and Ball, M. (ed) (2008) *From Sure Start to Children's Centres: Improving Services for Young Children and their Families*. London: Sage, p. 200.
46. Dowling, M. (1992) *Education 3–5*. London: Paul Chapman, p. 6.
47. Department for Education and Skills (DfES) (2007) *Early Years Foundation Stage (EYFS): Creating the Framework for Partnership Working, Statutory Framework*, London: DfES, p. 10.
48. Department for Education and Skills (DfES) (2007) *Early Years Foundation Stage (EYFS): Principles into Practice* 2.2, CD-Rom *in depth*. London: DfES.
49. Dowling, M. (1995) *Starting School at Four: A Joint Endeavour*. London: Paul Chapman, p. 148.
50. Athey, C. (1990) *Young Children Thinking*. London: Paul Chapman, p. 66.
51. Department for Education and Skills (DfES) (2007) *Every Parent Matters: Helping you to Help your Child*. London: DfES, ref. LKAW, p. 1.
52. Katz, L. (1995) *Talks with Teachers of Young Children*. Norwood, NJ: Ablex.
53. Edwards, E. and Knight, P. (1994) *Effective Early Years Education*. Buckingham: Open University Press, p. 111.

11

Being Alongside the Child

Summary of contents

- Certain experiences that feed young children's thinking and imagination can strongly influence their personal development.
- However, the quality of the adult is the key factor in helping the child grow up in the world. Children need practitioners who are committed, well trained, able and prepared to give a great deal of themselves.

We have already seen that giving scope for children to build on their interests releases their creative capacities (see Chapter 5). In this final chapter I touch on use of stories and storytelling as important influences and return to creative play as this is the fundamental glue which knits together all aspects of children's personal development.

THE INFLUENCE OF BOOKS AND STORIES

Literature plays a very important role in personal development for most people. We read books for relaxation, comfort and enlightenment. Reading a good book can reduce stress; we can often identify with a character and so recognise motives for our actions, or begin to understand how others operate. Stories also stick in the mind. We may listen to a lecture and strain to remember the facts but we will have no difficulty in remembering illustrations or anecdotes. We often tell ourselves a story as a way of making sense of a situation, or reliving an experience.

For young children books and stories play an even more crucial role. As we have seen, children have powerful feelings but may not be able fully to understand or articulate them – an appropriate story may help put their feelings into words and pictures. Cathy Nutbrown confirms this: 'Many books can help to support as well as challenge children's emotional development, reflecting and affirming their feelings, challenging their thinking and presenting characters who experience different emotions of fear, sadness, excitement, love and disappointment' (1).

Literature also plays a very important role in teaching. Books can help to introduce or reinforce for children important issues such as fairness, other ways of living and care for the environment. Of course, children need to experience these issues for themselves. However, if they have had only a very little experience of life, this first-hand knowledge will be limited; through stories and pictures they will encounter what they may later begin to know for themselves. All stories are valuable for children but the School Library Association emphasises the need for young children to have stories from their own families, communities and culture. 'The traditions of our cultural heritage conveyed through stories can be a strong part of our sense of identity and, thus, our sense of self' (2).

THE CONTEXT FOR SHARING BOOKS AND STORIES

At the beginning of the twenty-first century there is a wealth of information available for young children through television, film and computerised programmes. Some would consider that the attraction of sophisticated media approaches can mean that books pall in comparison. However, the power of story is age-old; it is simple, immediate and the method can be used flexibly. Young children will respond best if they share books and listen to stories with people they care for and in a comfortable environment. Babies love to have stories about themselves that reflect their day-to-day activities such as washing and eating. A sleepy young child knows that she is loved and secure when she shares a familiar storybook at bedtime while cuddling up to her parent or carer. At other times children can enter different worlds and experience excitement and danger in the safety of a group story. In a nursery setting the book area needs to tempt young children into selecting and tasting books for themselves and sharing them with friends. Many nursery settings transform their book areas into beautiful and imaginative spaces using furniture and soft furnishings and pictures. The illusion of privacy can be created through a den or cave. The continual presence of an adult in the book area can provide a lap for those children who most need this physical contact. Stories can also be offered 'on demand' and shared informally with small groups; in these cases children will select their choice of book rather than receiving one selected by the adult, which is more likely to happen in a set storytelling session. If children are given this type of provision and interaction then books come to offer much more than development in literacy. Stories will be associated with feelings of pleasure, intimacy and sharing thoughts, ideas and memories with others.

ENCOURAGING A PERSONAL RESPONSE FROM CHILDREN

Children invariably listen with rapt attention to a well-read story. Despite this, it takes careful planning to find out how much they have understood and what ideas they have about the characters and issues, and also to help them where possible to make links with their own experiences.

The Development Education Centre in Birmingham has produced useful publications which help children explore big issues in the world as they respond to stories. The authors of one publication argue that young children should be encouraged to talk about these issues as, among other benefits, it supports their social and emotional development, helps to break down ignorance, prejudice and fear and develops their self-confidence (3). Although the resource is intended for children at Key Stage 1, many of the activities are suitable for four- and five-year-olds. The suggestions below draw on some of this work.

- *Asking questions about the story*: sensitive questions from the adult can encourage children to share reactions and help them think about specific aspects of the story, e.g. I wonder how that little boy felt when he lost his cat?
- *Hiding the pictures*: this is best carried out in a small group with older nursery and reception-age children. The adult first reads the story without revealing the pictures but asks the children to think about the characters and describe or draw them. The children's descriptions and pictures can then be compared with the book illustrations, although it is important to avoid any notion of a 'correct response'.
- *Using speech bubbles*: this helps older children to empathise with the character. The story may encourage children to create their own dialogue. Photocopy and enlarge the pages of the story that encourage speech – draw a speech bubble coming out of the mouth of the character. The children can then discuss what they think the character is saying and the adult can scribe it in the speech bubble.
- *Drawing pictures*: children are asked to draw their favourite part of the story. Younger children may only be interested in talking about what they enjoyed; they may also need help to recall different aspects of the story. Older children's drawings will indicate what they think is most important.
- *Using visual aids*: storytelling can also involve the use of props, including puppets, miniature figures, models or figures on a magnetic board. If the adult initially demonstrates their use, children will enjoy using these to accompany the story.

Practitioners will all have a core of favourite 'situation' books which they call on as a resource to help children at important times in their lives. These books are best read with an individual or in a very small group, creating an atmosphere of intimacy. Young children's body language and comments will signal if the story has struck a chord as in these few examples:

1. *Look at You!* by Kathy Henderson (4). Beautiful illustrations capture everyday actions in a baby's life which culminate in the baby pulling itself up to stand. Ten-month-old Ben loved to hear this story and gazed at the pictures daily. As Carol, his key person, shared the story with him she made a personal link by saying 'Ben does that, clever Ben'.

2. *So Much* by Trish Cooke (5). A celebration of different ways of showing love for the baby from visiting members of the family. This affirms for very young children their widening attachments with different family members. Having listened to this story again and again, two-year-old Ned knew the sequence well. When his big sister kissed him, he hugged her and said 'So Much'.

3. *Just Like You Did* by Marjorie Newman (6). George doesn't want the new baby and would really like to return to the time before the baby was born. But mum and dad are able to reassure him that the baby will change 'just like you did' and will become a friend. This story leads naturally into talk about how young children feel about their position in the family. Having recently arrived with her family to live in England and facing the reality of a new baby sister, three-year-old Irma was feeling displaced on a number of fronts. She quietly listened to this story read by a bi-lingual assistant and then looked at the pictures and showed them to her mum who met her from nursery. Mum later reported that she had observed Irma whispering to her baby sister 'hurry up, hurry up to be big girl like me'.

4. *Once There Were Giants* by Martin Waddell (7). At the start of the story there is a family gathering around a new baby. The story follows the child as she grows, with the adult 'giants' shown on each page. The story ends almost as it started, but this time the baby has become one of the 'giants'; the new baby in the picture is her child. The story helps four- and five-year-olds deal with change and a sense of belonging in a family. Five-year-old Iram listened to the story on three occasions, entranced but without commenting. One morning he picked up the book and commented, 'I know about that book now. It's the way you start to grow and then it starts all over again'.

5. *Badger's Parting Gift* by Susan Varley (8). The animals grieve when old badger dies. However, they find that their friend has left them some wonderful gifts of skills that he taught them – these will always remain. They celebrate these in memory of their friend. A gentle and positive introduction to bereavement.

   Given an opportunity, children are often keen to share their experiences of death. Daniel's granny had always lived with him; now she was very ill and in pain. Daniel had visited her in hospital but had not mentioned it at school. After listening to Badger's final painless and joyful journey down the long tunnel, Daniel turned to his teacher and said quietly and confidently, 'My gran's going to be like that'.

STORYTELLING

Some believe that storytelling is the oldest profession; certainly there is a renewal of interest in this art and storytellers have sprung up all over the country. Long before books, stories were told to young children as a way of introducing them to the world; it is easier to remember a story than a rational explanations of events. The power of storytelling is immense: there is close contact between the teller and the audience, and a warm bond can be established. Children have no visual distractions; rather than providing ready-made images it encourages them to make pictures in their heads, to visualise and imagine.

Stories offer children phrases and words that literally 'catch' the ear and these they store to use later in their own stories and play. In stories where there are no right or wrong interpretations, children make their own moral judgements. Although most issues lend themselves to a story, traditional tales and fables contain particular treasure for personal development, gathered from the wisdom of many generations.

While all practitioners accept that reading stories to children is part of their job, some are less confident in telling stories. And yet everyone has the potential to become a compelling storyteller. Some of the important ingredients are to:

- create atmosphere: put on a story cloak, long gloves or hat to denote that you are the storyteller; sit on a special chair, draw children around you and invite them to sit on a special story floor covering
- develop a recognised story starter: 'Are you ready for a story? Are your ears open to listen? Well, here we go.'
- build in repetition: the more that children get to know key phrases in a story, the more they can participate and maintain their enjoyment and concentration
- build in sound effects: use your voice to the full – raise it, deepen it and use a whisper for good effect. Use one or two untuned percussion instruments to create different noises
- inspire: children, particularly the older ones, are not inspired by the bland and cosy but sometimes by what is a little disturbing. Once the group has got used to the conventions of storytelling and are well settled into the class you may judge that it is time to be a little more robust with stories; a little gratuitous fear can challenge thinking to the full. 'Don't go down into the woods today, Grandad', warned Peter, 'there may be a wolf there'. This enthralling introduction to *Peter and the Wolf* immediately draws children into the story
- build in a predictable ending to denote that story time is over: 'and now my story is ended'.

Although storytellers will have a repertoire of tales which they know back to front, stories can also be impromptu and tailor-made to meet a particular need. Skilled practitioners turn daily events into stories. Through observing children closely, staff will quickly identify what concerns them. Observations will reveal issues about children making and breaking friendships, feeling insecure about new situations or savouring pleasurable experiences. It may be insensitive and unhelpful to intervene at the time or even to refer directly to the observed behaviour, but a story can effectively pick up on the issue. Without a written storyline to follow the 'invented' story can be more easily adapted to meet children's particular interests and may be personalised: 'This is a story for Ahmed because it is his birthday'. Any child will warm to this gift. Stories which start 'When I was little … ' never fail to interest children. They are fascinated to learn that loved adults once experienced the dilemmas, joys and anxieties that they are faced with. The power of these stories again stresses the important model offered by the adult.

CHILDREN'S STORIES AND FANTASY PLAY

We all have a story to tell but young children slip into stories like fish into water. With increasing use of language children start to place their world into an understandable framework by using social scripts to describe daily events that they experience. This is the beginning of storying. While three-year-old Emily was with her childminder she had watched a video of Mickey Mouse with immense enjoyment. She was also aware that when she was at the childminder's her mother had been having driving lessons and had very recently passed her driving test. Emma lived by the coast where she often watched a Punch and Judy show with her mother during the summer months. Emma skilfully drew on all of these experiences as she portrayed a future scenario for herself.

> When I'm big I'm going to have a Mickey Mouse car and Mickey Mouse sunglasses and a Mickey Mouse lipstick. You can come in my car and sit in the front, but you must do up your seat belt. But first I must have driving lessons, lots and lots – to pass my test. We shall go … go to Punch and Judy. I like Mr Punch, but not the devil, he frightens me.

Scripts drawn from children's own experiences become embellished by stories they have heard and TV programmes and DVDs they have seen. They put these ideas into their script, experimenting with characters, settings and events. Young children's feet are not chained to the ground by common sense and their imaginations roam into far flung places. Although scripts are a form of story, they are essentially timeless accounts of personal experience; this is in contrast to stories which are told in the past tense, involve specific characters and have some sort of a beginning and end. Initially young children find this type of storytelling difficult and their stories will be relatively undeveloped. However, if they have plenty of adult models and learn that storytelling is a way of sharing things that are in their heads, children's stories will, over time, become more detailed and sequenced. Children's own stories are a valuable means of tuning in to their beliefs and concerns, as Vivian Paley, the eminent nursery teacher and author, found. Vivian had always made storytelling a regular part of her programme, but initially had little success with children sharing their stories. One day when Wally had spent a session in the 'time out' chair because he was always in trouble, Vivian, hoping to interest him, asked if he would like to write a story. When Wally protested that he could not write yet, Vivian offered to write the story down for him. Wally told her a story about a troublemaking dinosaur that ransacked a city and was put in jail. The story ended happily as the dinosaur promised to be good and when he was released from jail his mother was waiting for him (9).

Vivian Paley soon built her practice around storytelling and drama with young children. Throughout her teaching career she has been alert to the 'plots' that emerge from children's play. By highlighting these stories, offering to write them down and encouraging children to re-enact them, Vivian Paley enabled her children to communicate what was important to them. For her, drama has been an essential tool in examining the social and emotional worlds that are the foundations of learning (10). Children will rehearse their scripts and later their stories in dramatic play by themselves or with others, when the play becomes socio-dramatic. Through their play children use what they know or are interested in (their schema) and adapt or elaborate upon this information. Again the important factor is that the child is in charge of what happens. Erikson emphasises that socio-dramatic play helps children to cope with big issues in life such as disappointment, loneliness and anger (11).

Young children need regular and frequent opportunities to play, both for sheer pleasure and for more serious reasons as suggested by Singer and Singer: 'Imaginative play is fun, but in the midst of the joys of making believe, children may also be preparing for the reality of more effective lives' (12). Practitioners take account of both these aspects when they provide a context for play which gives plenty of scope for children's own initiatives.

Mary Jane Drummond describes children's imaginative play as 'allowing them to pass through invisible doorways into alternative worlds' (13). Nevertheless, while most children are natural players, some find it more difficult to 'pretend' and enter the world of fantasy. In these cases the adult has to take a more central role and find a way of enabling all to enter through the doorways. Children can be encouraged to build stories and recognise that even their simplest recount can be developed creatively. Sometimes it is helpful to provide them with tangible objects as story props. These are presented in story bags, boxes or attractively wrapped parcels. Children, in turn, pull an object out of a container or discover it in each layer of parcel wrapping. With help they knit the items into a story. The adult helps to link the story together, but the most important aspect is not the outcome but the experience of being imaginative together. Vivian Paley suggests that Lev Vygotsky's assertion that, in play a child stands taller than himself, above his age and normal behaviour, can also apply to practitioners as they listen and observe children and try to make sense of their play and storytelling (14) (see Chapter 1).

All practitioners recognise that children need play but the issue of super-hero play which occurs with boys taxes many staff. In some settings weapon and war play is banned usually because of the fear that such play encourages violence and aggression. In reality children continue their play and will use weapons surreptitiously. In one Camden nursery practitioners recognised that encouraging children to be deceitful was not good practice; moreover the ban on weapon play was to ignore and override what was important for children. When the nursery made a conscious decision to accept the play they were surprised to find that the level of aggression was reduced, interest in violent play lessened and the group ethos was more relaxed (15). Jackie Marsh in her edited book offers some very interesting perspectives showing how very young children engage with popular, media and digital cultures (16). The case study from Tachbrook Nursery (Chapter 5) offers an impressive example of how children can grow personally when their super-hero play is built on and supported.

Paley sums up beautifully the protection that pretending affords. 'Fantasy of course is the first line of defense against every sort of fear and in fantasy play the children discover the value of peer support as they dare to face and put the beanstalk to the test' (17).

SKILLED PRACTITIONERS ARE THE KEY INGREDIENT

'The single biggest factor that determines the quality of childcare is the workforce' (18). This belief is undoubtedly shared by all the leaders in the field of early years. And yet we still have a long way to go in gaining the highly qualified staff that are needed for the work and achieving the pay and conditions that they deserve. We have to seek out, appoint and reward the best people. Abbott's quote is passionate: 'I would fight to the death the view that anybody can look after young children and work with them; they have got to be the finest minds and the best trained people' (19).

Throughout this book the influence of modelling has been stressed. Young children are affected so strongly by the way in which practitioners behave, not only what they say or do – these are the outward signs; they also tune in to the way in which adults close to them think and feel. In fostering young children's personal, social and emotional development staff need to invest more of themselves than in any other aspect of work.

This final section is directed at the nature of the work and the qualities required to succeed as a high-quality practitioner.

Self-reflection

We all have our beliefs, values and attitudes which are based on our own experiences and which have served us well enough in our lives. When working with children and young families from a variety of backgrounds and cultures, these beliefs and assumptions may be shaken. Parents and carers may have very different ways of conducting their lives which are outside the experience of an early years practitioner. Children may not behave as they expect or respond to the practitioner's overtures. Colleagues may have different views about ways of caring for and educating children. All this can be discomforting, shake self-confidence and practitioners can become defensive. To avoid these negative feelings staff need to be prepared to be open-minded, re-examine what they believe, learn from others and sometimes adapt attitudes in the light of what they have learned. Once they are brave enough to reflect and learn from experience, practitioners can see how this helps them to grow professionally when they broaden, clarify and strengthen the underpinning for their work. It can be helpful to use a particular format to guide reflections. The SEAD document stresses the need for practitioners who genuinely contemplate the implications of their work. It includes a searching audit which is intended to support staff in making a judgement about how they look after and promote personal, social and emotional well-being for everyone in the setting. The important message is that practitioners need to take good care of themselves in order to care for others (20).

Flexibility

One of the joys of working with young children and their families is that it is dynamic. Edgington sums up the work as 'unpredictable and the best laid plans have a habit of going entirely awry'. She also points out that if control and predictability are what make you feel comfortable it is likely that such an adult will find working in the early years threatening (21). Practitioners need to have clear planned intentions for what they offer but must be prepared to adapt, or even abandon, plans in order to follow children's thinking and go with the tide of their motivation.

Emotional maturity

Involvement with young families and vulnerable children can mean sometimes dealing with powerful and harrowing issues such as family break-up and child abuse. Natural responses are to feel disturbed, upset, angry and frustrated. It is not easy to handle these emotions but practitioners need to learn the importance of remaining outwardly calm and in control, being able to cope with complexity.

Empathy

Goleman describes empathy as our 'social radar' (22). Effective practitioners who have this are able to see into a child's world and, when permitted, enter it. They tune in to the dilemmas experienced by families and parents and show that their feelings are acknowledged and respected. An empathetic response cannot in itself solve problems but it can help a person to feel that they are not alone. Goleman suggests that highly developed empathy goes even further than this by recognising the issues or concerns that lie behind another's feelings. When this happens it becomes possible for practitioners to offer families more tangible support.

Optimism

Practitioners work with children who have had different starts in life and who come into a setting at different stages of development. The exciting thing is that, although we can see what a child achieves today, we can never be sure of the potential she has for tomorrow. This must be a cause for optimism. Practitioners know that their work can make a difference. They understand that, regardless of children's different abilities, given the right climate (described in this book) their personal growth will flourish and this helps progress in all other aspects of their lives.

Communication

The ability to read young children's behaviour and to communicate with them is at the basis of successful practice. It is expressed so well in Colwyn Trevarthen's description of being able to 'dance with the children' (23). This implies harmony, recognising the steps that the child is taking, being able to anticipate the next move and adapting one's response accordingly.

Communication, we have seen, is so much more than talking or writing. Very young children are not concerned so much with words as with action. They represent and communicate their experiences through their bodies (Chapters 5 and 9) and the experienced practitioner will tune in to these expressions. Sign language gives children with speech and language difficulties access to communication. Where all adults and children are able to sign, the setting becomes more inclusive. And non-verbal communication does not stop once we can talk. Adults well know that the strong emotions of love and cold anger can be expressed clearly without words. Young children also understand the messages we give them through expression and gesture. Scot's mum abruptly left the family home at the weekend following a blazing row with her partner. Scot arrived at the nursery on Monday subdued and listless. The teacher felt that words would not be helpful at this stage; instead she kept close contact with Scot throughout the session through smiles and eye contact in group times; when going outside she volunteered her hand to Scot who (unusually for him) grasped it and continued to hold it, refusing offers from others to play with them. The next day, Scot's auntie thanked the teacher for her care and attention. Scot had apparently told her that, 'my teacher knows I'm sad and she said she loves me'.

Commitment

Practitioners will be variously qualified to work in early years and understandably will be at different stages of knowing about the theory of child development and the myriad ways of supporting young children. Many opportunities for training are fortunately now available to enable staff to acquire this knowledge and skill. And over time, work and life experience will add deeper perceptions to the role that they play.

However one disposition for the role is essential and that is commitment, an insatiable curiosity about babies and young children and a driving desire to get to know them. The work is often hard and unremitting; it requires huge physical and emotional energy, intellectual endeavour and it can easily lead to burnout. This job is not for the faint-hearted. And yet the commitment, creativity and passion tangible in good practitioners is there because they recognise the privilege of sharing the world of childhood and accompanying children in their very early stages of growing up.

REFERENCES 📖

1. Nutbrown, C. (2006) *Threads of Thinking*. London: Sage, p. 92.
2. Library Association (2008) *Riveting Reads plus Book Ahead 0–7*. Swindon: School Library Association supported by DCSF, p. 9.
3. The Development Education Centre Birmingham (2002) *Start with a Story: Supporting Young Children's Exploration of Issues*. The Tide Resource Base, 998 Bristol Road, Selly Oak, Birmingham B29 6LE.
4. Henderson, K. (2008) *Look at You!* London: Walker Books.
5. Cooke, T. (2008) *So Much*. London: Walker Books.
6. Newman, M. (2005) *Just Like You Did*. London: Bloomsbury Press.
7. Waddell, M. (2001) *Once There Were Giants*. London: Walker Books.
8. Varley, S. (1998) *Badger's Parting Gift*. London: Picture Lions.
9. Paley, V. (1981) *Wally's Stories*. Cambridge, MA and London: Harvard University Press.
10. Paley, V. (2004) *A Child's Work*. Chicago, IL: University of Chicago Press.
11. Erikson, E. (1965) *Childhood and Society*. Harmondsworth: Penguin Books.
12. Singer, D. and Singer, J. (1990) *The House of Make Believe*. Cambridge, MA: Harvard University Press, p. 152.
13. Drummond, M.J. (1999) Another way of seeing: perceptions of play in a Steiner kindergarten, in L. Abbott and H. Moylett (eds), *Early Education Transformed*. London: Falmer Press, p. 59.
14. Paley, V. (2004) op. cit. (note 7) p. 82.
15. Holland, P. (2003) War, weapon and superhero play: a challenge to zero tolerance. Summary of a paper presented at Tower Hamlets Early Years Conference, 6 June.
16. Marsh, J. (ed) (2005) *Popular Culture, New Media and Digital Literacies in Early Childhood*. London: Sage.
17. Paley, V. (1990) *The Boy Who Would be a Helicopter*. Chicago, IL: University of Chicago Press, p. 162.
18. Department for Education and Skills (DfES) (2004) *Every Child Matters: Change for Children*. Nottingham: DfES Publications, para 43.
19. Page, J. (2005) Working with children under three: the perspectives of three UK academics, in K. Hirst and C. Nutbrown (eds) *Perspectives on Early Childhood Education: Contemporary Research*. Stoke-on-Trent: Trentham, p. 110.
20. Department for Children, Schools and Families (DCSF)/The National Strategies Early Years (2008) *Social and Emotional Aspects of Development (SEAD)*. London: DCSF, Appendix 2, p. 53.
21. Edgington, M. (2004) *The Foundation Stage Teacher in Action*. London: Paul Chapman, p. 4.
22. Goleman, D. (1998) *Working with Emotional Intelligence*. London: Bloomsbury, p. 133.
23. Trevarthen, C. (1992) An infant's motives for thinking and speaking, in A.H. Wold (ed.) *The Dialogical Alternative*. Oxford: Oxford University Press.

Index